LATIN AMERICA - MERCOSUR

INTERNATIONAL HANDBOOKS ON ECONOMIC INTEGRATION

edited by:

Peter Coffey
University of St. Thomas
Minneapolis, MN 55403--2001
USA

Volume I
LATIN AMERICA-MERCOSUR
edited by Peter Coffey

Latin America - MERCOSUR

edited by

Peter Coffey

US West Chair,
University of St. Thomas,
Minneapolis, MN , U.S.A.

KLUWER ACADEMIC PUBLISHERS
BOSTON / DORDRECHT / LONDON

Distributors for North America:
Kluwer Academic Publishers
101 Philip Drive
Assinippi Park
Norwell, Massachusetts 02061 USA

Distributors for all other countries:
Kluwer Academic Publishers Group
Distribution Centre
Post Office Box 322
3300 AH Dordrecht, THE NETHERLANDS

Library of Congress Cataloging-in-Publication Data

A C.I.P. Catalogue record for this book is available from
the Library of Congress.

Printed on acid-free paper.

Printed in the United States of America

Table of Contents

Other Books by Peter Coffey

European Monetary Integration (with John R. Presley). Macmillan, London, and St. Martin's Press, New York, 1971.

The Social Economy of France. Macmillan, London, and St. Martin's Press, 1973.

The World Monetary Crisis. Macmillan, London, and St. Martin's Press, New York, 1974.

The External Economic Relations of the EEC. Macmillan, London, and St. Martin's Press, 1976.

Europe and Money. Macmillan, London, and St. Martin's Press, New York, 1979.

Economic Policies of the Common Market. Macmillan, London, and St. Martin's Press, 1979.

The Common Market and its International Economic Policies. Nuffic, The Hague, 1982.

The Main Economic Policy Areas of the EEC (editor). Martinus Nijhoff Publishers, The Hague, 1983.

The European Monetary System—Past, Present and Future. Martinus Nijhoff Publishers, Dordrecht, 1984; Second Edition, 1986.

The European Community and Mexico (editor). M. S. Wionczek (co-editor). Martinus Nijhoff Publishers, Dordrecht, 1987.

Towards a European Foreign Policy (editor), R. H. Lauwaars and J. K. DeVree (joint editors). Martinus Nijhoff Publishers, Dordrecht, 1987.

Europe and the Andean Countries, together with Ciro Angarita. Frances Pinter, London, and St. Martin's Press, New York, 1988.

The EEC and Brazil, together with L. A. Correa de Lago. Frances Pinter, London, and St. Martin's Press, New York, 1988.

The EEC and the Netherlands—Costs and Benefits, together with Menno Wolters. Pinter Publishers, London, 1990.

Main Economic Policy Areas of the EEC—Towards 1992. Kluwer Academic Publishers, Dordrecht, 1990.

The EC and the United States. Pinter Publishers, London, 1993.

Main Economic Policy Areas of the EC—After 1992. Kluwer Academic Publishers, Dordrecht, 1993.

The Future of Europe. Edward Elgar Publishing, Cheltenham, 1995.

The Future of Europe. Edward Elgar. Reprinting, 1996.

Europe—Toward 2001. Kluwer Academic Publishers, Dordrecht and Boston, 1996.

Special Note About this Book

This book marks the launching of a new series of books by Kluwer Academic Publishers. This series, the joint idea of Zachary Rolnik and the editor, is published in the framework of International Regional Economic Integration. Initially, it is planned to publish four volumes. These will deal with four different regions of the world: Latin America – MERCOSUR, NAFTA, Europe, and South-East Asia. Eventually, it is also hoped to include a volume on Africa. The editor is grateful to Zachary Rolnik, Vice President of Kluwer Academic Publishers, for taking this initiative.

Acknowledgements

Although all the views expressed in this book are exclusively those of the editor and authors, this work would not have been possible without the encouragement and assistance given by a number of friends and colleagues. The editor thus wishes to acknowledge this help individually.

He is particularly appreciative of the encouragement and help given by three Latin American friends and colleagues. Professor José Ares, formerly Dean of the Business School at the Universidad del Uruguay, and now Director of Human Resources at the Bank of Boston, in Montevideo, gave much encouragement. Equally, Professor Juan Carlos Torre, Director of the Center for Social Research at the Instituto Torcuato Di Tella, in Buenos Aires, encouraged the editor in his enterprise and introduced him to professor Lucangegelli. Very special thanks are due to Professor Antônio Salazar Brandão, Director of the Brazilian Institute of Economics at the Fundação Getulio Vargas, in Rio de Janeiro. Professor Salazar Brandão most graciously agreed to hold discussions with the editor as well as providing him with important documents about Brazil which proved to be indispensable in the preparation of the chapter on Brazil.

In Brussels, Mr. Andy Klom, of the European Commission most kindly agreed at short notice, to meet the editor and provided him with very useful documents.

At the University of St. Thomas, the editor is particularly grateful to Brian Hill who has so patiently transcribed the manuscript of this book. He is also grateful to his assistant Juan Molina, who prepared the index for this work as well as obtaining documents for the appendices.

Notes About the Contributors

Peter Coffey, a British national, teaches European and International Political Economy at the University of St. Thomas, where he holds the US West Chair. He has published widely on European and international issues.

Carlos Eduardo López-Rodriguez, a national of Uruguay, is a Professor of Integration Law at the Catholic University of Uruguay, Damaso Antonio Larranaga. He is also Professor of Commercial Law at the Oriental Republic of Uruguay University.

Jorge Lucángeli, an Argentine national, is Director of Argentine Foreign Ministry's CEI International Economy Centre. Before joining CEI, Lucangeli coordinated the UNDP "Integration of Argentina in MERCOSUR" project, also at the Foreign Ministry. After graduating in Economics at the University of Buenos Aires, he has been consultant to CEPAL, LAIA, INTAL, IBD, and the World Bank, with research on industrial economics, government-owned enterprises, and international trade. Formerly full professor of International Economics at the Salvador University, Lucángeli is at the present associate professor of International Economics at the University of Buenos Aires and also teaches at the Entre Rios National University's postgraduate course on MERCOSUR Taxation.

Dario Menanteau-Horta, a national of Chile, is a Professor of Sociology, Rural Sociology, and Latin American Studies at the University of Minnesota. He has undertaken research and taught in a number of Latin American countries as well as publishing widely. In 1985, he was awarded the title of "Professor Extraordinary" by the Austral University of Chile.

Robert Riley, a US national, is a Professor of Economics at the University of St. Thomas, where he specializes in International Trade and Regional Integration. He has taught in a number of countries, and has published widely.

Chapter 1
The Historical Background to Integration in Latin America

By Peter Coffey

ATTEMPTS AT INTEGRATION BEFORE MERCOSUR

Contrary to received wisdom, Latin America's experience with economic integration is almost as long as that of Western Europe. In contrast with

Western Europe, however, and until the more recent experience with MERCOSUR, Latin America has been only moderately successful with its record of integration.

The first attempt at economic integration on a wide Latin American scale started in 1960 with the creation of LAFTA - the Latin American Free Trade Association[1]. The aim of LAFTA was to create a free trade area over a period of 12 years. According to Lia Valls Pereira, the main force in creating this free trade area was to use the sophisticated concept (more linked to customs unions and/or common markets - according to the author) of economies of scale. Thus, the participating countries hoped to deepen their experience of import substitution, acquired during the Second World War. In turn, this would further foster the industrialisation process on the continent.

Despite the growth in the importance of regional experts as a percentage of total exports of these countries from only 7.7 per cent in 1960 to 13.7 per cent in 1981, LAFTA has not been considered to be a success. One can suggest many possible reasons for this.

One of the main reasons, listed by Lia Valls Pereira[2], is that these countries did not respect the timetable for the dismantling of tariffs. Also, because countries were at different stages of economic development, there were constant requests for waivers and special treatment. To the author, however, Lia Valls Pereira's view that the concept of important substitution at a national level militates against the idea of free trade is extremely important. Thus, the author would say that LAFTA appeared to be doomed to failure from the start. It collapsed in 1980.

In the same year, it was replaced by LAIA - Latin American Integration Association. This is a much more flexible organisation than its predecessor. It has no target dates for the removal of tariffs and simply seeks to encourage the signing of preferential tariff agreements between its members.

At a more sub-regional level, a group of Andean Countries[3] created the Andean Pact in 1969. These countries planned to create a free trade area. This was not successful. Thus, in 1992, they decided to free internal trade by 1993 (by 1995 for some). Then in March 1996, they agreed to form a customs union within 5 years. They also decided, surprisingly maybe, to create a directly-elected parliament.

Earlier, in 1960, a group of Central American countries decided to create a Central American Common Market.[4]

THE PRECURSOR TO MERCOSUR

According to Antônio Salazar P. Brandão, it was the return to democracy in Brazil and Argentina which was the key element in the diplomatic rapprochement between the two countries. To the author, it is important to remember that the military dictatorship in Brazil had started as far back as 1964. Also military fascist dictatorships had existed in most Latin American countries over a long period of time[5]. These regimes had been aided and abetted - or at the best, tolerated - by the United States and a few other Western Countries.

Apart from the dreadful and inexcusable persecution of innocent civilians which has been well documented[6], these regimes also indulged in economic wastage. There were, especially in the case of Brazil, high levels of protectionism. Also, since there was little or no effective democratic control, these regimes ran up major international debts. Following the 1982 debt crisis, countries indulged in competitive devaluations, protectionism increased and inter-regional trade decreased (see: Table 1). In the cases of most countries, there was an absolute, real decline in economic growth between 1982-86.

Table 1-1 Latin America – Intra-Regional Trade

Years	1980	1981	1982	1983	1984	1985	1986	1987	1988	1989	1990	1991	1992	1993
IAIA														
Share of Intra-IAIA Exports	13.8	14.3	12.3	8.5	8.9	8.0	11.0	10.7	10.6	11.0	10.9	13.6	16.8	19.2
Growth of exports to IAIA		8.9	-18.2	-28.4	16.6	-12.9	11.3	8.2	14.1	14.3	10.2	22.3	29.0	21.8
Growth of total exports		5.2	-5.3	3.6	11.6	-2.5	-19.4	10.9	15.3	10.8	10.6	-1.6	4.4	6.4
Andean Group														
Share of Intra-Andean Exports	4.0	4.9	4.6	3.3	2.9	2.6	3.4	5.1	4.7	4.1	4.2	6.0	8.0	9.7
Growth of exports to Andean Group		5.9	-7.3	-36.2	-3.5	-5.4	-8.9	65.5	-8.5	5.9	33.0	33.9	26.1	28.8
Growth of total exports		-13.5	-2.5	-10.7	10.8	3.8	-29.5	10.5	-2.0	22.5	30.5	-7.2	-4.7	5.7
MERCOSUR														
Share of Intra-MERCOSUR exports	11.6	8.9	8.1	5.9	6.3	5.5	8.6	7.4	6.6	8.2	8.9	11.1	14.3	18.5
Growth of exports to MERCOSUR		-11.6	-22.2	-22.0	25.4	-15.1	34.3	-3.6	16.4	30.4	7.6	23.6	41.4	38.9
Growth of total exports		15.0	-14.1	6.5	17.2	-3.2	-13.2	11.7	31.5	3.7	-0.3	-1.1	10.0	7.3

Source: CEPAL: Quoted from FGV Documents

To the credit of the newly elected democratic governments in Argentina and Brazil, moves were made at diplomatic levels to deepen the links between the two countries. In the 1970's one of the most important areas of controversy had been that of border disputes and the control of river waters. This problem area was the one that was immediately tackled by the new democratically elected governments. The next most important event in deepening relations was the signing, in 1986, of the Programme for Integration and Economic Co-operation (PICE) between Argentina and Brazil. This agreement comprised 24 individual sectors covering trade especially in capital goods, wheat and the automobile industry. It also included co-operation in technology and the supply of energy and other fields of activity.

Maybe surprisingly, only two years after the signing of the PICE Treaty, Argentina and Brazil signed a new treaty aiming at the creation of a common market.

This agreement, between the two most important countries in Latin America, was the real catalyst which led to the creation of MERCOSUR. In fact, with the agreement, Argentina and Brazil did hope to complete a common market by 1995.

Since Argentina and Brazil had therefore already embarked upon the road to creating a common market, it was both logical and simple for those countries to further extend this process by bringing Paraguay and Uruguay into the arrangement. Thus, the Treaty of Asunción, which created MERCOSUR, was signed between the four countries in March 1991. Subsequently, in December 1996, Chile became an associate member. In December 1996, negotiations were concluded to extend associate membership to Bolivia.

OTHER CONSIDERATIONS

The author cannot emphasise enough the two major factors which were indispensable to the creation of and subsequent success of MERCOSUR. These factors are the return to democracy by Latin American countries and the companying implementation of sober economic and monetary policies by these countries.

Without a return to democracy, a diplomatic rapprochement between Argentina and Brazil would have been unthinkable. Here, it is most important to bear in mind that the initiative for this rapprochement and for the creation of a common market did come from the governments and not from the business sectors.

In the field of economic and monetary policies, it should be remembered that these countries had experienced a period of "hyper inflation." In the case of Brazil, the annual rate of inflation had reached 2,400 per cent until the Plano Real Reform of August 1994. Thus, monetary reforms, some degree of privatisation and a reduction in the public debt were all indispensable policy changes if a deep degree of regional integration was to be achieved.

Argentina was really the first of these two countries to tackle the problem of "hyper inflation." This was done during the period 1989-91. Then, other reforms - especially concerning the reduction in the public sector - were introduced. Also, as from 1991, a "hard" exchange rate was introduced for the Peso which was linked with the US dollar.

Since 1991, Brazil had indulged in rather spasmodic attempts at fiscal and economic reforms. Then, in August 1994, with the introduction of a new currency, the Real, and the implementation of the "Plano Real", by Henrique Cardoso, the then Finance Minister, now the President of Brazil, things started to change. The new currency was expected to fluctuate in a relatively narrow band of fluctuation. According to Heinz-Georg Preusse[7], the new Brazilian currency had been revalued whereas the Argentine peso had, in fact, been devalued. It was, therefore, to be expected that Brazil would deflate, and, inflation would fall to between 2 and 3 per cent per month.

MERCOSUR: AIMS AND INSTITUTIONS

There is some similarity between the original European Economic Community (EEC) with its Six Founder Member States and MERCOSUR and its four Founder Member States. In 1958, in the case of the Six, France and Italy (and to a certain degree, the Netherlands) were interested in expanding their markets for their agricultural exports. In contrast, Germany wished to expand the export markets for its industrial products and manufactures. Belgium and Luxembourg, although, like Germany, industrialised societies, see themselves as major service centres. Italy also wished to export its unemployed nationals to its partners.

The similarity (at first sight, at least) between France and Germany in the old EEC and Argentina and Brazil in the MERCOSUR is striking. Argentina seeks export markets for its agricultural surpluses, Brazil for its manufactures. In turn, Uruguay sees itself as a service centre with a highly educated workforce. Paraguay sees itself as an entrepôt and a supplier of energy.

There are, however, major trade dissimilarities between Argentina and Brazil. Argentina, which does not have important domestic industries for capital and consumer goods, imposed zero import tariffs on such products. In contrast, Brazil is the most important producer of such goods in Latin America and has tended to protect her industries with relatively high tariffs. Consequently, these Brazilian sectors were not prepared to face the competition of free international trade.

In the negotiations leading to the signing of the Treaty of Asunción, both major partners compromised. Argentina did not demand a high Common External Tariff (CET) for its agricultural products. In turn, Brazil agreed to let Argentina gradually implement a reasonable CET over a period of time.

THE ECONOMIC AIMS OF MERCOSUR - TARIFFS

Clearly, the Member States of the MERCOSUR wish to enjoy the dynamics of regional integration. They wish to create a large internal market (somewhat similar to EU's Single Market) and thereby to enjoy economies of scale, standardisation and long production runs. In turn, their international negotiating power - particularly regarding trade issues - will improve.

In terms of tariffs, the final agreement reached achieved modest levels for the CET. The range is from 6 - 20 per cent - considered quite reasonable by international standards.

All four countries were allowed lists of exceptions for these products, it is expected that free trade between the Member States and the imposition of a CET will be reality by 2000.

Regarding capital goods, it was agreed that a CET of 14 per cent will come into force in 2001. For computers and some telecommunications products a CET of 16 per cent will be imposed in 2006. Consequently, MERCOSUR will only become a customs union in 2006. Currently, about 90 per cent of products move freely between Member States.

THE INSTITUTIONAL FRAMEWORK

Following the Signing of the Ouro Preto Protocol at the end of 1994, the MERCOSUR became endowed with a legal status, thus empowering the regional group to negotiate internationally.

As with the EU, the highest body is the MERCOSUR Council. This body is composed of the foreign and finance ministers of the four Member States. As with the EU, the presidency of the Council is held, on a rotating basis, for 6 months. The council must meet at least once every six months - with all the Presidents in session.

However, the real decision-making bodies are the MERCOSUR Group and the Trade Commissions. These bodies are made up of government officials. They are assisted by a number of technical sub-committees[8].

At a secondary level, there exists a parliamentary commission, composed of representatives of the four parliaments. Also, there is a consultative forum made up of private business leaders and representatives of trade unions. In some ways, this body is similar to the consultative Economic and Social Committee of the European Communities.

Finally, there is a modest secretariat, located in Montevideo. Unlike the EU, this body does not have powers similar to those enjoyed by the European Commission. In reality, the MERCOSUR Secretariat resembles more the EFTA Secretariat, in Geneva.

There exists an interesting complaints procedure. When a complaint is made, an attempt, using advice given by the technical committees, to reach a consensus. If this fails, then recourse is made to the Brasilia Protocol of 1991. Here a judicial panel is set up made up of one judge from each party to the dispute - plus one independent judge.

OTHER CONSIDERATIONS: DE-REGULATION AND PRIVATISATION

It is very important to note that Argentina and Brazil have undertaken important steps to deregulate their economies. Paraguay and Uruguay have both tended to link their de-regulation measures with those of their two more important neighbours. In all cases, de-regulation concerns agriculture the privatisation of state enterprises and banking.

AGRICULTURE

As with privatisation, it was Argentina which led the way in de-regulating (mainly price support) agriculture somewhat earlier than Brazil. Thus, in the late 1980's and early 1990's, Argentina de-regulated agriculture. Here, the author assumes that the Uruguay Round had some influence on these moves. Both Argentina and Uruguay opened up their agro-administration.

It is sometimes forgotten that Brazil had a heavily financed and important agricultural policy - similar to the Common Agricultural Policy (CAP) of the European Union. As with the CAP, the main mechanism was a policy of price guarantees. In the early 1990's, Brazil reduced this support to negligible levels.

In the early 1990's Uruguay introduced three levels of low tariffs on agricultural imports. Paraguay has tended, gradually, to align its agricultural reforms with those of Brazil.

PRIVATISATION

Argentina has led the way with major waves of privatisation. During the period 1990-93, Argentina privatised enterprises in 18 major sectors. The value of these privatisation's was approximately 17,972.6 million US dollars.

In contrast, Brazils' attempt at privatisation are fraught with greater difficulties because of national sentiment opposed to much sales - as well as the opposition of specific interest groups. The best example of this conflict has been the major opposition by citizens, legislators and lawyers to the privatisation of the giant iron ore mining company, Comanhia Vale do Rio Doce, in April and May, this year. Also it should be noted that the Brazilian constitution does demand that certain sectors of the economy remain under public ownership. This is especially the case for the oil industry. During the period 1991-95, Brazil nationalised enterprises in 9 major sectors with a value of approximately 12,259.1 million US dollars.

As with their major neighbours, both Paraguay and Uruguay are taking steps to privatise state enterprises.

BANKING

The banking legislation in the MERCOSUR is similar to that of the EU. In both cases, freeing capital movements requires the adoption of legislation about open-ness and basic liquidity requirements.

In this field, both Argentina and Uruguay had led the way by opening up their banking sectors between 1989 and 1991. Subsequently, at the level of the MERCOSUR, banking legislation guarding privatisation and liquidy requirements was codified in January 1994, in the protocol of Basiléia.

PROGRESS AND PROBLEMS

According to the statistics in Table 1, there has been a substantial growth in intra-MERCOSUR trade. The main growth, as was expected, has been between Argentina and Brazil. This has not been without problems. Shortly after the introduction of the Plano Real, the Brazilian currency appreciated by some 40 per cent. Whilst this provided a salutary deflationary impetus for Brazil, it made Brazilian exports less attractive price-wise. In contrast, Brazil, between 1991 - 94, had been enjoying a B.O.P. (Balance of Payment) surplus. Thus, in June 1995, Brazil announced it would impose car import quotas as from 1st January, 1996. Fortunately, Argentina and Brazil were able to solve this problem just as these quotas were to come into effect.

The outcome of this compromise was an agreement whereby a company located in one of the two countries may import (free of tariffs) vehicles and parts from the neighbour - so long as they match imports with exports. However, Argentina will enjoy a tariff-free export quota of vehicles of 85,000 until the end of 1998.

With this agreement, it is clear that the aim of the two countries is to create a world centre for vehicle production. To achieve this, they hope (and have, to a large degree succeeded) to encourage capital investment by discouraging imports of vehicles from third parties.

Subsequently, in July 1996, Brazil decided to impose, unilaterally, import quotas and tariffs on third party imports - notably on cars and textiles. This led the World Bank, in October of the same year, to criticise the world trade distortionary effects of MERCOSUR.

OVERVIEW: TOWARD THE FUTURE

In a relatively short period of time, MERCOSUR has achieved many of its aims. The majority of tariffs have been removed between the Member States and a CET had been imposed for many products. Trade has consequently increased between these countries. Signs of the economic success and the political potential of the MERCOSUR are the signing of a framework agreement with the EU and the association agreements with Chile and Bolivia. Also negotiations are in progress with Mexico to prepare a trade agreement. However, the organisation does find itself at a critical cross-roads.

There are signs that the basic infrastructure of the organisation will not be strong enough to sustain further economic growth and integration. In the specific case of Brazil, for example, it is doubtful whether there are enough educated and well-trained workers at an intermediate level.

Then there is the burning issue of co-ordination of economic and monetary policies. Whilst Argentina and Brazil have adopted hard monetary policies, they are applied in different ways. Here, one question is, should the Real be devalued? Also, is Brazil privatising its state-owned industries quickly enough?

Lastly, as the MERCOSUR Member States become more integrated, which is certainly a success story by Latin American records, the question must be raised whether it is desirable and necessary to transform the MERCOSUR Secretariat into an EU type Commission. The author believes that it will be necessary to set up some form of co-ordinating body.

SUBSEQUENT DEVELOPMENTS

During the month of April, this year, following the decision of Peru to withdraw from the Andean Pact (now known as the Andean Community), it was agreed to admit Panama as a new member. It is expected that it will take about 5 years for Peru's withdrawal to be fully effective. Since Bolivia will become an associate member of the MERCOSUR, a merger between that organisation and the Member States of the Andean Community can be expected. In a letter to the Financial Times, on 28th April, Ambassadors Gustavo Aliaga and Alfredo Pinoagote, pointed out that Peru's tariffs of 15 or 25 percent, on top of an 8 percent surcharge, were way above the tariffs of its partners.

[1] The members of LAFTA were Argentina, Bolivia, Brazil, Chile, Colombia, Ecuador, Mexico, Paraguay, Peru, Uruguay and Venezuela.[1]

[2]In "MERCOSUL - Perspectivas da Integração" edited by Antônio Salazar P. Brandão and Lia Valls Pereira, 1996, Fundação Getulio Vargas, Rio de Janeiro.

[3] The members of the Andean Group are Bolivia, Colombia, Ecuador and Venezuela. Chile had been a member but left for political reasons.

[4] The members are Costa Rica, Guatemala, El Salvador, Honduras and Nicaragua.

[5] The record of dictatorships in Latin America, as the following list indicates, is indeed a long one.

Paraguay: Alfredo Stroessner: 1954 - 1988
Ecuador: 1972 - 1979
Brazil: 1964 - 1985
Chile: 1973-1988
Argentina: 1976 - 1983
Uruguay: 1973 – 1985

[6]In particular, the case of the so-called "dirty war", is examined in some detail in Martin Edwin Anderson, "Dossier Secreto-Argentina's

Desaparidos and the Myth of the Dirty War" West Press, Boulder, Colorado, 1993. In a chilling lead article, the New York Times, on 6th October, 1996, examined the complicity of the United States in this repression, "Be all that you can be. Your future as an extortionist."

[7] Heinz-Georg Preusse, "Change in Development Strategies in Latin America - Another Transitory Move Towards an Open Market System?" in "Openness and Development," I.P Lang and R. Ohr (eds), Physica Verlag, Heidelberg, 1996.

[8] These technical sub-committees cover the following areas: communications, minerals, technical regulations, financial matters, transport and the infra-structure, the environment, industry, agriculture, energy, labour relations, business and social security.

Chapter 2
ARGENTINA AND THE CHALLENGE OF MERCOSUR

Jorge Lucángeli

INTRODUCTION

On March 26, 1991 in Asunción, Paraguay's capital city, the Treaty for the Establishment of a Common Market was signed by the Argentine Republic, the Federal Republic of Brazil, the Republic of Paraguay and the Oriental Republic of Uruguay. This agreement marks the crowning point of a process that began with the November 1985 Iguazú Declaration, by which Presidents Raúl Alfonsín and José Sarney expressed the will of the governments of Argentina and Brazil to accelerate the bilateral integration process.

Regional integration gained a renewed impulse and secured widespread backing, especially from the private sector, but also faced some resistance. This renewal of the integration vocation undoubtedly has its roots in political change underway in Southern Cone countries. The Latin American democratization process, spurning the national security doctrine, a loosening of the foreign debt tension, have all been factors with a positive influence on the renewal of this interest in integration and the renewed values attributed to its targets.

The central objective set down by the Treaty is the integration of Member States, through:

- The Free movement of goods, services and productive factors by, among other measures, the elimination of customs duties and non-tariff barriers and any other equivalent measures on the movement of goods.

- The establishment of a Common External Tariff and the adoption of a common trade policy for third party countries or groups of countries and the coordination of policy stances adopted in regional and international economic and trade forums.

- The coordination of macroeconomic and sectoral policies between Member States: in fields that include foreign trade, agriculture, industry, fiscal and monetary policies, foreign exchange and capital movements, services, customs, transport and communications, and others to be agreed on, in order to ensure adequate competitive conditions between member states.

- The commitment to harmonize legislation of member countries in pertinent areas, to reinforce completion of the integration process.

The final structure for the common market should have been achieved by December 31, 1994. During the transition period, lasting until that date, the member states adopted three basic tools. These were "General Rules of Origin", a "Dispute Settlement Procedure", and a "Safeguard Clause", all aiming to ease the definitive common market constitution.

Ouro Preto - a city in the Brazilian state of Minas Gerais which, on account of its attractive collection of Portuguese baroque art, in 1980 was declared by UNESCO to be part of the Human Cultural Heritage - was the venue chosen by the Brazilian Foreign Ministry for the seventh MERCOSUR Council meeting. The presidential summit conference of the four countries was held on December 16 and 17, 1994, and sealed the start-up of the Customs Union.

At this meeting, the Common External Tariff (CET) covering all of the tariff nomenclature was approved and became effective as from January 1, 1995. However, for capital goods it will only be fully applicable as from 2001, and for telecommunications and informatics full application must wait until 2006.

A List of Exceptions to the CET was also approved. Thus, for a number of tariff items, the CET was not applicable on January 1, 1995. The national tariff rates continue, with a timetable for convergence towards the AEC by 2001.[1]

At the Ouro Preto Summit another exceptional mechanism called the "Final Adjustment Regime towards the Customs Union" was also defined. At an earlier Common Market Council session held in Buenos Aires in August 1994 it had been agreed that member countries could submit a short list of products which would be excluded from the tariff liberation for intra-MERCOSUR trade. For this group of goods, after January 1, 1995 the tariff applied would be that charged on imports from the rest of the world - although, a 10 % tariff preference was granted for trade between member countries -. The aim of this adjustment mechanism was to preserve these products from free intra-regional trade.

At the Ouro Preto meeting it was also agreed that, until a common regime can be reached, the automobile, textile and sugar industries will remain subject to national rules laid down by each member country.

Together with the definition of a common external tariff and specific treatment for certain sectors, the MERCOSUR Council adopted a number of decisions to ensure a fluid trade in goods inside different national markets. A Technical Committee was set up to ensure that non-tariff barriers (NTB) - which are obstacles to fluid trade in goods - are dismantled and harmonized, by tracking the enforcement of decisions and also to maintain an updated list of NTBs.

Lastly, some public policies which mean granting subsidies or incentives to certain productive activities that imply spurious competitive conditions were also subject to review and harmonization between the partners. The presence of NTBs or other public policy tools bring about distortions and imply setting different rules of the game for economic agents operating in MERCOSUR. Based on their nationality, some firms are granted privileges. In this way, what is sought is to define a competitive regime in the broadest sense of the phrase. This ensures not only fair competition between private companies, but also restrains the management of public policies to grant incentives to firms from any country or to restrict market access.

It can be deduced from the comments above that the customs union established at Ouro Preto showed some imperfections and was also, to some extent, incomplete. The Customs Union also had exceptions to free trade in goods within the "enlarged market" because intra-regional trade was still subject to import duties on some products. As we will see below, after more than two years since the Ouro Preto Summit, further advances in the consolidation of the "broader market" have been quite poor and a number of restrictions on free movement of goods still prevail.

This contrasts with the accelerated integration process which took place after the Treaty of Asunción in 1991. Between March 1991 and December 1994 the integration process moved forward at an accelerated pace, but this dynamism fell off as from January 1995. The following pages try to examine factors that enabled an accelerated integration process in the Treaty of Asunción and the Ouro Preto Summit, and the factors which later delayed the deepening of the integration process.

HISTORICAL PRECEDENTS OF THE TREATY OF ASUNCIÓN

The LAFTA (Latin American Free Trade Association) was first established by a treaty signed in Uruguay's capital city, Montevideo, on February 18, 1960, and therefore known as the Treaty of Montevideo (As we will see below, 20 years later a 1960 suffix had to be added to the treaty's name in order to distinguish it from the

1980 agreement signed at the same venue defining the LAIA (Latin American Integration Association).

LAFTA aimed to build up a free trade zone within 12 years, a deadline which was later extended to 20 years. In this period all tariffs and restrictions that blocked commercial exchange between member countries had to be gradually eliminated. To carry out this process, negotiations had to be carried out on a regular basis with a mechanism which consisted in "National Lists" and a "Common List".

"National Lists" would include all concessions granted by each contracting party to the rest of the zone. It contained tariff concessions granted by each LAFTA member to its other partners, on the most favoured nation clause, but provided for the withdrawal of preferential tariffs from these lists should the country granting the concession be facing economic difficulties. The "Common List" was to be negotiated on a multilateral basis every three years. Products included on this common list couldn't be subject to non-tariff barriers, nor quotas.

The LAFTA member countries were unable to meet the targets laid down by the 1960 Treaty of Montevideo. LAFTA's failure may be traced, among other causes, to the ambitious objectives it had proposed. One must bear in mind that when the agreement was signed in 1960 Latin American countries were at the high point of the "import substitution strategy" and it could only be expected that dismantling tariffs between partners would be resisted.

At the beginning of the sixties, price instruments - based on import duties and additional taxes with a similar effect - were starting to replace foreign exchange controls and quantitative restrictions on imports with similar effect. Argentina had import duties of 91.5 %, as an average of all the tariff nomenclature. Other average rates were 40 % in Brazil, 41 % in Colombia; 49 % in Chile and 56 % in Venezuela. For manufactured consumer products, Argentina's average tariff rate was 110 %, Brazil 50.4 %, Colombia 100 %, Chile 83.4 % and Venezuela 111 %. (Macario, 1969).

Countries in the region - especially the larger ones - were each involved in a similar project: the development of their respective manufacturing industries. Therefore, they were unable to open their markets to competition by their regional partners. This meant that concessions granted in LAFTA were essentially concentrated on those products in which countries exhibited comparative advantages over their partners, and, therefore, weren't products which competed with those of other countries.

The poor capacity of LAFTA to recreate a free trade area led to a review of its legal instrument that culminated on August 10, 1980 when the LAIA (Latin American Integration Association) was founded by a new agreement also signed in Montevideo (commonly known as the 1980 Treaty of Montevideo, to distinguish it from the 1960 LAFTA precedent). [2]

LAIA set its final long-term target as setting up a Latin American common market. However, differing with LAFTA, it was more flexible. It lacked strict deadlines and also allowed for agreements between two or more countries which didn't have to be generalized to others. LAFTA applied the general most favoured nation clause that implied an automatic extension of concessions negotiated on a bilateral basis to the other member countries. LAIA, on the other hand, gave member countries the opportunity to negotiate agreements with a selective approach, allowing members to sign partial agreements in which not all countries are involved.

Although LAIA was valuable in promoting fluid trade between countries in the region, overcoming certain dissent in Argentine-Brazilian relations contributed enormously - as is only natural - to build the foundations of an integration agreement. The last great foreign policy issue which continued to affect bilateral relations was overcome with a Three Part Agreement on Corpus and Itaipú between Argentina, Brazil and Paraguay signed by the three countries in October 1979 which defined the levels for these hydroelectric dams.[3]

Conflict in the River Plate Basin had become more acute after 1966 as a result of the use of the water resources in the basin. The dispute revolved around the height at which the hydroelectric dams on the Paraná River were to be built. In order to reconcile the interests of the countries involved.

Argentina advocated a "prior consultation" mechanism that Brazil resisted. When Paraguay and Brazil signed the Itaipú Treaty in May 1973 to build the dam at that site, negotiations with Brazil had to be speeded up, because Argentina had already planned to build the Yacyretá and Corpus dams together with Paraguay downriver from Itaipú. Defining Itaipú's altitude became crucial for the feasibility of the two Argentine-Paraguayan hydroelectric projects. (Herrera Vegas, 1996) Cooperation continued with the signing of a nuclear cooperation agreement in 1980, which made reference to the exchange and training of technical staff, physical protection of nuclear materials, prospecting and developing uranium and nuclear security.

However, undoubtedly, the decisive factor favouring approaches by Argentina and Brazil was the return of both countries to democracy. Argentine military governments were always inclined to foster rivalry in the neighbouring country, to which they attributed an "imperial expansionist vocation". As a result, Argentine foreign policy during military governments stressed competition with Brazil instead of promoting cooperation and integration.[4]

Raúl Alfonsín, who was the Radical Civic Union party's candidate, became President in December 1983. The return to democracy after more than seven years of the cruellest military dictatorship Argentina has had led to significant economic and political changes. Argentina faced fierce isolation by Europe and the United States. In addition to complaints calling for the full application of human rights, was the scorn earned by the Argentine armed forces during the Malvinas war. President Alfonsín's government not only had to fight to rebuild democratic institutions, but also to strengthen Argentina's damaged international relations. But the "debt crisis" imposed severe limitations on the performance of the recently installed democratic government.

Although the Mexican government's decision to declare a unilateral moratorium on foreign debt payments in August 1982 is regarded as unleashing the Latin American debt crisis, this crisis had in fact been brewing since the 1979-1980 "oil shock". Argentina had to face both a foreign debt crisis as well as the consequences of defeat in the Malvinas war in 1982. The fiscal imbalance caused by the military conflict coincided with the end of external credit. When Alfonsín took office he had to face an enormous fiscal disequilibrium, with a public sector which had emerged as the Argentine economy's great debtor with neither internal nor external financing.[5]

The Radical administration's first year exposed the difficulties it had to face. In the third quarter of 1994 inflation had reached a 20 %

monthly rate, the gap between the "parallel" and official exchange rates was over 50 %. Also, and although it had been reduced, the fiscal deficit was still 7 % of GDP. It was therefore necessary to modify the economic policy which had been applied. On one hand, the need for a specific stabilization policy was acknowledged, beyond the mere call for a "price and wage agreement". On the other hand, upholding a disagreement with the United States was no longer feasible, as an agreement had to be secured with creditor banks on how to handle foreign debt. Both issues had mutual feedbacks: no agreement on foreign debt could be attempted without an adequate stabilization programme; but this wasn't feasible without an agreement with debtors that allowed for an orderly payment schedule.

The Austral Plan emerged from a review of the Radical government's initial economic strategy. It was designed with the immediate purpose of halting accelerating inflation, a process which was perceived as a serious threat to the continuity of a representative democracy which had only recently been secured. (Canitrot, 1992) It was understood to be a shock programme to rapidly bring the inflationary spiral under control, combining monetary and fiscal measures with a price and wage freeze and a system to convert contractual debts related to monetary reform. With an abrupt price deceleration, as was implicit in the plan, outstanding debts had suffered a sharp variation in their real value: the very high nominal interest rates had become equally high real rates when inflation halted. The Austral Plan included a debt conversion system to neutralize any wealth transfer which could have occurred as a consequence of disinflation. A new currency (the Austral) replaced the peso as the legal means of payment and debts in pesos were reexpressed in Australs according to a conversion scale that set the daily equivalence of both currencies. (Heymann, 1986)

The Austral Plan's results were soon visible in the falling rate of price growth. In the nine months after the programme was launched in June 1985 wholesale prices grew less than one percent per month, while consumer prices grew at a three per cent monthly rate. 1985 was a recession year, with a strong 4.6 billion dollar surplus in the trade balance, and the non-financial public sector's borrowing requirements were also lower. The following year GDP grew 5.7 %, gross fixed investment recovered, the current account again showed a surplus, although less than 1985, but the Consumer Price Index showed a 5% average monthly growth rate.

The Argentine-Brazilian integration process began, in this framework of a search for stabilization of macroeconomic variables. The initial instrument of the new integration scheme was the "Iguazú Declaration" signed at the border city of Iguazú on November 30, 1985 by presidents Raúl Alfonsín and José Sarney. "The permanent will of both peoples to grow increasingly close in their bonds of friendship and solidarity" was highlighted in this declaration. As a result of the declaration a Joint Committee was agreed on, with government and private sector representatives and presided by the foreign affairs ministers of both countries. As the product of the Joint Committee's labour, on July 29, 1986 the Argentine-Brazilian Integration Act was signed, establishing an Integration and Economic Cooperation Programme between the Argentine Republic and the Federal Republic of Brazil. On December 10, 1986 the Argentine-Brazilian Friendship, Democracy, Peace and Development Act was signed reflecting the unbreakable will of both nations to ensure success of the Integration and Economic Cooperation Programme.

The main tool in this first stage were "protocols"[6] that established mechanisms to reduce import duties and eliminate non-tariff barriers, through the inclusion of products in common lists agreed to on a mutual basis. On the occasion of six presidential meetings, the total number of protocols grew to 24.

The protocols signed between July 1986 and April 1988 covered a wide range of subjects and included trade agreements on a significant range of productive sectors. Among others, protocols covered Capital Goods, Wheat, Trade Expansion, Binational Firms, Energy, Biotechnology, Aeronautic Cooperation, Iron and Steel, Land and Ocean Transport, Nuclear Cooperation, the Automobile Industry and Food Industry (Castillo, 1993).

The Capital Goods Protocol was the "dynamic core" of the Integration Programme, from the outset. This was due to two basic reasons. Firstly, there was no primary sector allowing for an intrasectoral equilibrium between both countries. Secondly, in the capital goods sector, intensive use of flexible technologies and specialized manpower diminished Argentina's disadvantage against Brazil in scale economies and production costs. This sector also offered innumerable opportunities for joint investment and research, and had a considerable pull on other sectors of both economies.

In this protocol a universe of goods was agreed on, and then progressive negotiations of Common Positive Lists granted "national treatment", that is zero import duties and without non-tariff barriers, negotiating about half the universe. Starting with an initial list of 224 products in December 1986, 126 products were added in 1987; 129 in 1988; 640 in 1989 and 300 in 1990.

The aim of the Wheat Protocol was to ensure minimum sales volumes for Argentina. Export volumes were to be 1,375 million tons in 1987; 1,45 million tons in 1988; 1,55 million in 1989; 1,7 million in 1990 and 2,0 million tons for the 1991-1993 period. Wheat offered a strong base for mutual complementation, given Brazilian dependence on imported wheat. Brazil was on of the main customers for Argentine wheat and, viceversa, Argentina was one of the main suppliers of wheat to Brazil. This situation could correct part of the disequilibrium in trade between Argentina and Brazil.

The Trade Expansion Protocol proposed the gradual, sustained and balanced expansion of trade by the negotiation of tariff preferences for products, and the elimination of non-tariff barriers. Lists included on the protocol were Common Lists with zero duties. The main instrument was the LAIA Partial Scope Agreement that implied the renegotiation of mutual preferences which had already been granted. This renegotiation had a strong impact on trade which increased steadily from 1.4 billion dollars in 1987 to over three billion dollars in 1991, as most trade was channelled through this agreement. An equilibrium mechanism was also laid down, which would operate by granting larger preferences whenever the surplus of one party was more than eight percent of overall trade.

Through the Iron and Steel Protocol an enlarged market was sought to enable lower costs and a more intense exchange of goods to compensate mutual requirements of the industries located in both countries. A maximum tariff preference (zero import duty) was laid down for mutual supplies of iron and steel foundry products. After the protocol was applicable on December 10, 1987 trade in products negotiated showed a sharp increase in Argentine sales to Brazil, which grew from 652,000 dollars in 1987 to 59 million dollars in 1989.

Special characteristics of the sector delayed negotiation of the Automobile Industry Protocol which was finally concluded at the beginning of 1988. Its targets were to expand bilateral trade and production, reduce unit costs, increase percentages of national components, and stimulate investment in research and development in technology.

For the products negotiated (motor vehicles, car parts, and components manufactured in the territory of both countries) there was to be a zero tariff and no non-tariff barriers, with the exception of those negotiated by both countries. Annual quotas for trade in finished vehicles were agreed on, and also for the pertinent car parts included in common lists.

The Food Industry Protocol aimed at the growth at six-month intervals, from mid-1988 to the end of 1993, of a common list which began with 200 products. The elimination of tariff and non-tariff restrictions was agreed on, as were compatible plant health controls. The first extension included 115 additional products. In the first year this protocol was applied Argentine exports of food products to Brazil grew 18 %, especially for dairy products.

All these agreements enabled a significant increase in trade flows and laid the grounds to deepen the regional integration process.

THE TREATY OF ASUNCIÓN

The Integration, Cooperation and Development Treaty between the Argentine Republic and the Federal Republic of Brazil signed in

Buenos Aires in November 1988 consolidated the integration process between both countries. Its first stage envisoned removing all tariff and non-tariff barriers to trade in goods and services, a target to be secured over the following decade. A second stage, would proceed to gradual harmonization of all policies needed to establish a common market. This treaty was the first official statement of aims for a common market between both countries.

TABLE 2-1 ARGENTINA Trade with Brazil 1980 –1991 (million US $)

Year	TOTAL TRADE	Exports to Brazil	Imports from Brazil
1980	1,848.02	756.50	1,091.52
1981	1,466.79	586.58	880.22
1982	1,216.59	550.23	666.36
1983	1,012.68	358.07	654.61
1984	1,364.01	510.90	853.11
1985	1,017.10	468.87	548.24
1986	1,415.32	736.99	678.34
1987	1,406.47	574.69	831.78
1988	1,686.49	707.10	979.39
1989	1,961.10	1,238.99	722.11
1990	2,044.82	1,399.68	645.14
1991	3,090.17	1,614.68	1,475.49

Source: CTIC/DECEX/MEFP

The Buenos Aires Agreement was signed on July 6, 1990 and decided to establish a common market between the Argentine Republic and the Federal Republic of Brazil which had to be completed by December 31, 1994. The Buenos Aires Agreement is the closest precedent for the Treaty of Asunción, and the instruments and institutions laid down in the Act were later built into the MERCOSUR framework.

The Buenos Aires Agreement included two attachments. Attachment I detailed the methodology to build a common market. This was based on two fundamental pillars: the first was generalized, linear and automatic tariff rebates to arrive at December 31, 1994 with zero import duties; the second was the need to coordinate and harmonize macroeconomic policies between both countries.

Attachment II set up a Binational Working Group to Develop a Common Market between the Argentine Republic and the Federal Republic of Brazil with the task of debating and proposing all measures to enable compliance with the aims and deadlines laid down by the Buenos Aires Agreement.

With only a few changes, the Treaty of Asunción defined administrative and executive organs for MERCOSUR similar to those defined in the Buenos Aires Agreement. The Common Market Council (CMC) is the supreme organ in the common market. It has the political leadership and takes decisions to ensure that targets and schedules are met. Its members are the foreign affairs ministers -who are entrusted with coordination - and the economy ministers of each of the member states. The CMC meets whenever its members feel it is required, but at least once a year it must meet with the presidents of each of the contracting parties. Other ministers or authorities with a ministerial rank may also be invited to take part in meetings. The Council is presided on a rotary basis, changing every six months.

The Common Market Group (CMG) is the common market's executive organ and must see that the treaty's clauses are being met, propose concrete measures towards the application of the Trade Liberation Programme, coordination of economic policies and the negotiation of agreements with third parties, set the working schedule that ensures advances towards the common market, and establish Working Sub-groups to fulfil these objectives. The CMG is made up with four members and four alternate members who represent the foreign ministry -which coordinates the Group-, the economy ministry (in the fields of industry, foreign trade and/or economic coordination) and the central bank of each of the member countries. The CMG meets at regular or extraordinary sessions. Regular meetings are held on a rotary basis in alphabetical order every three months and extraordinary meetings are called at any time at the request of any contracting party at a venue to be agreed on.

During the transition period a set of instruments was designed to allow for facilitation of the transition towards a customs union as from January 1, 1995. These mechanisms were:

A Trade Liberation Programme that consisted in progressive, linear and automatic rebates of import duties, together with the elimination of non-tariff barrier or equivalent measures, to arrive at December 31, 1994 with no tariffs on intra-regional trade. Tariff rebates started in January 1990 with a 40 % minimum preference for the full nomenclature (and in some cases a higher percentage) and was increased seven percentage points every six months, until December 31, 1994 would reach a 100 % import duty reduction for intra-MERCOSUR trade.

- Each of the four member countries submitted a List of Exceptions to the Trade Liberation Programme which had to be reduced gradually, and disappear on December 31, 1994 (Argentina and Brazil) or December 31, 1995 (Paraguay and Uruguay).

- Coordination of macroeconomic policies was to be carried out gradually and converging with the tariff liberation schedules and the elimination of non-tariff barriers.

- Definition of a Common External Tariff which should stimulate the external competitivity of member states and applicable as from January 1, 1995.

- The adoption of common sectoral policies, with the aim of optimizing the use of productive factors and their mobility, and achieve efficient operating scales.

To ensure the development of a common market various Technical Sub-Groups (TSG) were set up, with the aim of advancing on the harmonization of different sectoral and macroeconomic policies. The following sub-groups were established:

1) Trade affairs.
2) Customs affairs.
3) Technical standards.
4) Fiscal and monetary policy.
5) Land transport.
6) Ocean transport.
7) Industrial policy and technology
8) Agricultural policy.
9) Energy policy.
10) Macroeconomic policies.
11) Labour relations, employment and social security.

Technical sub-groups carried out an intensive task in harmonizing rules, to dismantle different barriers that affected fluid circulation of goods in a broader market. The most significant TSGs have been Trade Affairs TSG 1 with the most important task of surveying non-tariff restrictions affecting intra-zone trade; TSG 2's task concentrated on harmonizing Customs rules; while TSG 10 had the responsibility of defining the Common External Tariff (CET).

During the transition period, which lasted until December 31, 1994 MERCOSUR members adopted three basic instruments. These were a regime about General Rules of Origin, a Safeguard Clause system and a Dispute Settlement procedure. These all aimed at easing the definitive establishment of the Common Market.

The General Rules of Origin stated that a change in the nomenclature position would qualify a product as originated in MERCOSUR, if the goods' raw materials had not originated within one of the member states. However, if there was no tariff hop, a product would be regarded as original if its imported inputs were not more than 50 % of the FOB value. In this aspect, MERCOSUR adopted the LAIA rules of origin.

The Safeguard Clause mechanism, which is common to all free trade agreements, was to be applicable whenever imports of any product caused injury or threatened injury to a market as a result of a significant surge of imports originating in other member countries in a short period of time.

The Common Market Group was the organ applying safeguard clauses. In the light of a consultation submitted by the importing country affected, the CMG had to come out with a ruling in about a month. Criteria employed to apply safeguard clauses made reference to the share of production levels and local productive capacity affected by the imports from a member country, market share and the level of trade between the countries involved. To avoid interruptions of intra-regional trade flows, in all cases the safeguard clause mechanism included import quotas in the framework of the Trade Liberation Programme to be granted by the country affected.

Finally, the Treaty of Asunción included as Annex III a Dispute Settlement procedure. This would later be further defined by the Brasilia Protocol, which contemplated the mechanism to be used to settle disputes which could emerge in the Treaty's application. Although the Brasilia Protocol was approved in December 1991, it only became applicable on April 24, 1993, after congressional approval by the four MERCOSUR member countries. The Brasilia Protocol sets up a mechanism to solve disputes between countries - private parties cannot submit a claim - by designating ad hoc arbitrators, without a court with a permanent seat and, above all, without the supra-national essence of a tribunal. Ultimately, it was an instrument designed for the transition period.

DIFFICULTIES IN THE TRANSITION PERIOD

During the transition period MERCOSUR had to define a common external tariff - which would be applicable as from January 1, 1995 - a common trade policy and coordinate macroeconomic policy, as already mentioned above. These plans were somewhat ambitious, one must admit, and several obstacles had to be overcome, after calling on the negotiating skills of the four member countries representatives.

First, a relevant factor to bear in mind is that the regional integration process began with fairly complicated macroeconomic situations in the two largest countries in the region. Argentina launched its Convertibility Programme immediately after signing the Asunción Treaty, after going through an intense hyperinflationary period. Brazil was attempting its own adjustment process. While Argentina was putting its macroeconomic situation in order, Brazil was slipping fast into an intense inflation process.

Domingo Cavallo was named Argentina's Economy Minister in 1991, after President Carlos Menem - who had succeeded Raúl Alfonsín in 1989 - had tried to defeat the hyperinflation process with two earlier ministers. Cavallo's policy laid its foundations on three pillars:

i) A stabilization programme, called the Convertibility Plan.

i) Public sector reform.

ii) The privatization programme.

At the time Cavallo took office, the situation was complex and his menu had visible restrictions in the options available. Devaluing the currency was considered out of the question - previous experience had shown that a devaluation was immediately transmitted to prices - . He thus accepted the exchange rate prevailing at the time, and accepted launching his stabilization programme with an overvalued currency, at a fixed rate which wouldn´t impact on the price levels. The nominal exchange rate was set by Congress.

The Convertibility Law requires money supply to have its exact counterpart in the Central Bank´s foreign exchange reserves, at the one peso per dollar fixed exchange rate. Therefore, the exchange rate "anchored" prices. Money supply could no longer be set, because it had to meet a strict relationship with the external balance of payments. Convertibility ended - in this way - any chance of financing public spending with fiscal credit. (Canitrot, 1992)

To reinforce the foreign exchange anchor, the programme included opening the domestic market to imports, through the adoption of a three tier import duty structure - at 22 %, 13 %, and 5 % - which led to a significant drop in protection levels. Starting from an average nominal tariff level of 18.4 % in 1990, the new average import duty was at a 11.6 % nominal tariff rate (Lifschitz & Crespo, 1995).

From an inflationary viewpoint, the Convertibility Plan had positive results. Consumer prices grew 19 % between July 1991 and June 1992. However, as happens with programmes that combine a sharp deceleration in inflation rates with a fixed exchange rate, there was a strong expansion of activity levels. After a 6 % fall in 1989 and stagnation in 1990, during the next three years GDP then expanded 8.9 %; 8.7 % in 1992 and 6.0 % in 1993.

Positive results of Argentina's stabilization plan highlighted discrepancies in performance between the Argentine and Brazilian economies. Macroeconomic asymmetries did not help to relieve the already traumatic moments of transition towards a customs union. A rapid recovery of activity levels in Argentina, together with a fixed exchange rate, which from the outset started with a relatively overvalued parity caused a swift deterioration of the current account. The trade deficit with Brazil also suffered a sharp increase. In addition, depreciation of the Brazilian currency helped to improve the competivity of Brazilian products and weaken Argentina's trade balance with Brazil.[7]

Macroeconomic coordination announced by the Treaty of Asunción was becoming impossible to achieve. On one hand, the Convertibility Plan adopted by Argentina limited coordination due to the rigidity shown in a number of policy tools (exchange rate policy, monetary policy). As regards Brazil, it was only after the Real Plan was launched in mid-1994 that the political will to restrain inflation became evident, after having lived with unprecedented persistent rates of monthly price increases of over 30 %.

During the transition period, it proved impossible to advance on the macroeconomic policy harmonization front. Attempts to coordinate policies were directed at exchange policies, but never went very far. Argentina wanted to harmonize nominal exchange rates, because its own exchange was fixed, and thus, hoped to launch Brazil on a similar venture. Brazil, on the other hand, tried to curb fluctuations in its real exchange rate because it thought the Argentine nominal exchange rate was impossible to sustain over time.

Frustrated attempts at macroeconomic coordination - an often ambiguous concept - did no more than confirm the paradox that is inherent in the concept. In times of substantial instability - which has been a characteristic of the region's countries until very recently - "demand" for coordination of macroeconomic policies is very high; but the opportunity to "supply" coordination is very poor by countries that face processes marked by profound instability (inflation, trade deficits, fiscal imbalance, etc.). On the other hand, during moments when stability is reigning, coordination "supply" is very strong, however "demand" is weak, because it is no longer called for. (Heymann & Navajas, 1992)

In second place, with this macroeconomic scenario in the background, in mid-1993 negotiations to define the Common External Tariff (CET) began. It was agreed that the CET would have a maximum 20 % rate, with 11 different rates starting at 0 % and with incremental steps, each of two percentage points. For a few items, an exceptional 35 % tariff would also be set.

Negotiating the CET was a tough task, because no precise methodology was laid down about how to go about establishing these rates. Each country wanted its own tariff structure to prevail. Both Argentina and Brazil had drastically reduced their tariff levels. In mid 1993 Argentina's average tariff had increased to 13 %, while Brazil was somewhat higher. Nevertheless, the Statistics Fee - which had been increased from 3 % to 10 % at the end of 1992 - had to be added to import duties in Argentina. The increase in the Statistics Fee - which was originally a fee earmarked to provide updated foreign trade statistics - was used to halt the strong increase in imports, especially from Brazil. This manipulation of the Statistics Fee led to some difficulties in MERCOSUR negotiations, which were overcome through goodwill shown by Brazil in admitting the hike.

The definition of the CET had to meet certain conditions:

i) An average tariff of about 11 %.

ii) Widely used raw materials were to be placed in the lower stages, between 6 % and 12 %.
iii) Consumer goods would be near the top of the range.
iv) The automobile sector would be granted special treatment.

Other sectors eligible for special treatment were capital goods, and informatics and telecommunications. In May 1993 Argentina brought down import duties for these products to 0 % and eliminated the Statistics Fee on these items. Therefore, capital goods, and data processing and telecommunications became duty-free items. This Argentine decision - based on the need to speed up the modernization and investment in the productive sector - led to serious difficulties in MERCOSUR negotiations because:

i) It perforated tariff preferences which had been granted to Brazil.
ii) It complicated CET negotiations with Brazil, which wanted a tariff level around 20 % for these products.

Brazil's capital-goods industry is in the middle stages of development, which is relatively efficient in some ranges of conventional capital equipment, such as agricultural machinery, tractors, buses and trucks, compressors and machine tools. For these products, Brazil is an important supplier to Argentina and other LAIA countries. This was the reason why it complained about "perforated preferences". Bringing down import duties to zero for the rest of the world placed Brazilian manufacturers on the same competitive footing as capital goods of any other origin. Argentina proposed, for such cases, granting a compensation to Brazilian manufacturers who had been harmed by its decision. However, in practice, this compensation never became really effective.

The Argentine measure hampered CET negotiations over capital goods. Argentina was not prepared to accept a CET which was far from zero, while Brazil wanted to continue protecting its "infant industry" in capital equipment and data processing.

In third place, completing the customs union involved harmonizing trade policy. This called to harmonize export incentives, to establish rules of origin for products with CET exceptions, to deal with free trade zones, to dismantle non-tariff barriers, among others. While Argentina proposed that the CET be defined as part of a package that would also include the full range of trade policy tools and the treatment of certain asymmetries stemming from government action (public sector subsidies), Brazil wanted to conclude CET negotiations independently from settling the other issues.

Argentina hoped that, in addition, certain manufacturing industry branches would be granted a special treatment in intra-regional trade, however. At the end of 1993 and throughout 1994, MERCOSUR was challenged fiercely, especially by the AIU (Argentine Industrial Union), an umbrella organization of chambers and business associations representing different manufacturing activities. AIU has traditionally been the spokesman of the interests of Argentina's large manufacturing and business groups.

What was AIU calling for? Leading businessmen in industry claimed that the MERCOSUR integration process had advanced at a very fast pace. Therefore, Argentine industry had been unable to achieve the competivity levels called for by an integration process. AIU's proposal was politically unacceptable because it called for application of the Customs Union to be delayed beyond the January 1, 1995 deadline.

Economy Minister, Domingo Cavallo didn't relish establishing the MERCOSUR Customs Union either. As integration advances, there are fewer degrees of freedom available to manage economic policy. A customs union presumes all member countries have declined indiscriminate management of trade policies, as all decisions must have the partners' consent. Cavallo's worry was that establishing a customs union also implied abdicating trade policy management, when, under the Convertibility Law he had already resigned exchange and monetary policies. The only remaining economic policy tool left to him was fiscal policy, a delicate instrument with Argentina's past history of chronic fiscal deficits. Nevertheless, despite having shown a preference for a free trade area rather than a customs union, the MERCOSUR timetable still went ahead.[8]

At this stage, the question to answer is, What was moving manufacturing executives to oppose the integration process? The answer must be traced to the poor competitive conditions shown by Argentina's manufacturing industry. This low degree of efficiency was widespread, but was especially evident in the relationship with Brazil and, especially, in sectors producing widely used raw materials, such as iron and steel and pulp and paper.[9]

The pulp and paper industry had gone through a long period of stagnation in the eighties - when production grew at a 1 % yearly rate -, which had left it technologically backward. Most capacity had been installed in the 1958-1975 period. In this manner, when demand began to grow in the early nineties, and MERCOSUR tariff preferences began to show their effect, the sector started to suffer serious trade imbalances, especially with Brazil. Until 1990, the sectoral foreign trade balance for pulp and paper had shown a surplus for Argentina - of about US$ 123 million -, but by 1993 the balance had become negative by about US$ 400 million, of which about 40 % was due to Brazil.

Brazil had aimed to improve the competivity of its pulp and paper industry through modernization. As well as considerable investment in new plants, substantial efforts were made to improve training in technology, and product and process management, leading several firms to obtain their ISO 9000 certification. Investment on stream by 1991 led to a new pattern for the sector, by increasing concentration in production and improving overall scales in the sector (Fontanals, 1994).

The case of Argentina's iron and steel industry was slightly less pressing than that of the pulp and paper sector. Industry restructuring had started in the mid-seventies with two direct reduction plants, the incorporation of new technologies to increase productivity and steel quality, the disappearance of semi-integrated firms and a strong concentration in supply (only three firms accounted for 80 % of production). But until the early nineties it was still a sector subject to strong regulations, high levels of protection and significant export incentives.

When the Convertibility Plan started up, and its dismantling of regulatory frameworks ensued, the iron and steel sector had to face a new situation with more competition. The outlook changed abruptly for industry, with the privatization of SOMISA - the government-owned company producing pig-iron which was awarded to the Techint group - owners of Siderca, a firm producing seamless tubes for the oil industry, and Siderar, a manufacturer of rolled products, - the elimination of non-tariff barriers to imports - which called for authorization by a government body, - a sharp fall in import duties and the elimination of price preference for domestic companies in public sector procurement.

The Brazilian iron and steel industry is one of the largest in the world - ranking eighth among leading producing countries at the start of the nineties - making over 20 million tons a year, a volume six times the size of Argentina's total capacity. Towards the end of the eighties a profound transformation of the regulatory framework and government presence in the sector began. Together with the privatization of state-owned companies, the deregulation of iron and steel production began, and import duties dropped. Opening up the market to imports ensured that firms wouldn't take advantage of the end of price controls to abuse with monopolistic practices.

Although iron and steel sectors in both countries had undertaken a major effort to gain efficiency, Brazil continues to hold certain advantages in products with little added value where access to iron ore is significant - the country has one of the most important reserves in the world - and scales of production marked by market size have an influence on average costs - for example, cold and hot rolled flat products -. Argentina has competitive advantages as a producer of seamless tubes, where Siderca has an international level efficiency, and in the production of special non-flat steel products, where scale and raw material costs are less signficant (Fontanals, 1994).

Pausing to examine some details of the performance of the pulp and paper industry and the iron and steel industry is justified as a requisite to understand the stance adopted by the Argentine government during the transition period. As the Trade Liberation

Programme included in the Treaty of Asunción went forward, competitive difficulties started to appear in some sectors. In the first place, Argentina's officials fell back on the safeguard clause mechanism, allowed for by the treaty during the transition period. Between mid-1992 and mid-1994 16 applications for safeguard clause rulings were approved. Five were for the paper industry, two for tyres, four for refrigerators and compressors, while the others were for wood, bolts, aluminium kitchenware, porcelain insulators and high density polyethylene. The following table lists the safeguard clauses approved.[10]

Other requests were rejected, including filings for wood products, vinyl fabrics, polypropylene products, farm products, footwear, among others. It may be noted from the table that iron and steel products were not subject to safeguard clauses, a situation that also calls for an explanation. The Trade Liberation Programme, as mentioned above, included a number of exceptions, whereby each country was entitled to set a list of tariff items which remained excluded from the tariff reduction schedule. Argentina included 394 items and, together with Brazil, its list had to be reduced 20 % each year. The final 20 % tranche of about 80 items was largely (around 60 products) steel products. Therefore, excluded from free intra-zone trade, producers did not call for safeguard clauses.

Under pressure from some industrial sectors, prior to the Ouro Preto summit, the Argentine government proposed three mechanisms to the

TABLE 2-2 Products with Argentine Safeguard Clause Approval 1992-1994

Products	1993 Imports (1,000's US dollars)			
	# items	MERCOSUR	Rest of world	Total
Corrugating medium paper	4	14,551	5,570	20,121
Glassine/Tytanium bioxide papers	1	4,437	187	4,624
Kraft paper	7	8,127	11,743	19,870
Bond paper	3	13,626	209	13,835
Coated papers	7	2,530	8,351	10,881
Car tyres	1	12,582	10,073	22,655
Tractor tyres	1	2,121	478	2,599
Household refrigerator compressors	1	31,670	5,355	37,025
Porcelain electricity insulators	1	1,778	205	1,983
Household compression refrigerators	1	23,512	15,761	39,273
Horizontal freezers	1	9,906	519	10,425
Vertical freezers	1	7,913	637	8,550
High density polyethylene	1	27,532	10,682	38,214
Screw nuts	1	3,298	3,246	6,544
Aluminium kitchenware	1	4,785	1,185	5,970
Wooden furniture	1	5,252	1,171	6,423

Source: Trade and Investment Secretariat, Economy Ministry

VI Common Market Council meeting which took place in Buenos Aires on August 5, 1994, which could be enforced together with the Customs Union:

i) Structural Adjustment Agreements.
ii) Intra-MERCOSUR Safeguard Clauses.
iii) A MERCOSUR Trade Commission.

Structural Adjustment Agreements were designed to ease the reconversion process of specific productive sectors, by spurring specialization policies, sub-contracting policies, eliminating asymmetries and ensuring the defence of competition, technological development and extension and access to improved levels of competitivity.

Intra-MERCOSUR Safeguard Clauses were to be a complementary instrument to the structural adjustment agreements, whereby, during the duration of the latter a country could fall back on safeguards whenever imports from a member country affected in a noticeable manner production in a sector included in the agreements.

Both these instruments were flatly rejected by the Brazilian delegation, who claimed that they were a severe distortion to the essence of a customs union. Once again, differences that had been with a large part of the MERCOSUR transition period emerged: Argentina was reluctant to establish a customs union, while Brazil exerted pressure to achieve this customs union at any cost.

Where there was agreement was to set up a Mercosur Trade Commission (MTC), an organization which would later be approved at Ouro Preto. The MTC proposal came from Argentina, who felt that for the Customs Union to work an agile organization was needed in MERCOSUR to oversee the application of common trade policy tools agreed on by the contracting parties. The MTC has been a fundamental component in MERCOSUR's institutional framework. Among its tasks and scope it has been acknowledged as the first stage in a claim submitted either by member states or by private parties (persons or legal entities).

SOME CONSEQUENCES OF THE INTEGRATION PROCESS DURING THE TRANSITION PERIOD

Economic theory hasn't been generous in providing a tool kit to measure the benefits of economic integration in an adequate manner. This section tries to measure the impact of the integration process through intra-regional trade performance, although, as some authors suggest - trade may not necessarily be the most relevant variable by which one can assess an integration process -. In fact, an integration process is essentially a political process and, therefore, it is from this viewpoint that it should be examined.

It is important to examine what occurred with the integration process in the transition period because, as we have mentioned, and despite the difficulties and obstacles highlighted in the previous section, some indicators show the MERCOSUR project maturing fast during the 1986-1994 period, and especially in the four years 1991 to 1994.

Total exports of MERCOSUR countries to the region grew more than 350 % between 1986 and 1994. This result is in marked contrast with the increase of exports to other destinations: between both years, where growth in exports was only 80 % (See Table 7).

Of course, if the incidence of intra-MERCOSUR trade is compared to all trade, it is still far from being considered satisfactory. Thus, in 1995 intra-MERCOSUR exports were 20.5 % of all exports, but in 1986 the percentage of intra-MERCOSUR exports was less than 9 % of the total, while imports were about 12 %. As we can see, although these are still somewhat low percentages, in recent years the share has grown considerably. The regional market now has a noticeable dimension.

However, it is also important to note the differential impact of MERCOSUR trade for each of the member countries. For smaller countries - Paraguay (57 %) and Uruguay (47 %) - MERCOSUR is a significant export destination. Brazil emerges with the least "dependency" on this alliance, as only 14 % of its exports are to MERCOSUR destinations.

Argentina is in an intermediate position. In 1996, a third of all its exports were shipped to MERCOSUR partners. But MERCOSUR's share in Argentine exports has grown vigorously since the first agreements with Brazil. In 1985, member countries absorbed 8 %, less than a tenth of all Argentina's exports; by 1990 the share had increased to 14.8 % and in 1994 was already about 30 % (See Table 8).

Another relevant aspect emerging from an analysis of intra-regional trade refers to the growth shown by trade in manufactures. While in the mid-eighties manufactures were somewhat less than half all intra-MERCOSUR trade, at the start of the nineties this share was approaching two thirds of all commerce. The strong trade growth was therefore concentrated in manufactured products.

This statement is especially significant for Argentina's trade with MERCOSUR. In 1995 and 1996 exports of manufactures averaged 62.5 % of shipments to the region. Nevertheless, what stands out is that in 1996 exports of manufactures of industrial origin (MOI) were 44 % of all exports to MERCOSUR, whereas their share in sales to the rest of the world had dropped to 19 %.[11] In 1985, the mix of exports to MERCOSUR had been 29 % of MOI and 26 % of manufactures of agricultural origin (MOA). The latter dropped to a 17 % share in 1996.

Another process worth noting in the regional integration experience is intra-industry trade (IIT), defined as two-way commerce between two countries - i.e. simultaneous exports and imports of products pertaining to the same industry - as distinct from inter-industry trade where trade exchanges are between different industries. As an indicator of IIT intensity, a coefficient ranging from 0 % to 100 % is used, indicating the share of intra-industry trade related to all trade within a given industry branch. When the value of imports exactly matches exports this coefficient is 100 %, while the absence of intra-industry trade would indicate a zero value.

Since the mid-eighties, intra-industry trade between Argentina and Brazil has been growing, although with some ups and downs. Between 1984 and 1991 IIT for manufactures has more than doubled: the coefficient was 49, which means half of all trade in manufactures was intra-industry trade.[12]

However, the IIT coefficient dropped sharply in 1992. With the exception of chemical products, the setback in the IIT indicator is fairly general for all industry. For the manufacturing sector as a whole, the coefficient fell to 32.8, while machinery and transport equipment show the sharpest drops with the IIT coefficient dropping by almost half. But, once again in 1993, intra-industry trade recovered the levels of earlier years, and the total for manufactures rose to 50.

1992 was an atypical year, because Brazilian exports to Argentina showed an increase of about 120 %, while Argentine exports to Brazil only expanded a mere 5 %. The growth in exports of Brazilian manufactures was somewhat higher than the aggregate, thus reaching an 84 % share. On the other hand, Argentine exports recorded a fairly even growth between manufactures and other goods, maintaining a 40 % share. This situation changed in 1993, a year when Argentina's exports of manufactures to Brazil grew 70 % over the previous year and, as a result, the share of industrial products in the export mix expanded to 42 %.

Bilateral trade in the automobile industry complex (AC) - finished vehicles, motors and car-parts - undoubtedly explain a significant part of the trade dynamics and shifts in intra-industry trade. The strong expansion of domestic demand eroded the grounds for "managed trade" in the automobile sector during 1992. AC imports were about a billion dollars, compared to 275 million dollars in 1991. But Argentine exports to Brazil also grew: from 144 million dollars in 1991 to 250 million dollars in 1992. In 1992, a quarter of all Argentine-Brazilian trade was in the automobile complex. But is also clear that the AC IIT coefficient dropped from 69 in 1991 to 40 in 1992.

In 1993, the AC IIT coefficient made a marked recovery and surpassed the 1991 figure, as it grew to 76. Causes must be traced to the smaller disequilbrium shown in the sectorial trade balance as a

TABLE 2-3 ARGENTINE-BRAZILIAN TRADE 1986-1996 Intra-Industry

Trade by SITC Sections

SITC Section	1988	1990	1991	1992	1993	1994	1995	1996
5 Chemical products	32.4	67.0	65.7	58.7	49.6	52.0	57.1	62.0
Other manufacturers classed by raw materials	13.6	34.4	25.7	16.9	27.9	27.3	42.6	44.1
7 Machinery and Transport equipment	45.0	63.2	60.2	34.4	60.9	64.3	70.7	63.3
8 Manufactured articles	51.4	37.6	73.5	32.3	37.9	37.8	58.2	56.2
Automobile industry complex	S/d	S/d	68.8	40.0	76.1	79.2	79.1	72.3
All manufacturers	32.2	54.5	49.0	32.8	49.7	51.6	60.4	58.5

Source: Lucángeli (1993) and own information based on INDEC data

result of strong growth in Argentina's AC exports towards Brazil (which grew 140). The need to meet commitments engaged as part of the improvement automobile industry agreement undoubtedly helped to improve the sectorial trade balance. But expansion in Brazilian demand for cars shouldn't be ignored either.

During the years 1994 and 1995, IIT continued to grow, and for manufactures as a whole the series peaked. 60 % of all commerce in industrial products is two-way trade. Despite these variations, the pattern shown by Argentine-Brazilian trade reflects a considerable degree of maturity, as befits countries which have arrived at a threshold of development and industrial diversity: Trade in manufactures prevails, and, of this, a major part is intra-industry trade.[13]

The European Economic Community's experience is an eloquent example. In the mid-eighties, EEC countries recorded - for all manufactured goods - IIT coefficients ranging between 50 % and 65 %. It is also in chemical products and machinery and transport equipment where we find the sectors where the intra-industry trade phenomenon appears as most intense. According to several authors (B. Balassa, D. Greenaway and P. Krugman, among others) in these industries both scale economies and product differentiation prevail, characteristics which are touted as the fundamental determinants of intra-industry trade. Whether it is due to the presence of lower costs or differentiated products, the goods exchanged are easily substituted in consumption and/or use similar inputs or stem from joint production techniques.

What has enabled this rapid expansion of intra-regional trade and intra-industry specialization? As we have mentioned in the introductory pages of this chapter, one of the relevant factors in the MERCOSUR transition period has been its impact on trade expansion. The integration process advanced very fast. The reply to the question has to be traced to two processes that occurred at the same time: together with the MERCOSUR Trade Liberation Programme, countries in the bloc opened up unilaterally to world trade.

During the transition period, MERCOSUR member countries agreed to grant tariff preferences to conclude in December 1994 with a full free trade zone, as mentioned in another section. This would mean zero import duty rates covering trade between member countries for all the tariff nomenclature. This tariff preference timetable was linear and automatic, starting with a minimum 40 % preference, and concluding with 100 % in December 1994.[14]

However, the incremental tariff preference schedule coincided with an unilateral trade liberalization process by the member countries to the rest of the world, which deepened the regional integration process even more. As can be observed in the table below, between the end of the eighties and the beginning of the nineties, the market opening of both Argentina and Brazil was significant.[15]

In the decade between 1985 and 1994, Argentina slashed its average import duty in half. Brazil's trade liberalization process was even more drastic, as its average import duty fell from a mean of 51 % in 1985 to 13.2 % in 1994. This meant that, after applying the tariff

TABLE no. 4 NOMINAL TARIFF DEVELOPMENTS (%)
Argentina & Brazil - 1985-1984

Year	Argentina	Brazil
1985	30.3	51
1988	30.0	38.5
1990	20.0	30.0
1991	11.6	23.3
1992	11.6	15.4
1994	14.3	13.2

Source: Lucángeli (1989), Lifschitz & Crespo Armengol (1995) and Kume (1996)

preference in MERCOSUR, import duties between partners resulted in a net tariff which was almost nil. Therefore, once barriers were dismantled, trade flows became very fluid.

What happened, to a certain extent, was that *de jure* integration did no more than provide an institutional content to *de facto* integration which had advanced with vigour. The successful decisions adopted by the governments of the member countries was precisely to ratify through political agreements a process that was underway naturally.

Paul Krugman (1991) has pinpointed the matter of spatial localization of production, a topic which had been almost forgotten by economists. In *Geography and Trade* he claims that simplifying models had led to suggest that production was carried out in an ideal space and that costs of transport are irrelevant. But, as soon as economies of scale are introduced and the effects of lower transaction costs are considered, production localization emerges as a relevant issue. In short, what Krugman and some other authors claim, is that geography, and space, matter.

This view is supplemented by what some authors claim are *natural blocs*. In so far as international trade is also influenced by transport costs and communications - as "geographical" factors underlying trade - there would be a strong tendency to engage in a more intense trade with neighbouring countries. Dismantling trade barriers and non-tariff barriers between neighbouring countries would thus result in a significant increase in commercial exchange between these neighbours. This theoretical framework is maybe the most appropriate to understand the fast growth of intra-regional trade during the transition period to MERCOSUR.

THE CONSEQUENCES OF OURO PRETO

The presidential summit meeting of the four MERCOSUR countries in the city of Ouro Preto, on December 17, 1994, defined the characteristics of the Customs Union which became applicable as from January 1, 1995. Basically the agreement included a CET for the full tariff nomenclature, although for capital goods it will only be applied as from 2001, or 2006 in the case of informatics and telecommunications. For Argentina, applying the CET also implied lower tariff protection regarding other countries, as the 10 % Statistics Fee was no longer charged.

The import duty structure defined at Ouro Preto had 11 levels, with a minimum duty of 0 % and a maximum tariff of 20 %, with intermediate steps increasing two percentage points. The average tariff was 11 % - disregarding capital goods - and import duties on widely used raw materials produced by the iron and steel, chemical and petrochemical, pulp and paper industries ranged below the average, between 5 % and 10 %. Fuel also had a fairly low import duty level - almost zero -. Final consumer goods, whether durables or non-durables, were close to the top of the range with average duties of 18 % or 19 %. Products in the food chain, especially processed foodstuff, were also above the average, at about 14 %.

The drop in average protection was fairly widespread, as has been mentioned above. On average, and disregarding capital goods and transport equipment, the average tariff dropped from 16 % before the CET was applied to 10.4 % after adopting common duties. For the so called widely used inputs the fall in protection is especially marked, especially for basic industrial supplies. Major reductions also occurred for consumer goods, especially semi-durables. On the other hand, for capital goods, parts and accessories and for transport equipment, nominal protection increased; although in the case of capital equipment, the new tariff schedule will only be applied as from January 2001[16] (See Table 10).

For *capital goods* a 14 % CET rate was set, while the CET for *data processing and telecommunications* was defined at 16 %, but in the latter case only applicable as from January 2006. For both capital goods and data processing and telecommunications a convergence mechanism towards the CET is applied, in some cases ascending (Argentina, Paraguay and Uruguay) and in the other case descending (Brazil). Meanwhile, for several capital goods and data processing and telecommunications tariff items, imports below the respective 14 % and 16 % duty levels were set.

The CET design allowed for certain products to be excluded from the common tariff. Argentina, Brazil and Uruguay could each submit a list of 300 items, while Paraguay was granted up to 399 items.

Argentina submitted a *List of Exceptions to the CET* for 231 tariff items which would converge towards the CET in the year 2001. In some cases the list is ascending, as the national import duty must increase to meet the CET in 2001. This segment includes 80 chemical products, which from tariff rates of 2 % and 8 % must increase to an average of 12 %.

For another significant group of tariff items, convergence is descending. Noticeable in this collection are paper and board (10 items), iron and steel products (37 items), electric household goods (17 items) and footwear (17 items) (See Table 11).

The Common Market Council also approved the list of products which would benefit from another exceptional mechanism known as the *"Final Adjustment Regime towards the Customs Union"*. In the meeting held in Buenos Aires on August 5, 1994 it had been agreed that member countries would submit a short list of products to be exempt from tariff preferences for intra-MERCOSUR trade. For this group of goods, the nominal tariffs applied for imports from the rest of the world as of December 31, 1994 would be applicable as from January 1, 1995 for trade between member countries - although a 10 % tariff preference was granted -. The aim of this mechanism was to shelter these products from free regional trade.[17]

How was the *Final Adjustment* list made up? As has already been mentioned, Argentina had proposed the signing of Structural Adjustment Agreements with its partners, aiming to support those sectors which were not able top compete in an enlarged market. The adjustment mechanism was thus the result of negotiations to provide a special treatment to some sectors with difficulties to compete with their MERCOSUR counterparties. The list was therefore made up with products which had been excluded from the final tranche of the Trade Liberation Programme during the transition period (80 tariff items) and products which had been subject to safeguard clauses, also during the transition period. Products included in the Adjustment Regime would have a final tariff liberation deadline in 4 years time.

The Argentine list had about 220 tariff items, where garments stand out (with approximately 40 items); sporting footwear; iron and steel sheets, cross sections, strips, bars, wire and tubes (about 100 items); some classes of paper (about 20 items); tyres and certain refrigerators. Garments started with an import duty of 27 % as of January 1, 1995; steel products paid 18 % (or 23 % in some cases); papers and tyres 23 %. The remainder ranged between 14 % and 23 %.

As can be noted from the list of products, as both exceptions to the CET and the Adjustment Mechanism, the iron and steel, paper, footwear (especially sportswear) and household goods managed to secure a preferential treatment both for extra-regional and intra-regional trade.

Textiles, garments and sporting footwear were subject to special treatment. Until a common import policy could be defined for the sector, each of the MERCOSUR member countries could apply measures against imports from the rest of the world. This implied that Argentina continued to apply specific import duties still applicable - and disputed within the WTO - but these duties are not applicable on intra-regional trade.

At the same time the Common External Tariff was being defined, with a special treatment for certain sectors, the MERCOSUR Council adopted a number of decisions to ensure fluid movement of goods within the broader market and allow free access to different national markets.

To ensure that non-tariff barriers (NTB) which hamper fluid goods shipments would be dismantled and harmonized, a Technical Committee was set up to follow-up on rules and also to keep an updated list of NTBs. Some NTBs which had already been identified ceased to be applicable as from January 1, 1995. In the case of *Argentina*, the most important NTB which was eliminated was the 10 % Statistics Fee applied to intra-regional trade. Another restriction that was eliminated refers to prior authorisation to import poultry and eggs for breeding purposes. *Brazil* promised to lift the ban on imports of recreational vessels, and authorisations to import wheat-flour, petrochemicals and some other products. *Uruguay* dismantled the prior import permits for wheat, flour and fertilizers and *Paraguay* lifted bans on the import of other products.

At Argentina's proposal, the establishment of a Technical Committee on *Public Policies Distorting Competition* was approved, with the purpose of identifying those public sector policy measures applied in any member country which could distort competitive conditions within the region due to their discriminatory character. This is the case of supply - by government-owned companies - of certain inputs at prices below the market level (iron ore, naphtha, or methanol), tax exemptions, credit lines at subsidized rates, etc.

The presence of these NTBs or public sector policies that affect competitivity introduces distortions and implies different rules of the game for economic agents within MERCOSUR. Some firms, on account of their nationality, are entitled to obtain certain privileges. In this manner, what is pursued is a competitive regime in a very broad sense, that ensures not only fair competition between private firms but which also represses the management of public policies that grant incentives to business from any specific country or restrict market access.

Another major achievement at Ouro Preto was the promise member countries made to work out a common automobile industry regime before December 31, 1997, to be applicable as from January 1, 2000. The mechanism to be laid out had to contain three basic elements: liberation of intra-zone trade, the definition of an import tariff structure for the sector, and the absence of national incentives distorting competitive conditions within MERCOSUR.

However, in addition to the commitment undertaken by all four countries by Decision 29/94, an agreement between Argentina and Brazil was also reached in order to consolidate access terms to the respective markets. For the purpose of computing the local content coefficient, Argentina acknowledged Brazilian car-parts as national within the Argentine automobile regime. On the other hand, for compensation of car parts to be imported, Argentine exports to Brazil would be multiplied by a 1.2 factor.[18]

Brazil, meanwhile, would grant national treatment to Argentine made car parts to meet the local content requirements under the then applicable "carro popular" (people's car) and Argentine vehicles meeting the "carro popular" standards would be regarded as Brazilian. Free trade in cars, trucks and buses between assembly lines was also established (with no quotas and zero import duties). Finally, Brazil acknowledged Argentina's automobile industry regime until December 31, 1999, while Argentina would accept the Brazilian "carro popular" until the end of 1996.

The Ouro Preto meeting adopted other decisions, and in many cases decided that pending issues had to be solved during 1995. As regards the former items, a Rules of Origin system was defined for goods exempt from the CET. The general rule was defined as a "change in tariff position", while in some cases (data processing, chemicals, telecommunications) specific requisites were applied. If there was no tariff change, 60 % regional added value was required.

Mechanisms to ensure competition, protection against unfair trade practices by third party countries and a common safeguard policy, non-tariff barriers and the definition of a common policy for the sugar sector, would all be dealt with by ad hoc working groups following guidelines laid down by the Common Market Council and had to be defined throughout 1995.

Lastly, the Ouro Preto Protocol approved the MERCOSUR institutional structure. As a novelty, this structure introduced the establishment of a MERCOSUR Trade Commission (MTC), an organization requested by Argentina to keep track of the commitments undertaken by member countries to act as the initiator of claims submitted by the contracting party countries or by private parties. The institutional framework was completed with a Joint Parliamentary Committee, formed by congressmen from the four countries and the Economic and Social Consultive Forum, a consultive body with representatives of the private sectors from the four countries.

MERCOSUR PROGRESS AFTER OURO PRETO

There were several attempts to deepen the MERCOSUR integration process after Ouro Preto. As mentioned in the previous section, the Ouro Preto summit meeting left many issues unsolved. Setting up a MERCOSUR Trade Commission to be followed by the establishment of Technical Committees implied acknowledging that issues were still pending where agreements would be needed.

The Asunción Summit, as the eighth meeting of the Common Market Council (CMC) in August 1995 was called, took place in Paraguay's capital city, and was of key importance. Argentina's aim at Asunción was to ratify commitments undertaken at Ouro Preto, especially those referring to free market-access to other member countries. For the enlarged market to be effective, it was felt that the Council should renovate the MERCOSUR wager by issuing a document - The "Asunción Mandate" - which would ratify commitments undertaken in Ouro Preto related to the integration process.

"Measures to Favour Intra-zone Trade" was the name given to CMG Resolution 21/95, approved in Asunción. Briefly, this text set a 30-day deadline for the Common Market Group to meet and plan solutions, which meant - in plain words - that all partners - including Brazil - had to define how to change barriers it couldn't justify and which were affecting intra-zone trade. The importance of Resolution 21/95 was difficulties found in market access due to decisions Brazil was adopting at the time, as import licenses and cash payment for imports in a number of tariff items.[19]

The Asunción meeting also aimed to identify tasks to perfect the integration process. Argentina decided to push for the deepening of the integration scheme. The Asunción Mandate was originally thought to be a strict confirmation of commitments which had already been agreed upon. But it was also expected to advance in a number of fields which had not yet been negotiated. This is how the

Presidential Summit in Paraguay arrived, with the idea of setting firm targets and deadlines to achieve a number of targets.

However, negotiations in Asunción concluded with a commitment to define - by the next presidential meeting at the end of 1995 - a task plan. The Asunción Mandate to Consolidate MERCOSUR, adopted as Decision 6/95, was an invitation to intensify efforts to build the Common Market "with the aim of carrying out concrete advances by the year 2000".

At the Punta del Este meeting in December 1995 a "MERCOSUR 2000" programme was approved. This was an action plan targeting two different levels. On one plane it identified subjects which had to be solved to improve the integration process with reference to intra-MERCOSUR free trade. The other level showed obligations which would require an engagement to deepen the integration process, for access to higher stages, and with greater commitment.

The consolidation of free intra-MERCOSUR trade and competitive conditions called for harmonization tasks and the adoption of a number of rules and technical standards, similar issues in the sanitary and plant-health fields and advances on competition defence codes and consumer protection. The analysis of distortive public policies ranked among the subjects to be harmonized or progressively eliminated.

With reference to trade policy instruments, duties related to the timetables to achieve the CET had to be identified, as also adequate customs procedures, a key element in the Customs Union, especially concerning the drafting of rules to apply the Customs Code. There were also tasks for the final design of rules against unfair trade practices and safeguard clauses, as common disciplines to adopt regarding the rest of the world. Also included at this level were undertakings already acknowledged regarding the automobile, sugar and textile industries, cases where complementary actions, productive specialization and the harmonization of trade policies needed to be promoted.

Bringing services into free intra-zone trade was also attempted as another post-Ouro Preto issue, as the subject had been set aside at this meeting. The first meeting of the *Ad hoc Services Group* to renew negotiations between member countries was only held in September 1995. A first stage consisted in the preparation of a regulatory framework to put order in the market-opening process of different services (deregulation between members). This started a task which brought about major difficulties because the starting points were substantially different.

Nevertheless, after this first meeting, negotiations on an agreement on services were repeatedly postponed and only regained some impulse towards the end of 1996, although without any definite agreement. The ad hoc Group restarted its tasks aiming to set rules of the game that would provide a legal status and backing for any business which could be developed in the region. The task carried out by the ad hoc Group defined four fields for analysis: the articles of a Draft Framework Agreement (FA) which had to include the definition of general disciplines and the Liberation Programme; Institutional Aspects, which tackled an order to manage the Framework Agreement and trade in serices; a survey to identify Initial Commitments, which consists in establishing which sectors will be the first to open up to the regional market; and lastly MERCOSUR External Negotiations, as FTAA Free Trade Area of the Americas negotiations proceed.

Nevertheless, services do not appear to be the most serious delay. What is more worrying is the slow advance in what has been called the consolidation of free intra-regional trade, and in defining common regimes (for automobiles, sugar and textiles). Delays in defining these issues is significant and important, while in some cases there have even been setbacks.

This is the case of negotiations carried out within the Technical Committee (TC) about "non-tariff barriers" (NTBs). There appears to be a difference between non tariff *measures* and non-tariff *restrictions*. If a national rule is defined as a *"measure"* this means it is not a *"restriction"* and, therefore, it is not negotiable between partners. Brazil submitted to the last meeting of the TC on NTBs a document with a proposed method to classify non-tariff measures and non-tariff restrictions. In a first stage, rules had to be grouped according to a number of categories. 16 groups have been identified, linked to health protection, environment, protection against unfair trade practices, conservation of natural resources, arms controls, etc. Brazil is steadfast in a position that states that most of its domestic rules are not, in general, *restrictions.*

The automobile sector has been another very conflictive issue. At the Ouro Preto summit meeting, Decision 29/94 - *Adjustment to a Common Automobile Industry Policy* - was the means for member countries to promise not to introduce unilateral changes in their respective national policies running against the spirit of the basic elements of a future Shared MERCOSUR Regime, namely: free intra-zone trade, a common external tariff and the absence of national incentives which could distort competitivity. It also obliged member states not to modify bilateral agreements in such a way that market access or trade flows would be restricted. The Argentine-Brazilian agreement included as an objective, progressively achieving free trade for the automobile sector.

Nevertheless, in June 1995 Brazil spurned the Ouro Preto agreement with PM Provisional Measure 1024. The new regime allowed for the possibility of import duty exemptions for raw materials, inputs, parts, components and capital goods for companies making cars, trucks, buses, tractors, harvesters, road-building machinery, bodyworks, trailers, parts and components and assemblies and subassemblies. It also enabled the executive branch to establish export incentives, freeing imports of inputs and finished vehicles, and also capital equipment if certain export targets were met or for the purchase of Brazilian capital goods. It also relaxed local content rules in part, especially in those cases where automobiles would be shipped to foreign markets.

On the other hand, the executive branch could also set up quantitative restrictions on car imports (except for assembly lines) and until the end of 1995 imports were limited to half the quantity imported from January 1995 to the date of the Provisional Measure (PM) in June 1995.

This PM adopted by the Brazilian government aimed at both designing a new automobile industry regime that would improve international competitivity of the industry, and also to discourage the strong growth in imports of finished vehicles that was threatening the trade balance.

Argentina reacted fiercely against the Brazilian decision which effectively ignored the Ouro Preto agreements. Argentine pressure enabled slacker restrictions on intra-zone car imports, although there had been little advance on the definition of a common automobile industry regime, as Decision 29/95 provided for. At the end of November 1995, Argentina and Brazil agreed on guidelines aiming to define the common policy which would be deal with at the Punta del

Este summit in December. However, discussions were postponed until mid-January 1996.

The main aspects analyzed during the negotiations had the basic purpose of drawing up a common MERCOSUR regime. Although the agreement bears in mind benefits granted under the Argentine regime, Brazil upholds the status of some incentives included in its PM 1024 system, such as the possibility of lower import duties for inputs for the motor vehicle industry. But, perhaps, one of the most important aspects of the agreement is to include "trade in car-parts" in the compensation scheme.

The agreement foresees that imports to Argentina from Brazil and vice versa which are compensated with exports to any destination can be introduced without paying import duties. Trade in vehicles will be ruled by a countertrade mechanism, and will be duty-free if values are balanced. Brazil also acknowledges a quota of 85,000 finished vehicles of Argentine origin which can be freely imported until December 31, 1998, as a result of the compensation deficit the Argentine automobile industry had built up.

Meanwhile, in the 1996-1999 period trade in a given number of finished Argentine vehicles could be imported without restrictions and paying zero import duties, for automobile assembly lines without a counterparty in the other country and would not be subject to compensation.

As regards local content criteria, national guidelines would be respected. In the case of Brazil, the FOB value of imported parts cannot be more than 40 % of the total value of parts used, while Argentina allows up to 40 % of imported parts, but measured against the final value of the vehicle, before taxes, and this percentage will drop to 32.5 % by 1999. Brazil will recognize a vehicle or part as of Argentine origin if it meets the required maximum percentage of imported parts, while Argentina acknowledges Brazilian origin if a maximum of 30 % of imported car parts is used, measured on the ex-works price. So that parts and components may be admitted as national, they must be compensated with exports to any destination.

The Argentine-Brazilian automobile industry agreement, together with PM 1024/95 system, clearly reflect how multinational firms are adapting to new forms of competition on the world market. At the bottom line, multinational assembly lines are preparing to achieve higher levels of efficiency and develop a regional automobile pole in MERCOSUR.

Building the “single market” can be seen to have been delayed too long. Perhaps one of its most relevant failings is that several non-tariff barriers still prevail, and hamper the free movement of goods in the larger market.

The MERCOSUR Trade Commission (MTC) has played a key role during this period in this respect. Although the MTC has been entrusted to watch over the application of a common intra-MERCOSUR trade policy, its task was largely concentrated on solving matters related to free access within the enlarged market. A survey until the XII MTC meeting shows the number of inquiries was about 150, of which Argentina has filed about 100. In general, consultations filed can be grouped in four main subject areas:

i) MERCOSUR rules which have not been included in national legal system.
ii) Restrictions to authorize imports.
iii) Tax policies, fiscal treatment and special import regimes.
iv) Application of the Common External Tariff and the Final Adjustment Regime.

The MTC has essentially concentrated, to a certain extent, to solve problems stemming from the absence of full applicability of the "single market". Although, as we have mentioned, this is in fact one of its main tasks, it has apparently spent too much time on these problems and, in fact, has become a preliminary stage for the dispute settlement mechanism.

In contrast to the slow advances in consolidating "free access to the enlarged market", MERCOSUR advanced at a fast pace in its links with other regional blocs. Only a few months past the second anniversary of the Ouro Preto meeting, MERCOSUR has signed an agreement with the European Union, free trade arrangements with Chile and with Bolivia, it is negotiating with the Andean Pact and Mexico and is proceeding with negotiations to establish a FTAA Free Trade Area of the Americas in 2005. Despite this "unequal progress" there can be little doubt that "external relationships" have contributed to strengthen the integration process. To a certain extent, these agreements impose some discipline within MERCOSUR.

On December 15, 1995 an agreement between MERCOSUR and the European Union was signed in Madrid. This treaty gave an institutional backing to the political dialogue between heads of state and agreed on a commitment to undertake preparatory tasks to build a free trade zone between both regions in the future. This has been a significant political event, in the recognition by the world's most important regional agreement that MERCOSUR is an integration agreement. The agreement is a commitment to identify the tools for progressive and reciprocal liberalization of all trade, including sensitive products, as is clearly the case of farm produce.

After two years of tough negotiations, on October 1, 1996 the MERCOSUR-Chile agreement became effective. The agreement is a so called second generation instrument, and contains many aspects, although the most substantial part is nevertheless the Trade Liberation Programme. This identifies different categories of products and their respective tariff liberation schedules. These classes put an order on different product groups, according to their sensitivity regarding exposure to market opening.

Once the free trade agreement was applied, Chile's average import duty for MERCOSUR products was about 6 %, and this includes about 65 % of purchase from MERCOSUR. An equivalent percentage will be applied for purchases MERCOSUR makes from its new partner and the share of imports from Chile is about 50 %. This is decidedly a substantial change in trading frontiers.

By January 1, 2004 all products not included in exception lists (which identify goods with special treatment) will be free for regional trade. The rest of the products, classified according to their sensibility for different countries, have different liberalization schemes. Most products have an initial 40 % tariff preference which will drop to zero duty in 10 years time. The exception lists -products with the highest degree of sensitivity - include products which start the market opening process in 10 years, to become free in 15 years time (rice and olive oil, among others). Tariff liberation for wheat and wheat flour includes a provision so that at the end of the 18 years agreed to free trade as well as import duties, other mechanisms like specific import duties included in Chile's price bands, will also be abolished.

Negotiations on Rules of Origin within the Free Trade Zone were the most difficult. In fact, it is not yet clear what impact on regional trade the terms negotiated will have. These rules grant origin according to the composition of the products, and specific requirement details place a cap on free trade. Thus, for food, a product could cease to be regional origin, according to the source of its packaging.

As regards Temporary Admission, which was another source of conflict, it was agreed that the mechanism would be allowed for a short period. It was authorized for five years for intra-zone trade, and this is a critical aspect: the impact of this clause on regional free trade is unpredictable.

Although Argentina was one of those most insistent on closing a deal with Chile - with the political aspiration of setting aside many decades of friction over border problems - the agreement was somewhat questioned as some Chilean products are competitive with Argentina on the Brazilian market. This situation includes pears and apples, vegetables, wine and other agroindustry products.

As regards the FTAA, negotiations have stagnated after the meeting held in Florianapolis, Brazil in September 1996, preparing for the trade ministers meeting to be held in May 1997. That meeting had very positive results for MERCOSUR as the proposal submitted by the regional group was well received by the other delegates, including Mexico. The MERCOSUR proposal consisted in gradual advances in negotiation. A first stage, would agree on matters related to "business facilitation", such as, for example, customs procedures, goods transport, certificates of origin, and others. A second stage would start when the tasks entrusted to working groups are concluded. This would cover other subjects including sanitary and plant-health measures, technical standards, and rules of origin.

Once this stage is concluded, the final stage would begin, with substantive negotiations to discuss market access and related issues, starting with goods and proceeding to services and government procurement.

The FTAA programme, as may be noted, is still carrying out its initial studies, and continuity of the negotiation process is not very clear. Advances in negotiations and setting up the FTAA will obviously be largely dependent on the pace United States wants to set, although it now appears that the administration is trying to speed up approval of a "fast track" mechanism. If this fails, it would delay the establishment of a hemisphere free trade zone.

On the other hand, MERCOSUR has shown some reluctance in starting negotiations, especially by Brazil. The reason is that two different geopolitical plans are at stake. Brazil seeks to negotiate the FTAA as a bloc, after consolidating a South American free trade agreement with MERCOSUR and LAIA countries (with the exception of Mexico), which would give it more bargaining power. On the other hand, until now United States tries to speed up negotiations to complete a hemisphere-wide free trade area as soon as possible.

Underlying this difference is the fact that FTAA is not fully compatible with MERCOSUR. The region's external trade policy will be substantially affected, once a hemispherical free trade zone is established. The essence of a customs union is its capacity for trade discrimination against third parties. In so far as such discrimination is not effective against a significant share of the rest of the world, the customs union loses its appeal. And this is especially so, if one of the partners is the United States.

A close review of the integration process since Ouro Preto shows the presence of two issues which have not been clearly solved. The first refers to the emphasis to be placed on deepening the integration process before extending the scope of its external relationship. Prior to including other countries or regional arrangements, would it not be better to go about a more profound MERCOSUR integration process, deepening mechanisms which aim to achieve a single market? The reply is neither unanimous, nor clear cut.

External relationships reinforce, as has been noted, the partners′ commitment to the integration process. But one issue which appears to be beyond discussion is the effect on the customs union of a proliferation of free trade areas with other countries or regional agreements. Ultimately, preferences between customs union partners will gradually be diluted. If one admits the hypothesis is of a FTAA continental free trade agreement starting in 2005, with a free trade agreement with the rest of LAIA countries and the European Union, to which countries will MERCOSUR apply its common external trade policy? It cannot be stressed too much that a "regional agreement" is above all a discriminatory mechanism against the rest of the world.

In any case, despite what may be agreed upon on the issue examined above, there is still the matter of free access to a larger market. In the current state of MERCOSUR, this appears to be a matter of the first order. The "proper working" of the Customs Union calls for the "single market" to be applicable, and this means dismantling all restrictions affecting free movement of goods between member countries, and this calls for the full application of the free trade zone.

CONCLUSIONS

We have mentioned in the preceeding section that, since the Ouro Preto summit in December 1994, further advances in the MERCOSUR integration process have clearly been sparse. This is with reference to consolidating rules for an "enlarged market" and bringing in other aspects of the integration process. At the risk of becoming repetitive, it should also be noted that the Customs Union must be built up on the foundations of a full free trade area, containing minimal restrictions to free movement of goods. And, in this respect, MERCOSUR suffers from severe limitations that we have already mentioned.

However, despite these limitations, the integration process as an economic and social factor continued its progress. Information regarding intra-regional trade, albeit with figures for 1996 which are still provisional, show that growth continued as intra-zone exports reached 21.4 % of all trade. And, in Argentina's case, MERCOSUR exports and imports both continued growing.

The same can be said about intra-industry trade. In 1995 and 1996 the highest values were reached for manufacturing industries overall. 60 % of trade in manufactures between Argentina and Brazil is intra-industry trade, and even after excluding the automobile industry and its satellites from these estimations, the intra-industry trade coefficient is still 50 %.

Another process which may be worth highlighting refers to the impact MERCOSUR has had on the development of joint investment projects. According to a study carried out by the Argentine embassy in Brazil, until mid-1996, about 300 joint Argentine-Brazilian undertakings had been undertaken. Many are in food (33%), automobile (13 %) and car parts (9 %) industries and in the financial system (9 %). (Embajada Argentina en Brasil, 1996).

Nevertheless, during these two recent years there have been systematic complaints about Brazil coming from the other partners - especially by Argentina - insisting on a more fluid access to the Brazilian market. Undoubtedly, for MERCOSUR, the Brazilian market is very tempting. Of about 200 claims filed with the MERCOSUR Trade Commission until the end of 1996, Argentina accounted for about two thirds - mostly complaints about Brazil -, and a significant part refer to claims about difficulties in market access caused by bureaucratic problems and, basically, on the application of technical or health standards.

Consolidating the "single market" led to a more efficient allocation of productive resources, in terms of comparative advantages or locational advantages prevailing. The latter is an important matter. In so far as restrictions to intrarregional trade are dismantled, relocation of economic activities bearing in mind relative costs in different countries is a process which will tend to become more intense. According to the basic postulates of "economic integration" theory, as the integration process prevails, there should be benefits as a result of the "trade creation" effect.

Nevertheless, it is clear that the transition towards a "single market" has lost its dynamism. The common regulatory framework ruling over the behaviour of members of the "broader market" has not had any significant new incorporation since Ouro Preto. The questions that emerge are, what is this lack of dynamism of the "formal" integration process due to? Which are the reasons explaining this difficulty or resistance to continue with progress in building an enlarged market?

Until Ouro Preto the "easy stage" of the integration process was transited. Dismantling trade barriers - both tariff and non-tariff - between partners in the regional agreement accompanied the unilateral trade opening process which had started at the end of the 1980s and the beginning of the 1990s. The MERCOSUR integration process was scarcely resisted, as it was based on another, more general process, like the unilateral integration process with the rest of the world.

But once this first stage in the bloc's history was over, deepening the integration process implied not only more open trade, but also the need to harmonize, coordinate and dismantle a wide spectrum of rules and policy tools which hampered the establishment of a common economic space. At this new stage, government areas not dealing with economic policy directly become increasingly important.[20]

Starting at Ouro Preto, the toughest stage of the integration process began. Deeper commitments to the regional agreement imply ceding more degrees of freedom, not only of economic policy, but also in other public policy fields. This seems to be the most significant limitation to advance in the integration process. The two largest partners, especially, resist ceding sovereignty in handling their public policy tools.

The lack of an adequate institutional framework may also have conspired against the good working of a single market. In many cases, both a lack of consensus about which rules to apply, and the design of the rules itself affect their application. It is often argued that MERCOSUR rules suffer from ambiguous texts allowing for non-uniform interpretations.

The paradigm of recent behaviour between the larger MERCOSUR partners has been Argentina's permanent complaints about Brazil systematically using economic policy tools regarded as discriminatory against its partners. At the same time, Brazil upholds its legitimacy in applying these tools. This diverging interpretation of the limits that constrain management of domestic public policies is not unconnected to different concepts in both countries on the role of government and public policies. Brazil still believes the state has a key part to play in economic and social management, and that its regulatory and economic promotion activities are important. In Argentina, on the other hand, the state role and government policies are said to be subsidiary to private initiative; therefore, state action should be minimized.[21]

Is it possible to advance in the integration process with different economic policy models? Undoubtedly, these differences make it more difficult to deepen the integration process. But this is not an unavoidable impediment if there is a firm political decision to assign a proper priority to integration strategies.

The limitation to full applicability of the broader market has been linked to a difficulty to interpret and build-in rules issued by the MERCOSUR organs. The single market's existence basically depends on the impact of such common rules. In this way, the challenge is to design institutional mechanisms that ensure national legislation will be incorporated into rules issued by regional organizations.

An overall demand for a more polished institutionalization of MERCOSUR exist. "Institutional flexibility" is justified in the transition stage, when the integration process had a "heterodox" style, with political negotiations dominating a somewhat diffuse and lax institutional framework. Deepening the integration process called for strengthening MERCOSUR institutions, although this means discussing of an extremely thorny issue on supranational or inter-government action.

In short, a single interpretation of rules is needed, so that decisions adopted by MERCOSUR institutions can become included in member's national legislations in an agile fashion. An adequate institutional framework would contribute to overcome obstacles that appear in the road to consolidate a "single market".

Table 2-5 Argentina Macroeconomic Indicators

Year	GDP growth rate Total Change %	Per capita %	Price index Consumer %	Wholesale %	Exports (millions US$)	Imports (millions US$)
1980	2.1	0.4	100.8	75.4	8,020	10,539
1981	-6.9	-8.3	104.5	109.6	9,143	9,430
1982	-5.8	-7.1	164.8	256.2	7,626	5,337
1983	2.6	1.1	343.8	360.9	7,836	4,504
1984	2.2	0.8	626.7	575.2	8,107	4,585
1985	-5.1	-6.4	672.2	662.9	8,396	3,814
1986	5.2	3.8	90.1	63.9	6,852	4,724
1987	3.1	1.8	131.3	122.9	6,360	5,818
1988	-1.8	-3.0	343.0	412.5	9,135	5,322
1989	-6.3	-7.5	3,079.5	3,432.6	9,579	4,203
1990	-0.1	-1.5	2,314.0	1,606.9	12,353	4,077
1991	9.5	8.0	171.7	110.5	11,978	8,275
1992	8.4	6.9	24.9	6.0	12,235	14,872
1993	5.3	3.9	10.6	1.6	13,118	16,784
1994	6.7	5.3	4.2	2.3	15,834	21,590
1995	-4.6	-5.9	3.4	6.5	20,963	20,122
1996 (*)	4.4	---	0.2	3.2	23,811	23,699

(*) Estimated

Source: Economic Commission for Latin America and Caribbean and INDEC

TABLE 2-6 Argentina & Brazil (Peso-Real)

Year	Real Exchange Rate Argentina	Brazil	Peso-Real Ratio
1980	37.9	68.7	55.1
1981	46.5	64.5	72.1
1982	90.2	66.7	135.2
1983	109.8	89.7	122.4
1984	99.5	102.5	97.1
1985	116.0	109.9	105.6
1986	100.0	100.0	100.0
1987	100.0	91.0	109.9
1988	101.6	81.1	125.4
1989	146.8	69.4	211.6
1990	90.6	54.5	166.3
1991	58.6	62.5	93.7
1992	50.0	66.7	74.9
1993	46.8	60.3	77.7
1994	46.2	46.9	98.5
1995	46.0	34.9	131.7
1996	47.3	33.3	141.8

Source: Based on BCRA. INDEC. IESP. IMF

Table 2-7 Foreign Trade of MERCOSUR Countries (Million US $)

Year	EXPORTS			IMPORTS		
	Total	MERCOSU	Others	Total	MERCO	Others
1986	30,565	2,636	27,929	21,536	2,593	18,943
1987	34,148	2,530	31,618	24,148	2,621	21,527
1988	44,829	2,927	41,902	23,076	3,075	20,001
1989	46,355	3,838	42,517	26,061	3,935	22,126
1990	46,419	4,132	42,287	27,276	4,101	23,175
1991	45,935	5,103	40,832	32,214	5,147	27,067
1992	50,683	7,136	43,547	38,705	7,323	31,382
1993	54,058	10,373	43,685	40,964	8,678	32,286
1994	62,080	11,940	50,140	59,460	11,976	47,484
1995	70,335	14,350	55,985	75,400	14,666	60,734
1996	75,100	16,100	59,000	s/	s/d	s/

Source: ALADI Secretariat. CEI International Economy Centre

TABLE 2-8 ARGENTINA Trade with Mercosur (Million $)

Year	Exports Million de	%*	Imports Million de	%
1980	1,137	14.2	1,306	12.4
1981	892	9.8	1,106	11.7
1982	828	10.9	827	15.5
1983	522	6.7	795	17.6
1984	656	8.1	980	21.4
1985	668	8.0	698	18.3
1986	895	13.1	832	17.6
1987	769	12.1	1,003	17.2
1988	875	9.6	1,170	22.0
1989	1,428	14.9	869	20.7
1990	1,833	14.8	875	21.5
1991	1,977	16.5	1,805	21.8
1992	2,327	19.0	3,755	25.2
1993	3,684	28.1	4,214	25.1
1994	4,804	30.3	5,147	23.8
1995	6,770	32.3	4,594	22.8
1996	7,919	33.3	5,774	24.4

(%) As share of all trade to/from the World

Source: INDEC

TABLE 9 ARGENTINA ARGENTINE EXPORTS BY MAJOR PRODUCT GROUPS (In million US dollars)

Year	Primary Products			M,O,A,			M,O,I,			Fuels and Energy			TOTAL		
	Mercosur	Rest of World	Total	Mercosur	Rest of world World	Total	Mercosur	Rest of world	Total	Mercosur	Rest of world	Total	Mercosur	Rest of world	Total
1985	188	3421	3609	171	2433	2603	196	1353	1549	113	522	636	668	7729	8396
1986	333	2173	2506	230	2457	2686	261	1234	1496	71	94	165	895	5958	6852
1987	230	1512	1742	148	2678	2826	361	1334	1695	29	68	97	769	5592	6360
1988	227	2175	2402	131	3812	3943	478	2155	2633	39	118	157	875	8260	9135
1989	372	1673	2045	306	3700	4006	675	2511	3186	76	267	343	1428	8151	9579
1990	582	2757	3339	364	4299	4663	777	2588	3364	108	877	985	1833	10520	12353
1991	622	2679	3301	402	4525	4927	797	2186	2984	155	611	766	1977	10001	11978
1992	773	2727	3500	359	4470	4829	906	1917	2823	289	793	1082	2327	9908	12235
1993	917	2362	3279	510	4414	4924	1569	2110	3679	677	559	1236	3684	9434	13118
1994	1139	2601	3740	865	4936	5801	1971	2676	4647	780	871	1651	4804	11035	15839
1995	1426	3391	4816	1234	6240	7474	3094	3410	6504	946	1223	2169	6770	14193	20963
1996	1539	4271	5810	1320	7106	8426	3502	2954	6456	1546	1537	3082	7906	15868	23774

Source: INDEC

TABLE 2-10 ARGENTINA Nominal protection and Common External Tariff

	Common			Nominal		
Categories	Avg	Ma	Min	Avg	Ma	Min
Basic food and beverages	8.0	16	0	10.2	20.0	0.0
Processed food and beverages	13.4	20	0	16.3	30.0	2.5
Basic industrial raw materials	4.8	20	0	10.3	30.0	0.0
Processed industrial raw	9.9	20	0	14.9	30.0	0.0
Basic fuels	0.2	2	0	1.7	15.0	0.0
Processed fuels	0.4	6	0	0.0	0.0	0.0
Gasoline	5.2	14	0	6.4	15.5	0.0
Capital Goods (KG)	12.9	20	0	6.0	30.0	0.0
Parts and components for KG	12.4	20	0	17.8	30.0	0.0
Automobiles	20.0	20	0	16.0	20.0	0.0
Car parts	15.0	20	0	20.3	30.0	0.0
Consumer durables	17.7	20	0	23.1	30.0	0.0
Consumer semi-durables	18.4	20	0	26.6	30.0	0.0
Consumer non durables	13.7	20	0	18.3	30.0	0.0
TOTAL	11.0	20	0	14.3	30.0	0.0
TOTAL without KG and	10.4	20	0	16.0	30.0	0.0

Source: Author's survey

* Includes Imports Duties and Statistics Fee

TABLE 2-11 ARGENTINA Exceptions from Common External Tariff
(CET)

SITC Gro	Product Description	National Tariff (%) Ave.	Max	Min.	CET % Avera	Tariff items
5	Fruit and vegetables	19.0	19	19	14.0	2
11	Beverages	2.0	2	2	16.0	1
23	Rubber (unprocessed)	2.0	2	2	14.0	1
29	Animal and vegetables prods	14.0	14	14	9.3	3
51	Organic chemicals	2.0	2	2	12.8	65
52	Inorganic chemicals	8.0	17	2	7.6	5
53	Dyeing. tanning and coloring	2.0	2	2	12.0	1
54	Medicinal and pharmaceutical	2.0	2	2	13.2	10
58	Plastics in nonprimary forms	22.0	22	22	16.0	4
62	Rubber manufactures	23.3	24	22	16.0	3
64	Paper and paperboard and articles	24.0	24	24	13.0	10
65	Yarn and textiles	6.0	6	6	16.0	2
67	Iron and steel	23.3	24	19	14.7	37
68	Non-ferrous metals	19.3	22	17	10.7	18
69	Metal manufactures N.E.S.	22.8	29	6	15.8	10
74	Industrial machinery and	28.2	29	24	20.0	6
76	Telecommunications eqpt.	29.0	29	29	20.0	3
77	Electrical equipment N.E.S.	27.8	29	24	18.9	17
78	Road vehicles	29.0	29	29	20.0	2
82	Furniture and parts	24.0	24	24	18.0	4
85	Footwear	29.0	29	29	20.0	17
89	Other manufactures N.E.P.	24.0	24	24	18.4	10
	Total	17.4	18.4	15.6	15.3	231

Source: Author´s survey

TABLE 2-12 ARGENTINA Final Adjustment Regime - Intra-MERCOSUR

Tariff (%)

SITC Gro	Product description	January 1, 1995 Ave.	Max	Min.	Tariff items
5	Fruit and vegetables	14.0	14	14	2
7	Coffee, tea, cocoa, spices and	23.0	23	23	1
24	Cork and wood	16.0	16	16	1
57	Plastic in primary forms	18.0	18	18	1
62	Rubber manufactures N,E,S,	23.0	23	23	4
63	Cork and wood manufactures	18.0	18	18	3
64	Paper and board	23.0	23	23	24
67	Iron and steel	19.7	23	16	123
69	Metal manufactures N,E,S,	23.0	23	23	3
77	Electrical equipment N,E,S,	26.0	27	23	4
82	Furniture and parts	23.0	23	23	1
84	Articles of apparel and	27.0	27	27	43
85	Footwear	27.0	27	27	13
	Total	21.6	21.9	21.1	223

Source: Author's survey

BIBLIOGRAPHY

Canitrot, Adolfo (October-December 1992): *"La macroeconomía de la inestabilidad"* (Macroeconomics of instability), in Boletín Informativo Techint N° 272, Buenos Aires.

Castillo, Luis A. (1993): Mercosur: Antecedentes y Situación Reciente (Mercosur: Precedents and Recent Situation), mimeo, Buenos Aires.

Embajada Argentina en Brasil (Argentine Embassady in Brazil) (1996): Argentina-Brasil, Comercio, inversiones e integración física, (Argentina-Brazil, Trade, investment and physical integration), Brasilia.

Fontanals, Jorge (November 1994): Industria del papel y celulosa e industria siderúrgica en el Mercosur (Pulp and Paper and Iron and Steel Industries in Mercosur), UNDP Project PNUD-ARG 92/025, mimeo.

Herrera, Vegas, Jorge Hugo (1996): *"Las políticas exteriores de la Argentina y Brasil: Divergencias y convergencias"* (The Foreign Policies of Argentina and Brazil: Divergence and Convergence), in Felipe A,M, de la Balze (comp): Argentina y Brasil enfrentando el Siglo XXI, CARI-ABRA, Buenos Aires.

Heymann, Daniel (February 1986): *"El Plan Austral: Una Experiencia de Estabilización de Shock"* (The Austral Plan: An Experience in Shock Stabilization), in Daniel Heymann, Tres Ensayos sobre Inflación y Políticas de Estabilización, Working Paper Nº 18, CEPAL Buenos Aires, Buenos Aires.

Heymann, Daniel and Navajas, Fernando (1992): *"Aspectos conceptuales de la coordinación de políticas macroeconómicas con referencia al Mercosur"* (Theoretical aspects of the coordination of macroeconomic policies with reference to Mercosur), in Ensayos sobre coordinación de políticas macroeconómicas, CEPAL, Santiago.

Krugman, Paul (1992): Geography and Trade, Leuven University Press and The MIT Press, Cambridge.

Kume, Honorio (February 1996): A política de importacao no Plano Real e a estructura de protecao efetiva (Import policies in the Real Plan and the structure of effective protection), FUNCEX, Rio de Janeiro.

Lifschitz, Edgardo and Crespor Armengol, Eugenia (July-September 1995): *"Evolución de la protección arancelaria 1990-2001"* (Tariff protection developments 1990-2001) in Boletín Informativo Techint Nº 283.

Lucángeli, Jorge (September-October 1989): *"Política comercial y desempeño industrial - La experiencia argentina de los últimos cuarenta años"* (Trade policy and industrial performance, The Argentine experience during the past 40 years), in Boletín Techint No, 259.

Lucángeli, Jorge (July-September 1993): *"La presencia del comercio intra-indsustrial en el intercambio entre la Argentina y Brasil",* (The presence of intra-industry trade in commerce between Argentina and Brazil) in Boletín Techint, No, 275.

Macario, Santiago (1969): *"Proteccionismo e Industrialización en América Latina"* (Protectionism and Industrialization in Latin America), in Hacia una Tarifa Externa Común en América Latina, INTAL-IDB, Buenos Aires.

Yeats, Alexander (February 1997): Does Mercosur's Trade Performance Raise Concerns about the Effects of Regional Trade Arrangements?, Policy Research Working Paper 1729, The World Bank.

[1]. Argentina included 232 tariff items on its National List of Exceptions to the CET; Brazil listed 232 items, Uruguay 212 and Paraguay 253. Nevertheless, a deadline was set at April 30, 1995 to complete national lists of 300 items, except for Paraguay which was allowed 399 items.

[2] LAIA members are the following countries: Argentina, Bolivia, Brazil, Colombia. Chile, Ecuador, Mexico, Paraguay, Perú, Uruguay and Venezuela.

[3] The history of relations between Argentina and Brazil reveals that conflicts have been present on several occasions. Both countries were born with opposing geographic and historical polarities and struggles to enforce a regional leadership have been numerous. Nevertheless, these have gradually converged until a regional integration agreement was signed (Herrera Vegas, 1996).

[4] Avoiding a possible Brazilian invasion had extremely negative consequences for the Mesopotamian provinces (Misiones, Corrientes and Entre Ríos). Because the region borders on Brazil, they were left behind in their physical integration with the rest of the national territory. The reason waved by the military was that in the face of a potential Brazilian invasion through the Mesopotamian provinces, the lack of fluid communication with the rest of the country was a means

to ensure territorial integrity. It was only at the start of the 1970s that bridges were built to link Mesopotamia with the rest of Argentina, and also from the former region to Uruguay.

[5] Argentina's public and publicly guaranteed long-term foreign debt had grown from 10.2 billion dollars in 1980 to 25.4 billion dollars in 1983 and 35.7 billion dollars by 1983 (See The World Bank: **World Debt Tables.** 1988-1989 Edition).

[6] "Protocol" in this context refers to a supplementary international agreement.

[7] After a positive trade balance of US$ 3.7 billion in 1991, the balance was negative by US$ 2.6 billion in 1992, US$ 3.7 billion in 1993 and US$ 5.75 billion in 1994. Part of this negative balance was originated in trade with Brazil.

[8] In 1994, the Argentine economy started to show signs that despite privatizations and public sector reform the fiscal situation remained unsolved. Tax revenues were not enough to match levels required by public spending that continued proving it was inflexible downwards. While in 1993 public accounts had closed with a primary surplus of 6.4 % of GDP, in 1994 the surplus had dropped to 2.9 %.

---

[9] Businessmen from the iron and steel and paper industries had always carried considerable weight in Argentine Industrial Union decisions, occupying key posts in its Board Council.

[10] Safeguard clauses for the paper industry in most cases included various tariff nomenclature items.

[11] Manufactures of industrial origin is a classification used by the INDEC Census Bureau to group those manufactures which are not based on the processing of agricultural raw materials. In this category one finds chemicals, plastics, rubber manufactures, leather goods, paper and board, textiles and garments, footwear, base metals and their manufactures and machinery and transport equipment.

[12] Intra-industry trade between Argentina and Brazil is considered, because this is where this form of exchange is most intense.

[13] This statement is not by A. Yeats (1997) who considers the MERCOSUR integration process as favouring intra-regional trade being more intensive in activities which do not fit the comparative advantages of the region's countries. The issue is the subject of a heated debate, but is outside the scope of this chapter.

[14] The tariff preference implies that duties on imports from partner countries are lower than those from the rest of the world in the proportion corresponding to the preference.

[15] Market opening not only consisted in lower import duties but also y dismantling several non-tariff barriers.

[16] The import durt timetable for capital goods was brought forward by Cavallo in 1995 when he needed to increase Treasury revenues as a result of the effects of the Mexican crisis. The duty rate was first set at 14 % and then at 16 %.

[17] In fact, as the products are excluded from free regional trade, the Final Adjustment Regime for the Customs Union is a mechanism to adjust to the free trade zone.

[18] The Argentine automobile industry regime has a basic one-to-one ratio between imports and exports, with an imported content of up to 40 % of the price of vehicles.

[19] "Import licenses" are a bureaucratic procedure required to carry out an import. They are not prior permits, but - under certain circumstances - delays in their issuing operates as a non-tariff barrier.

[20] Anything concerning harmonizing technical or plant health standards, for example, involves a very broad range of public

administration fields, to refer to some cases which have had most impact on intra-regional trade.

[21] Two issues reinforce this difference. On one hand, the Brazilian government system, - basically since the 1988 constitutional reform - has been marked by a marked federalism, which gives a large degree of autonomy to the states, especially in fiscal affairs. In this way, states may adopt investment promotion regimes, for example, which are extremely attractive, quite apart from any federal government decision. On the other hand, in the Argentine case, the Convertibility law has noticeably restricted the economic policy tools to which the executive branch may resort. In practice, it has to fall back on fiscal policy, but with restrictions in the way the deficit is financed.

Chapter 3
BRAZIL

Peter Coffey

THE HISTORICAL BACKGROUND

Brazil is quite different from all other countries in Latin America. This difference is not only based on the sheer size of the country and its Portuguese ancestry, but it is a product of a major chance development in its history which gave it a degree of self confidence not generally shared by most other countries in the region. But, we shall come to this important development in a moment. At the outset, the two metropolitan powers, Portugal and Spain, were set on seeking gold and other precious materials in Latin America. They were major rivals, and, thus, at the end of the fifteenth century, they sought the mediation of the Pope in their territorial disputes on that continent. The outcome was that in 1494, in the Treaty of Tordesillas, Pope Alexander VI, decreed that the dividing line between the two parties would be on a longitude 375 leagues west of Cap Verde. Subsequently, following further disputes, borders were, once again, settled, this time, in 1750, with the Treaty of Limits. Eleven years later, Portugal unilaterally abrogated the treaty, and, Brazil continued to expand in all directions.

The sheer size of this country – ruled by a relatively small and distant metropolitan power – had a number of consequences which remain with us to the present day. First, Portugal could not police such a large country with its relatively small army. Thus, the Portuguese Monarch relied on Nobles who managed the so-called “captaincies” on his/her behalf. This, coupled with the size of the country, conferred a certain degree of independence on the different regions – which subsequently became federal states. This development has tended to create a problem, i.e. tensions between the federal government and the states which remain with Brazil to the present day.[1]

The other development was the relative lack of racism which is such an attractive feature of Brazilian society. This is the result of the inevitable intermarriage between the Portuguese, Indians and Africans. This was inevitable because the small number of Portuguese could not possibly people such a large territory.

But the really important historical development which has tended to make Brazil so very different from other Latin American countries was a direct result of the Napoleonic Wars, in Europe. When Napoleon invaded Portugal, the British Royal Navy, in 1807, escorted the Portuguese Royal Family to Brazil, where they arrived in 1808. Now, the metropolitan power was Brazil and not Portugal, and Brazil, linked hitherto exclusively to the Mother Country, opened up to the world.

This historical event had a number of consequences which could not have been foreseen at the time. When the King, Dom João III, returned to Portugal, in 1821, he left behind the Crown Prince, Dom Pedro, who, in 1822, declared the independence of the Empire of Brazil – a kind of constitutional monarchy. He became Emperor Dom Pedro I. His son, also Pedro, was born in Brazil. When, in 1831, the Emperor abdicated and returned to Portugal, his son became (though, still an infant, he did not assume power until 1840) the Emperor Dom Pedro II. This Great Emperor ruled until 1889, when he was ousted in a revolution which declared Brazil a republic. Pedro II was arguably the first great royal environmentalist. Some historians would argue that it was a combination of his concern for the environment and his abolition of slavery[2] that led to the coup which removed him. Under his long reign, Brazil developed greatly with a national system of education and communications and a national railway system. The economy experienced booms based on different tropical products, sugar, rubber and coffee. During the period, 1875 until the end of the 1950's, about 5 million Europeans migrated to Brazil.

SUBSEQUENT DEVELOPMENTS

This brief historical introduction tends to show that, apart from its size and Portuguese ancestry, Brazil is very different from other countries in Latin America. Subsequent developments, however, tended to emphasise the similarities rather than the differences with her neighbours.

During the period from the declaration of the Republic, in 1889 to 1930, the political system can be described as a constitutional democracy. Political power alternated between the two most powerful states, São Paulo and Minais Gerais. Despite the continued rivalry between these two states, the poor Nordeste, has, in recent years, become the third most important player in the national presidential stakes.

This (by Latin American standards) relatively long period of constitutional democratic rule, was halted in 1930, when a military coup brought the civilian Getulio Vargas, to power. He served as a dictator until 1945. Like the developments described earlier, the rule of Getulio Vargas, who is still revered by the poorer sections of Brazilian society, had important influences on the country and its economic policies which remain with Brazil to the present day. In its attempt to integrate Brazil more effectively into MERCOSUR, the present Brazilian Government is trying to change some of these policies.

Getulio Vargas is such an important figure in twentieth century Brazilian history that some reference must be made to his policies. His name is closely linked with social security, wage indexation and tenure in the civil services. Although is philosophy of "Étatisme" and the policy state ownership of certain key sectors are not exclusively his, he is closely linked with state management of the economy.

As with other Latin American countries, the Second World War had the most profound effect on Brazil. Unable to import manufacturers from Europe and the United States, Brazil was forced to adopt a policy of import substitution and develop its own industries. However, Brazil was also very different from the other Latin countries in that she entered the War on the side of the Allies. This meant that she had really entered the international diplomatic stage as an important country.

economic stagnation and political radicalisation which marked the rule of President João Goulart.

The coup, covertly supported by the United States, brought to power Humberto Castello Branco. He was succeeded, as President, by a series of senior army officers Arthur da Costa e Silva, 1967-69; Emilio Garrastazu Medici, 1969-74; and Ernesto Geisel, 1974-79.

Despite the harsh and ruthless nature of the régime, which, due to the relatively smaller numbers of its victims, has earned much less publicity than similar but more sinister regimes in Chile and Argentina, a policy of liberalisation started in the early 1980's. Under Geisel's successor, General José Baptista de Oliveira Figueiredo, who ruled from 1975-85, political exiles were allowed to return, and, in 1982, they were also allowed to run for state and federal office.

ECONOMIC DEVELOPMENTS

According to Antônio Salazar P. Brandão and his colleagues, at the FGV, the policy of import-substitution, introduced in the Second World War, continued after the cessation of hostilities, and led to trade and internal policy intervention in national economic management by the State. This continued until the 1980's. On the positive side, this led to a big wave of capital investment in the 1950's and high economic growth and a great diversification of the industrial sector.

Unfortunately, however, according to the same economists, there was also "overvaluation of the exchange rate, quantitative controls of imports and exports and high import tariffs" which "produced an anti-export bias to industrial and agricultural products". There was also a negative inflationary financing of this policy of import substitution.

On the positive side, the military régime of 1964 embarked upon a series of economic, fiscal and monetary policies which reduced inflation and stimulated growth. On the exchange rate side, a "crawling peg" series of very small devaluations was adopted. Also, credit subsidies and tax incentives led to a growth in the export of manufacturers.

Interestingly, the first oil crisis of 1973 – 76 does not seem to have much effect on economic growth and the emphasis on the national capital goods sector. Instead of retrenching, the State simply borrowed on the international finance markets. In contrast, the second oil crisis of 1979, the steep rise in interest rates and the international debt crisis was a very different matter.

Although the Brazilian economy continued to grow during the period 1982-86, it did not do so between 1987 and 1991. Also, attempts at deflation were only temporarily and partly successful. On the plus side, however, Brazil was particularly successful in producing trade surpluses in manufacturers. Despite this success, according to the experts at the FGV, "the import-substitution model had exhausted its role as the engine of growth and was only producing distortive effects upon the economy. There was also an urgent need to reform the role of the State which had acted as a player shaping the market forces during the import-substitution strategy."

THE RETURN TO DEMOCRACY

The author cannot emphasise enough the capital importance of the return to democracy in both Brazil and Argentina as the indispensable catalyst in the diplomatic rapprochement between the two countries and the subsequent creation of the MERCOSUR. In both countries, colleagues have constantly stressed this fact with the author.

The Brazilian Electoral College, made up of all the members of the Congress and six delegates from each federal state, had, surprisingly, maybe, continued, under the military régime, to choose the president. Thus, in January 1985, this College voted the veteran and much respected Tancredo Neves, of the opposition PMDB (Brazilian Democratic Movement Party), as President. When, in March, of the same year, Tancredo Neves, died suddenly after a brief illness, Senator José Sarney, the Vice-President, became President.

Subsequently, in 1989, Fernando Collor de Mello, won the directly contested Presidential elections. The demise of Collor de Mello was an unexpected as it was proof of the surprising strength of the newly-found Brazilian democracy. In 1992, a major corruption scandal erupted and the President was impeached in Congress and forced to resign. He was replaced by Vice-President Itamar Franco. Subsequently, in January 1995 Fernando Henrique Cardoso, the successful finance minister, became President, having won the presidential elections in October of the previous year.

BRAZIL AND MERCOSUR

As has been explained in the previous two chapters, MERCOSUR is built on the foundations of agreements (including the creation of a common market) which had been concluded between Argentina and Brazil – before the signing of the Treaty of Asunción.

At first sight, there seems to be some degree of similarity between the interests of France and West Germany when negotiating the treaty of Rome which led to the creation of the European Economic Community (EEC) and the negotiations between Argentina and Brazil for the creation of a common market. In the former case, France had mainly (though not exclusively) agricultural interests, whilst the German interests were mainly industrial. In the latter case, Argentina was very interested (though not exclusively) in expanding its exports of wheat and beef to Brazil (which has a shortfall for both products) whilst Brazil was interested (though not exclusively) in securing a major part of the Argentine market for its exports of capital goods. There, however, the comparison with the old EEC ends because both Argentina and Brazil do have important agricultural and industrial sectors, though the Argentine agricultural sector is greater than that of Brazil.

The negotiations leading to the creation of a common market have been succinctly analysed from the viewpoint of Argentina, by Jorge Lucángeli, in the previous chapter. Now, let us turn to the Brazilian side.

Before examining more specifically the Brazilian side, it is important to bear in mind three facts. First, as has been repeatedly stressed to the author by Antônio Salazar Brandão, the initiative for the rapprochement between Argentina and Brazil, came from the two governments and not from business leaders. It was, therefore, the initiative of the governments which led to the signing of the PICE (Programme for Integration and Economic Co-operation), in 1986. It is this Programme, in fact, an agreement based on 24 economic sectors that is the indispensable forerunner of the Treaty of 1988, establishing a Common Market. Furthermore, according to Roberto Lavagna[4], the PICE represents a desire to consolidate Brazil's inustrialisation process - particularly in the capital goods sector. Also, according to Roberto Lavagna, these agreements lay down trade balance goals, which, hopefully would encourage business leaders to support a regional integration process.

Second, Brazil, had, until the application of the 1988 Treaty, been a highly protectionist country when one compared its tariffs with those of other countries. In particular, Brazil was determined to protect its capital goods industry - especially in computers and telecommunications. This differed strongly with Argentina (and with Uruguay) which having a negligible presence in some of these sectors imposed zero or very low tariffs on imports of capital goods.

Third, Brazil was (and still is) very interested in creating an internal MERCOSUR market for capital goods. In turn this would *) tend to encourage investment flows into the region from third parties.

Consequently, Brazil and other Latin American countries (also, Mexico) did not sign the protocol of the Uruguay Round, in April, this year, which would have liberalised trade in telecommunications in January, 1998.

A further consideration is that Argentina had already started its liberalisation process at the end of the 1980's, and, in comparison with Brazil, was successful with its stabilisation process.

For Brazil, apart from the very short transition period for the implementation of the main part of the Treaty of Asuncion, major tariff reductions were involved. Thus, in introducing a tariff reform in 1990, the aim was to reduce the average tariff from 32 to 14 per cent in only three years.

The negotiations about the common external tariff (CET) proved to be very difficult in some sectors. Surprisingly maybe, except for some capital goods. Brazil was not, in principle, opposed to a low CET. Thus, Argentina could not demand high tariffs for its traditional agricultural commodities. The final agreement on a CET ranging from 6 to 20 per cent must be considered reasonable by international standards.

According to experts at the FGV, there were areas of contention in the negotiations, which, to the author still demand clearer solutions. One major issue, which still rankles (bitterly, to the author, in view of Brazil's unilateral action in imposing import controls) is the lack of clear legislation in case of unfair trading practices. Also, further legislation for the safeguards for certain products seem necessary.

It was Brazil's concern over the future development of an internal MERCOSUR market for capital goods, especially for computers and telecommunications, that led to the final special compromise. Here, it was agreed that for capital goods. an average CET would enter into force in 2001. However, for computers and some telecommunications goods, the CET of 16 per cent will only come into force in the year 2006. In the meantime, the Member States will gradually converge their external tariffs on these goods. Thus, the customs union will only be fully effective in 2006. As has already been discussed in the previous two chapters, all four Member States were given lists of exceptions for "sensitive" products which have been gradually phased out. Also, rules of origin agreed for goods not subject to the CET, were 60 per cent for all products , but 80 per cent for capital goods.

OTHER CONSIDERATIONS

Although MERCOSUR is more important to Paraguay and Uruguay as a percentage of their total export market[5], both Argentina and Brazil know that the future potential for MERCOSUR lies in their joint markets. Equally, since for internal domestic reasons, the governments of both Argentina and Brazil understood that the control of inflation, tax reforms and privatisation are critically important, co-ordination here is indispensable. Unfortunately, this co-ordination, at the time of writing, is difficult, if not impossible to achieve. The problem is twofold.

In the case of Argentina, currency reform, privatisation and reforms of the public sector started earlier than in Brazil and have been successful. In comparison, In Brazil, these reforms came later and only the currency reforms can be seen as being successful.

In fact, in Brazil, as the Economist noted, in May this year[6], changes in State ownership of assets and conditions of employment for civil servants, both State and federal, require changes in the constitution. These changes are very difficult to achieve.

> But the government's main hopes of fiscal reform lie in two constitutional amendments. One would allow governments (federal, state and municipal) to sack workers when payroll expenses amount to more than 60% of their revenues, and would cap individual earnings. The other would reform a public-pensions system which is out of control: federal-government

spending on pensions has increased from 5.5 billion in 1992 to 16 billion last year. Officials hope that between them, these reforms could shave up to 3% of GDP from government spending within three years of approval (though others think this is optimistic because the proposed pension reform is timid and because the problem is not so much the size of Brazil's civil service, as its perks and inefficiencies which the government is only starting to address).

Almost two years after they were introduced into Congress, both constitutional amendments remain bogged down. The drama Mr. Cardoso repeatedly faces in his efforts to modernise his country is that changing Brazil's constitution requires 60% support in both houses of Congress. Though in theory the centre-to-right alliance which supports his government commands such a majority, attacking the privileges of public employees strikes at the heart of the patronage system which sustains many of Brazil's traditional political bosses. In practice, Mr. Cardoso makes progress in his legislative agenda only after time-consuming horsetrading.

The other major problem concerns the currency reforms themselves. In Argentina, the hard peso is linked to the US Dollar and is backed and supervised by a Currency Board. In Brazil, the hard Real fluctuates in a narrow band.

Again, in the case of Brazil, whilst MERCOSUR is a growing market, it will be observed from the following statistics, that Brazil has important trading interests in other parts of the world. This fact will, from time to time, inevitably cause tensions for the Real. In fact, writing in Carta Capital[7], in January, this year, Delfim Netto, a former minister, advocated the devaluation of the Real. He supported his case by citing the example of the United Kingdom which left the Exchange Rate Mechanism (ERM) of the European Union (EU) in 1992 and devalued the Pound Sterling. Subsequently, the British Economy has boomed.

RESULTS FOR BRAZIL IN THE MERCOSUR

The author believes that it is still too early to make definite assessments for Brazil's experience with MERCOSUR. There are a number of reasons for this view. These reasons mainly concern internal economic and currency factors. At the beginning of the 1990's, Brazil was experiencing a recession, the reverse was true of Argentina. Also, in the case of Argentina, the currency reform and stabilisation policy had taken hold.

Thus, it can be said that the peso was overvalued. Consequently, the terms of trade were very much in Brazil's favour and there was an upsurge in Brazilian exports to Argentina. More recently, Brazil's currency reform and stabilisation process have tended to make Brazilian products overpriced in Argentina and the former trade surplus has disappeared. It is therefore indispensable that this possible influence of tariff reductions on intra-regional trade creation be placed in this framework. Nevertheless, the following trade statistics, supplied to the author by the FGV do show the increasing importance of MERCOSUR (especially that of Argentina) to Brazil.

Table 3-1. Brazil's Exports: Geographical Regional Direction 1991-94

Regions	Share % 1994	Share % 1991	Average Annual growth 94/91
LAIA	22.37	15.55	25.60
MERCOSUR	13.59	7.28	36.99
LAIA - MS (*)	8.78	8.27	13.50
United States	20.24	19.58	12.49
European Union	27.12	30.89	6.52
Asia	16.21	18.01	7.40
Africa	3.10	3.27	9.23
Others	10.96	12.69	5.95
Total	100.00	100.00	11.25

Source: Balança Commercial – DTIC – Brazil.
(*) – LAIA, except MERCOSUR

It is clear from Table no. 1 that Brazil's geographical direction of trade has shifted quite appreciably in a very short period of time. Thus, whilst both the United States and especially the European Union continue to occupy important places, Latin America and notably MERCOSUR have increased their share of brazil's export market.

If we dissect Brazil's trade flows inside the MERCOSUR, Table no. 2, we note, that, as was expected, Argentina occupies the most important place among the three partner countries. Interestingly enough, however, both Paraguay and Uruguay have a strong showing – particularly when one takes into account the relatively small size of their populations.

Table 3-2. Brazil's Exports to MERCOSUR Countries.

Country	Average growth		Share
	1989/1991	1991/1994	1994
Argentina	44.15	40.98	69.85
Paraguay	24.32	28.54	17.79
Uruguay	0.52	29.50	12.36
Total MERCOSUR	30.07	36.87	100.00

Source: BACEN – Brazil

According to experts at the FGV, it is the composition of the bi-lateral Argentine-Brazil trade flows that is of the greatest interest to analysts. Furthermore, to the author, it is in these tables where it is possible to note the potential internal dynamic effects of the MERCOSUR Common Market as described by Scitovsky[8] and others when examining the infant EEC in the 1950's.

When we examine Tables no. 3 and 4, we note the important place occupied by manufacturers in this bi-lateral trade. Whilst, as was expected, Brazil does export large quantities of coffee and iron ore to Argentina and Argentine sales of wheat and corn to Brazil are very substantial, manufactures (especially for Brazil) are very important in these trade flows.

Table 3-3 Main Brazilian exports to Argentina 1994 and 1993

Products	Share % 1994	Growth % 94/93
Parts, Tractors, Motor VeH	9.37	10.26
Passenger Cars	5.96	-13.55
Goods Vehicles	4.74	70.56
Piston engines and parts. Nes	3.61	13.17
Iron ore mining	2.28	-1.35
Flat-rolled plated iron or steel	2.25	-17.53
Semi-finish, iron or steel	2.08	86.23
Manufacture of chemical products n.e.c.	1.95	10.92
Coffee, not roasted	1.64	81.31
Pumps and compressors	1.58	-4.99
Other products	64.55	13.99
Total Argentina	100.00	13.04

Source: Balança Commercial – DTIC – Brazil. Courtesy: FGV

Table 3-4 Main Argentine Exports to Brazil, Jan-Oct, 1995 and 1993

Products	Share & 1994	Growth % 94/93
Oil	15.49	45.42
Wheat	14.13	-11.42
Gear box	6.20	23.28
Vehicles	4.54	-8.00
Corn	4.03	-12.08
Gross Cotton	2.78	600.68
Other leathers and skins	2.23	-4.88
Piston Engines and parts, nes	2.20	-23.09
Soya oil	2.11	115.20
Frozen fishes	1.63	37.46
Other products	44.65	15.77
Total	100.00	14.29

Source: INDEC – Argentina. Courtesy: FGV

Of particular interest to analysts are the statistics, in Table no. 5, elaborated by analysts at the FGV, which stress the role of intra-industry trade. Also, as has been noted by the same experts, there is the development of "strategic trade", i.e. the development of a few products, e.g. processed food products, which find a MERCOSUR – wide market. Similarly, there is a movement of firms between all the four Member States. Here, one well-publicised example has been the move into Argentina by the famous Beer producer, Brahma.

Table 3-5 Intra-Industry trade – 1992

Country	Developed Economies	Developing Economies	USA	E_U	LAIA	Brazil	Argentina
Brazil	0.58	0.42	0.64	0.55	0.50	-	0.73
Argentina	0.27	0.63	0.30	0.23	0.70	0.56	

Source: Commodity Trade Statistic.
Elaboration: FGV/IBRE/CEEG.

CONCLUSIONS: OVERVIEW

The return to democracy in Argentina and Brazil and resulting diplomatic rapprochement between the two countries were indispensable pre-conditions for
The creation of MERCOSUR. These developments also made possible a number of necessary changes in the management of the economies of the two countries. Among the most notable of these were currency reforms and the control of inflation, de-regulation and privatisation plus reforms (mainly fiscal) in the public sector. In all these areas, Argentina has been swifter and more successful than Brazil.

In the specific case of Brazil, two major problems have been the necessity of changing the Constitution and the competition between the Federal Government and the States. In the former case, privatisation of State assets and changes in the contracts of civil servants necessitate changes in the Constitution. In the latter case, at the time of writing, according to the Financial Times[9] the federal Government had signed re-financing deals with 17 of the 27 States. In the fiscal area, a value added tax (VAT) system will be introduced in 1998.

One area, where major progress has been made is in agriculture where state financial support for farmers has been dramatically reduced. In turn, this has made the creation of free trade between the MERCOSUR countries in agricultural products much easier.

Similarly, banking reforms being undertaken (which had been done early by Argentina and Uruguay) will facilitate the creation of a MERCOSUR-wide banking and financial markets. Here, Paraguay tends to align its reforms with those of Brazil.

There are, inside Brazil, major social problems. At the lower levels (not at university levels) there is a crying need to make education and training accessible to all.

Then, there is the crying problem of income disparities and poverty levels. These disparities have always existed but were exacerbated by the international debt crisis of the 1980's. More recently, some experts have estimated that there is much poverty in rural areas with many young people living in absolute poverty.

Finally, it should be stressed that Brazil is deeply committed to the diplomatic rapprochement with Argentina and to the construction of MERCOSUR. However, her links with other trading blocs and the great difficulties encountered in applying necessary internal economic and fiscal reforms imply that the transitional period until the final completion of MERCOSUR in 2006 will not be an easy one. In the meantime, Brazil has made it clear that she prefers first to consolidate MERCOSUR before seriously considering special links with NAFTA.

---

[1] There have, in fact, been several attempts at secession. The most important and successful one (for the secessionists) was the secession of the most southern state, which, in 1827, became Uruguay.

[2] Slavery had, in fact, been abolished the pervious year, 1888, by the Regent Princess Isabel, when the Emperor had been away in Europe.

[3] The coup of March 1964, is admirably documented in René Armano Dreifuss, "A Conquista Do Estado Ação Politica, Poder e Golpe De Classe'" 1981, Vozes, Petrópolis.

[4] Roberto Lavagna, "As Perspectivas do MERCPOSUL", in Perspectivas do Economia Brasileira. 1994, IPEA, Rio de Janeiro, 1993.

[5] According to the FGV, 1991, MERCOSUR accounted for 35.2 per cent of total exports of Paraguay and Uruguay. The equivalent figures for Argentina and Brazil were 4 per cent and 16.1 per cent, respectively.

[6] The Economist, "Reforming Brazil:, 17th – 23rd May, 1997, London.

[7] Antonio Delfim Netto, "Onhenhenné E Os Fatos," Carta Capaital, 22 January, 1997, Rio de Janeiro

---

[8] Tibor Scitovsky, “Economic Theory and Western European Integration,” Unwin University Books, 1958, London

[9] Financial Times, “Brazil to Refinance Sâo Paulo State Debt,” 24/25 May, 1997.

Chapter 4
Present and Future - Uruguay

Carlos Eduardo López Rodriguez

"...and they will be united in perfect union between themselves, not in that mean union forcing each people to lose a part of its trust in exchange of a subservient obedience, but in that union that makes to the interest itself, not in detriment of the rights of the peoples and their free doing and will"

José Gervasio Artigas,
Statement made to the Corrientes City Council,
March 29th, 1814.

INTRODUCTION

The Oriental Republic of Uruguay, the second-smallest nation in South America, is situated on the eastern (hence "oriental") shore of the Uruguay River, across which lies Argentina. To the east is the Atlantic Ocean, to the north and northeast Brazil, and to the south the widest estuary in the World, known as the Rio de la Plata.

Uruguay has no significance mountain ranges or mineral resources. However, its rolling grassland hills hold abundant livestock and agricultural activities, with nearly 90 percent of agricultural land. Wildlife has diminished with the growth of human and livestock populations.

Table 4-1 Comparative table of agricultural land.

	Agricultural Land Percentage of Land area
Argentina	65.1
Brazil	29.4
Paraguay	57.9
Uruguay	84.8

Source: Food and Agriculture Organization (F.A.O.) Trade Yearbooks 1991-1992.

Uruguay's boundaries are almost totally demarcated by water. The excellent hydrographic system gives the country plenty of hydroelectric power. A dam at Paso de los Toros on the Rio Negro has created a reservoir (Embalse del Rio Negro), the largest artificial lake in South America. The Montevideo harbor, the country's capital, is the best in the Rio de la Plata, a geostrategic resource that may become even more important as the Southern Common Market (MERCOSUR) comprising Brazil, Argentina, Paraguay, and Uruguay becomes fully operational.

Situated in the mild zone, Uruguay does have well marked seasonal changes in weather, although snow is unknown and a hard freeze is rare.

In terms of population, Uruguay is not much more than the Federal Capital of the Argentinean Republic or a neighborhood of the city of São Paulo. Represents the 1.6% of the total population of the MERCOSUR.

Montevideo is home to nearly 45 percent of all Uruguayans and, not surprisingly, is the political, economic, and cultural hub of the country. Almost 90 percent of the population is of Spanish or Italian descent. The small Indian population either fled, was killed or intermarried, leaving the country with no full-blooded Indians by the 1850's. A small black population of about 50,000 to 60,000 is a product of slavery and proximity to southern Brazil. A low birthrate and the out-migration of economically active individuals under the age of 40 gives Uruguay the oldest population profile in Latin America. The population is nominally about 66 percent Catholic.

The educational system is free through to university level. Literacy rate: 96%; ages of compulsory education: 6-14; educational budget: 3% of gross national product (G.N.P.) or 15.5% of total government expenditure.

Uruguay is characterized, together with Argentina, by higher social modernization and living standard levels than the other

Table 4-2 Income distribution in the MERCOSUR. Comparative table of income's distribution in the countries that form the MERCOSUR. Only Metropolitan and urban areas were considered.

	Poorest 40%	Next 30%	Next 20%	Wealthiest 10%
Argentina	15.2	25.0	28.2	31
Brazil	9.6	19.3	29.4	41
Paraguay	16.2	24.8	29.8	29
Uruguay	21.9	26.2	26.0	25

Source: E.C.L.A.C.

Labour Force: 1,355,000; civil servants 25%, manufacturing 19%, agriculture 11%, commerce 12%, utilities, construction, transport, and communications 12%, other services 21%.

Foreign Debt: $4.2 Billion. At present, there is a stand-by agreement in force, that enabled a "contingent" loan – in eventual adverse situations – for 100 million of Special Lights of Draft (approximately US$ 141

Million), but Uruguay has not resorted to this credit yet. Recently, the Uruguayan government has suggested to the International Monetary Fund (I.M.F.) the signing of a stand-by agreement until 1999.

Investment: 12.8% of G.D.P. It is expected that private investment will continue to increase during 1997 and public investment to 10%.

Budget: Revenues $2.9 billion, expenditure $3.0 billion, including capital expenditure of $388 million. During the last months a certain deterioration was noted in the fiscal goals, partially due to the cost of the retirement reform and to the incentives for public employees' retirement. For 1997 a deficit of 2% of the G.D.P. is expected.

HISTORICAL, POLITICAL AND ECONOMIC BACKGROUND

Historical Aspects

The Rio de la Plata eastern shore entered lately in the Spanish empire's history, but it was mentioned for the first time early in the 16th century, due to a strange event. 1516 Solis' expedition watered somewhere along the coast in its search for a passage to the Pacific Ocean. The captain himself landed only to be stabbed to death and, according to witnesses, eaten by a number of bellicose natives.

After a futile search for mineral wealth the Spanish left the area on the eastern bank of the Uruguay River largely alone for the next century. It was the decision of a Spanish colonial governor in Asunción, Hernando Arias, to release cattle and horses on the fertile plains that led to the commercial viability of the area known as the Banda Oriental. Ranchers and cowboys (gauchos) began to make frequent forays to gather hides and capture horses. In 1680, Portuguese settlers moving south from Brazil established an outpost at Colonia del Sacramento on the Rio de la Plata. As a consequence, Montevideo was founded in 1726.

Colonial life was dramatically shaken by an English invasion at the dawn of the nineteenth century. Such an event could be explained by the fact that English exporting economy was being worn down by Napoleon's continental blockade. After Trafalgar, Britannia ruled the seas and was seeking for new markets among Napoleon's allies' colonies even by violent means. In a clash during over a year, in 1806-07, both Montevideo and Bs. As. Surprisingly outmatched the threat. Such loyalty was to have many consequences. Firstly, colonies realized they could defend themselves much better than a far away empire with a non-existing fleet could. The Spanish "debacle" of 1808 didn't make things look better. Secondly, seducing trade prospects, with no "Impuesto de

Circulo" (abhorred importation tax of 53%), seemed to be assured by an ubiquitous English fleet. And thirdly, a long-term social transformation began, fed by circumstances all over the 19th century, from mostly civilian colony to militarized nation.

In fact, independence movements spread all over Spanish colonies from 1810 on. Viceroyalties structures were blown up in behalf of previously existing provincial ones. Confederate (later Federal) and Unitarian tendencies tried to face such fragmentation.

Confederate tendency prevailed in the Banda Oriental. Towards 1813, José Artigas formulated a political programmés with clearly regional pretentions, (interprovincial) of confederate integration and of balance between free trade and protectionism, that allowed the provinces to participate in the international commerce without surrendering to Buenos Aires's centralism. Under his leadership the provinces of Entre Rios, Corrientes, Santa Fe, Misiones, Córdoba and the Banda Oriental performed a "Federal League", also known as "the system of the Free Peoples", which geopolitical center would be in the Misiones.

In its Regulation of September 9, 1815, José Artigas proposed to create some kind of customs union among the then called Provincia Oriental and five other Argentinean provinces known as Artiguist Protectorate.

The Regulation established the internal tariffs' release and the establishment of a common tariff with regard to third countries.

Portuguese invasion of the Provincia Oriental put an end to artiguist leadership. His fall meant the whole project of provincial integration's fall.

In 1825, a group of men, later known by nationalistic historiograghy as "33 Orientals", started a "liberating Crusade", that caused a war for the Argentinean Confederation, against the Empire of Brazil which was expanding at that time.

The war ends in 1828, with British mediation in a Preliminary Convention. A buffer state was established between the two rivals, and Montevideo became its capital. After the pledge allegiance to the Constitution it was named "Republica Oriental del Uruguay".

Political independence did not economically separate Uruguay from the surrounding regions. The port of Montevideo continued to be, as in colonial times, an alternate port in respect to that of Buenos Aires. A great part of south Brazil as well as Argentinean Mesopotamia's production flowed away through Montevideo's seaport. Such a thing as the existence of a regional market since that moment cannot be stated, but Montevideo was one of the main capitals of trade of a region much wider than the one formed by the Uruguayan state territory.

Moreover, Uruguay just starts to consolidate itself as an independent state by the end of the Guerra Grande war (1839-1852). After two decades of political and economic stability, Uruguay went through a military stage that rationalized production and brought economic growth. This century finished after a stage of oligarchic civism. It is not until then that a certain economic, social and democratic policy is established, which constitutes the contemporary Uruguay.

In 1903, José Batlle y Ordoñez of the Colorado party was elected president. His centralizing instincts and bold ideas quickly provoked another civil war that Batlle won in 1904. He went on to make the country a model of political and social reform, eventually earning the title of "Switzerland of South America." Serving two separate terms as president (1903-07, 1911-15), he eventually achieved legislation creating social security, unemployment insurance, divorce on demand, and, most important, a series of state corporations in such areas as insurance, mortgage banking, and utilities. Despite the dislocations caused by the Depression of the 1930's, including the dictatorship of Gabriel Terra (1933-38), the Batllista legacy and ideology (Batllismo) have endured.

World War II brought renewed prosperity to Uruguay as the need for wool and beef by the Allies seemed insatiable. The dominant politician in the postwar period was Luis Batlle Berres of the Colorado party, a grandnephew of Jose Batlle. His industrial populism was based on a differential exchange policy that overtaxed agricultural exportations. Uruguay enjoyed unrivaled prosperity and political stability. At this time Uruguay experimented with a multiperson executive power – the colegiado – a form of plural presidency proposed by Jose Batlle and used in modified form from 1919 to 1933. The pure colegiado (colegiado integral) was in use from 1952 to 1966.

From the mid-1950's on, a drop in international demand for Uruguayan exportations produced economic stagnation, inflation, and increased political paralysis. Responding to the electorate need for changes a Blanco Government took office in 1959 after a whole century of parliamentary opposition. The disassembling of industrial protectionism came far too late and brought social unrest. The country rushed into the first steps of a would be endemic external debt. Recognizing the seriousness of the situation, the country returned to a single-person presidency.

Uruguay's most recent constitution, adopted in 1967, continues a tradition of concurrent election of the president, all members of the legislature and all local government officials for 5-year terms. The legislature is made up of 30 senators and 99 representatives.

President Jorge Pacheco Areco (1967-72), of the Colorado Party, ruled by emergency decree during much of his term. He did so in the face of significant labour unrest and a creative but increasingly violent guerrilla movement known as the Tupamaros.

Since 1971, a leftist coalition known as the Frente Amplio, or Broad Front, has been able to win the support of about 20 percent of the voters. Today, this support surrounds 30 percent.

In 1973, Pacheco's handpicked successor, Juan Maria Bordaberry led the country into a military dictatorship. The military ruled for nearly 12 years (taking total control in 1976), arresting and torturing hundreds, driving others into exile, and suppressing all independent forms of cultural and political expression. The population's refusal to accept a military dominated government and the regime's inability to produce sustained economic growth finally brought the regime down.

Political Changes: Return to Democracy

Since the return to democracy, two political parties have rotated in the government. Both of them have made very important efforts to constitute a coalition government. These efforts finally succeeded in the last three years between one of the main leaders of the Blanco Party – Alberto Volonté – and the present leader of the Colorado Party – Julio Maria Sanguinetti.

Julio Maria Sanguinetti of the Colorado party won the 1984 elections, taking office on March 1985. Working with his legislature, he pardoned the remaining political prisoners, restored civil liberties, and reestablished Uruguay's credibility in the international arena. The economy rebounded in 1986-87 from the near depression levels of the early 1980's. The last two years of the administration saw a flat economy and a bitter debate and national plebiscite on a pardon for human-rights violations committed by the military during the dictatorship.

The ruling party split over its presidential candidates for the 1989 elections. The result was a victory for the national party and its leading candidate, Luis Alberto Lacalle. Montevideo mayoralty was won by Tabaré Vázquez, a socialist medical doctor who ran for the Frente Amplio. The Lacalle administration sought to privatize state-owned companies and to reform bureaucracy. A 1992 plebiscite halted its efforts and left Lacalle increasingly unpopular.

The Colorado party and Sanguinetti won the 1994 elections. On the 8th December 1996, the 1967 Constitution was partially reformed, especially on that concerning electoral systems. This reform brought about a second round or ballotage at presidential election, which will confirm future presidents with over 50% support (art. 151).

Concluding, it must be said that democratic transition helped the country to reestablish its contact with the outside world. This contact had been narrowed during the dictatorship, just when the world was experimenting serious changes affecting science, technology and production as well as distribution of world power and its new ability to organize and explain ideologies. As from 1989, voting-on-tradition crisis, pressured towards the revision of leadership, growth of the left wing and autonomy of public opinion regarding political parties, led to a significant mutation in Uruguay electoral history. We must bear in mind that ever since the dictatorship years, there has been a tendency towards a permanent government heading the deepening of a liberal opened economy based on freedom of exchange and capital flow.

Current Economic Policies

Economic development has been held back by excessive government regulation of economic detail and 50% to 130% inflation.

However, from 1990 on, the Uruguayan government - the same that signed the Asunción Treaty and the Protocol of Ouro Preto - gave a strong impulse to the liberalizing tendencies of national economy. This impulse laid on the following tripod: commercial opening of Uruguay to the World, by a fast unilateral tariff cut and a drastic reduction of the non-tariff protections; deregulation of some industrial activities (automobile industry, abattoir industry and tannery, for example) and exchange delay. The combination of the referred tripod damaged competitive capacity and even challenged the survival of some industries, because it made exports more difficult and caused the imported products to be cheaper, compared to the national products in the internal market. Its result was the increasing substitution of local products by imports, regarding consumers' goods and production assets, as an important number of enterprises changed their source of supplies towards abroad, looking for lower costs, better quality and wider variety. We witnessed an intense industrial restructuring, of a mainly defensive character. Only the service sectors, offer and work expanded.

However, after several years of sluggish growth, real gross domestic product (G.D.P.) jumped by about 8% in 1992. This rise is attributable mainly to an increase in Argentinean demand for Uruguayan exports, particularly agricultural products and electricity. In a major step towards greater regional cooperation, a referendum on December 1992 overturned key portions of the landmark privatization legislation, seriously affecting President Lacalle's broad economic reform plan.

Table 4-3 Gross Domestic Product & Unemployment Rate. Table of the evolution of the G.D.P. (Búsqueda, January 30, 1997) and the unemployment annual average, expressed in percentage of population economically active. (Búsqueda, January 2 and 30, 1997

	GDP Millio n US$	GDP per capita US$	GDP Variatio n %	Montevideo unemploy-ment	Rest of the country	Total unemploy-ment
1983	5,079	1,710	-	-	-	-
1984	4,829	1,616	-1.09	13.9	-	-
1985	4,719	1,569	1.48	13.1	-	-
1986	5,859	1,937	8.86	10.7	9.3	10.1
1987	7,330	2,409	7.93	9.3	8.9	9.1
1988	7,583	2,478	-0.01	9.1	8.2	8.6
1989	7,992	2,598	1.29	8.5	7.4	8.0
1990	8,355	2,700	.88	9.2	7.7	8.5
1991	10,041	3,226	3.22	8.9	8.8	8.9
1992	11,849	3,785	7.88	9.0	9.0	9.0
1993	13,806	4,385	3.00	8.4	8.2	8.3
1994	16,204	5,116	6.76	9.2	9.2	9.2
1995	17,837	5,599	-2.43	10.8	9.7	10.3
1996	18,671	5,834	4.80	12.6	11.4	12.0

Source: B.C.U. and N.I.S.

In 1996, Uruguay freed itself from the economic turbulence registered in 1995. The economic staff registered in its credit having recovered from the tendency to growth. In 1996 the G.D.P. increased by 5% in respect to

1995. The government expects that in 1997 this growth will maintain, but at a lower pace.

The devaluation pace during 1996 got to 27% annual and the inflation reached 24.3%. At the end of 1997 the devaluation pace is expected to be around 15% annual and the inflation to align this percentage.

Although exports and imports of assets raise, the government is aware of the fact that it faces other problems in its economy, high unemployment rate and higher fiscal deficit than expected.

Table 4-4 Prices. Table of annual variations of prices (in percentage). Búsqueda, January 2, 1997

	1993	1994	1995	1996
Inflation	52.9	44.1	35.4	24.6
Production	31.1	41.0	27.7	23.5
Devaluation	26.6	27.4	26.5	22.7

Source: N.I.S.

THE COUNTRY'S INTERESTS IN THE MERCOSUR

Production

Uruguay's G.D.P. per capita places the country among the higher income nations in Latin America. However, Rio Grande do Sul and Minas Gerais

G.D.P.'s are three and five times higher respectively than Uruguay's. That of the State of Sao Paulo is one of the twenty highest in the World. Uruguayan G.D.P. represents only 1.5% of MERCOSUR's

The average sector participation in 1991-1993 G.D.P.'s was as follows: farming 11.3%, manufacturing industry 23.1%, construction 3.9%, electricity 3.1%, commerce, restaurants and hotels 12.8%, transport, warehousing and communications 7.7%, banking and other financial services, insurance, real estate goods and services given to enterprise 22%, communal, social and personal services 17%.

Natural Resources: soil, hydropower potential, minor minerals. Land use: arable land 8%; meadows and pastures 78%; forest and woodland 4%; other 10%; includes irrigated 1%.

Livestock and agriculture are the historic foundations of Uruguay's economy. Beef, wool, textiles, and leather make up the bulk of exports.

In recent years dairy products and tourism have added to the country's income. Industrial activity represents about a third of economic activity, and services (including tourism and banking), nearly 45%.

Figure 4-1 Agriculture in MERCOSUR. Comparative table, cow milk, rice, wool, mutton & lamb, and honey.

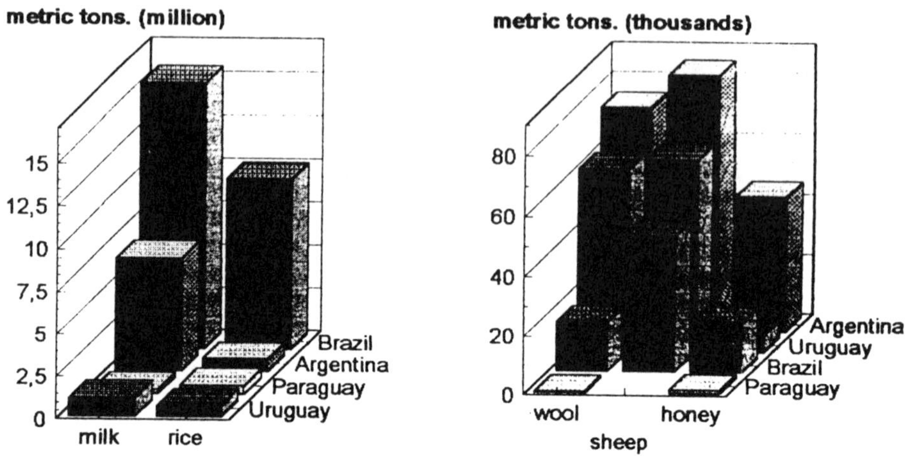

Source: F.A.O. Trade Yearbooks 1991-1992. Mindscape World Atlas MPC

Industries: Meat processing, wool and hides, sugar, textiles, footwear, leather apparel, tires, cement, fishing, petroleum refining, cigarettes, paper, particle board, wood, wine.

Trade

Since the treaty of Asunción's signing, in 1991, trade between members of the MERCOSUR grew more than 3 times. Figures for 1994 were of US$ 11,940 millions. The Subregional trade's growth is faster than each country's global foreign trade, a reason why, gradually, the countries are more and more dependent on each other.

Exports and Imports

Between 1988 and 1995, total Free on Board (F.O.B.) exports in Uruguay grew from US$ 1,404.6 millions, to US$ 2,105.9 millions. A 6% growth is expected for 1997.

The 1988 and 1995 total import figures in Uruguay, cost insurance & freight (C.I.F.), are of US$ 1,176.9 and US$ 2,866.9 millions respectively. A lower rate of import growth is expected for 1997.

Total exports composition is as follows; 17% corresponds to hides and leather goods, 10% to beef, 9% to wool, 7% to fish and 4% to rice.

Table 4-5 Exports & Imports. Table of Uruguayan exports, imports and commercial due balance. (C.D.B.) in millions of dollars. Búsqueda, January 30, 1997.

	1988	1989	1990	1991	1992	1993	1994	1995
Traditional exports	539.1	593.0	623.8	470.7	514.4	432.6	562.0	648.7
Non traditional	865.5	1,005.8	1,069.1	1,134.0	1,188.1	1,212.8	1,351.5	1,457.2
Total exports	1,404.6	1,598.8	1,692.9	1,604.7	1,702.5	1,643.5	1,913.4	2,105.9
Total imports	1,176.9	1,202.8	1,342.9	1,636.5	2,045.1	2,325.7	2,786.1	2,833.9
CDB	227.7	396.0	350.0	-31.8	-342.6	-680.4	-872.7	-781.0

Source: B.C.U.

From the total imports, 23% were of consumption goods, 17% of capital goods, and 60% of production assets. Major imports include fuel, oil, metals, machinery, transport equipment and chemicals

Trading Partners

In the 1991-93 triennium, the MERCOSUR countries bought 38% of the Uruguayan exports, the North American Free Trade Agreement (NAFTA) bought 13%, the European Union (EU) 23% and the Asian countries 11%. In 1994, Uruguay placed 46.8% of its exports in the MERCOSUR.

In addition, during the same period, 45% OF THE Uruguayan imports were from MERCOSUR members, 13% from NAFTA, 17% from the

Figure 4-2 Graphic with the annual rates of variation of Uruguayan exports and imports. Búsqueda, January 2, 1997. ALONSO, La problematica social en el proceso de integracion, Economia's participacion social en el Mercosur

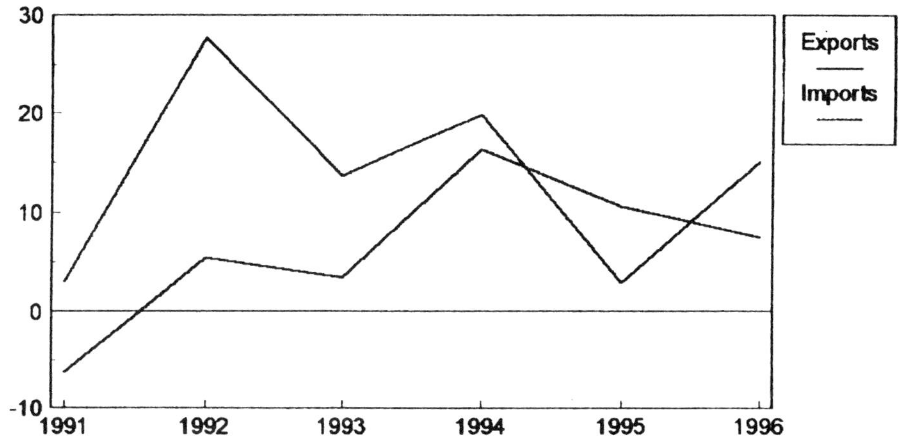

Sources: N.I.S., E.C.L.A.C. and U.N.D.P.

EU, and 11% FROM THE Asian countries. In 1994, 50.2% of Uruguayan imports came from MERCOSUR.

As far as countries are concerned, main export partners were Brazil, USA, Argentina and Germany. Import partners: Brazil 23%, Argentina 17%, USA 10%, and EU 27.1%.

Table 4-6 Comparative table of Sub-regional and international trade of the MERCOSUR (in millions of dollars) in 1994.

Subregional Trade

	Argentina	Brazil	Paraguay	Uruguay	Mercosur	Mundo
Argentina		3.595	495	650	4.470	15.659
Brazil	4.136		1.053	732	5.921	43.000
Paraguay	71	304		9	384	804
Uruguay	377	494	24		895	1.913
Mercosur	4.584	4.393	1.572	1.391	11.940	61.376
Mundo	21.555	38.00	1.848	2.773	64.176	

This high share of MERCOSUR countries in Uruguayan foreign trade, could be explained by the stimulus of the celebrated bilateral pacts and certain structural factors. Among these, we must highlight the role of geographic proximity, relative small size of Uruguayan industry and the way they complement each other.

Argentina as well as Brazil have, due to their geographic location, a high natural protection, reflected in high freight costs for imported goods. This protection does not apply to those entering from Uruguay, which allows this country an almost exclusive access of products with a low unitary transport cost. Buenos Aires – main consumer market of

Argentina – is very close to Montevideo, which is the main Uruguayan supplier of manufactured goods.

The small size of Uruguayan industry, in relation to huge Argentinean and Brazilian markets, determine a marginal character that facilitates the granting of concessions for the entrance to these markets. This smallness generates an opportunity for development of certain levels of regional specialization, through the insertion in small segments of the markets of the neighbouring countries. Supply in such a small scale would be of no economic sense for the large productive units installed.

Uruguayan foreign trade with Brazil is strongly complementary. Natural resources and advantages in the production of certain agricultural items (rice, barley, and milk) enabled a trend in competitive conditions. On the other hand, Brazil laid out an industrial specialization pattern with a higher added value and of larger scale economies.

As far as Argentina is concerned, Uruguayan trade is constituted by products with a medium or high index of industrialization (between 40 and 55% of exportations). These products are generally composed by raw materials of national source, especially agricultural. However, an increasing proportion of Uruguayan exports belongs to industrial accounts (synthetic and artificial textiles, paper, plastics, paints and other chemicals) which process imported raw materials.

Finally, Uruguay was given an additional advantage to its foreign trade with Argentina and Brazil. This consists in allowing Uruguayan enterprises to have access to raw materials in "temporary admission," what supposes their following exportation once industrially elaborated. Price advantages attained in this way allowed some exports expansion: chemicals, as an example

TIMETABLE AND MODALITIES OF THE TREATIES OF ASUNCIÓN AND OURO PRETO

Latin American reorganization and economic cooperation process had its main impulse in the ECLAC papers, published by the United Nations in 1949. The expression "integration" may have been used for the first time in the Latin American environment in these publications.

In 1960 the Central American Common Market (MECC) and the Latin American Free Trade Association (ALALC) were created. The ALALC established a programmés of commercial liberalization consisting in the elimination of all import taxes, within a period not longer than 12 years, as from 1960. This programmés should materialize through the periodic and collective negotiation of a "common list" of products that would be free of customs charges and of any other tax to imports with equivalent effects. Unfortunately, after 10 years of the ALALC being in force, not even an approximation of the "common list" had been reached. This and other causes brought negotiations to a halt. Resolution no. 370 started the restructuring mechanism of this organization, which ended up in 1980 with the signing of another treaty that originated the Latin American Integration Association (ALADI).

Figure 4-3 Diagram of the Latin American integration processes.

ALADI	
Argentina	2,777,000 km
Bolivia	1,099,000 km
Brasil	8,512,000 km
Columbia	1,139,000 km
Chile	757,000 km
Ecuador	284,000 km
Mexico	1,973,000 km
Paraguay	407,000 km
Peru	1,285,000 km
Uruguay	187,000 km
Venezuela	912,000 km

Groupo Andino	
Bolivia	3,099,000 km
Columbia	1,139,000 km
Ecuador	284,000 km
Peru	1,285,000 km
Venezuela	912,000 km

MERCOSUR	
Argentina	2,777,000 km
Brasil	8,512,000 km
Paraguay	407,000 km
Uruguay	187,000 km

At this stage, among the Latin American additional protocols and pacts, whose aims are those of cooperation and integration, three levels could be distinguished: Latin American, subregional cooperation and subregional integration. ECLAC, the Latin American Economic System (SELA) and the ALADI stand as examples of associations at a Latin American Cooperation and integration level. At a subregional level we can highlight four agreements aiming at integration: the Central American Common Market (MECC), the Caribbean Common Market (CARICOM), the Andean pact and the MERCOSUR

At the subregional cooperation level a heterogeneous group of cooperation treaties appears: the Cuence del Plata Agreement, the Hydroway the URUPABOL and various agreements of economic complementation, such as the Argentinean-Uruguayan Convention of Economic Complementation (CAUCE) and the trade Expansion (PEC).

Uruguay joined Brazil, Argentina and Paraguay in forming the Southern Common Market (MERCOSUR) on March 26, 1991, by signing the Asunción Treaty. This treaty was framed within the ALADI on November 19, 1991. An agreement on economic complementation was then signed with the same contents (Economic Complementation Agreement #18).

Figure 4-4 Comparative table of the Territorial extension of three of the main agreements of Latin American integration.

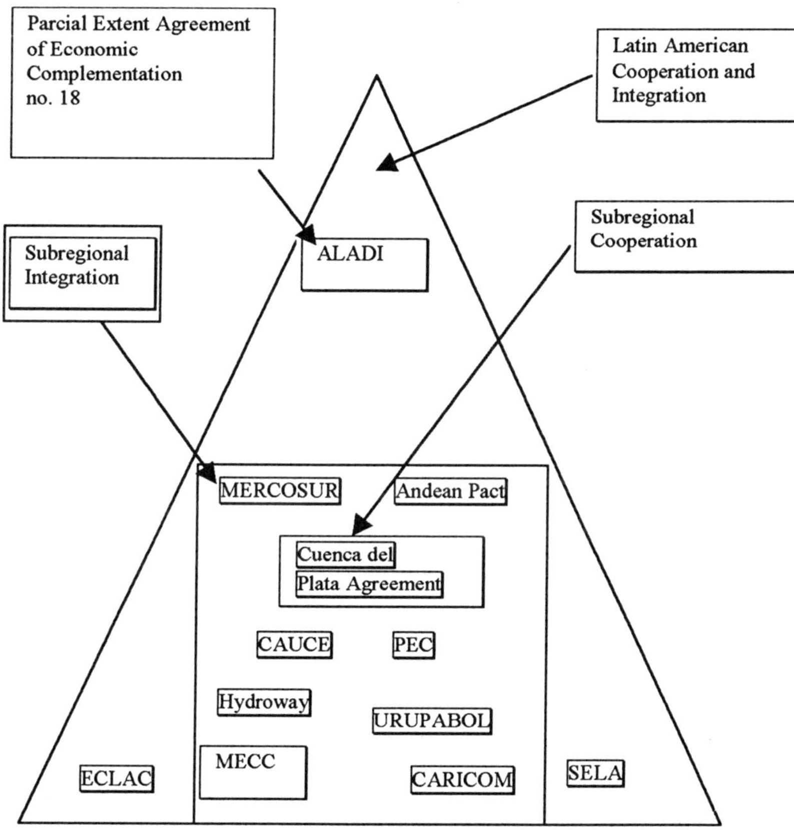

Source: ALADI en Cifras

CAUCE and PEC

Uruguayan subregional economic integration with Brazil and Argentina had started fifteen years before the signing of the Asunción Treaty. In the frame of a deep economic restructure, Uruguay searched for a new international role by signing two bilateral agreements of special importance: CAUCE and PEC. In the aftermath, various complementary agreements were summed up.

All these treaties were exceptions to ALALC's agreements system. Its bases are in Resolution #204 of the Ministers Council of the ALALC (September 2, 1967) and in resolution #354 of the Conference of the Contracting Parts of the ALALC (December 16, 1975). In the former it was declared that Uruguay was in the position to ask the special treatment foreseen in the Montevideo Treaty for countries of minor relative economy. In the latter resolution Uruguay was provisionally authorized to give concessions to Argentina and Brazil, not extended to the rest of the ALALC members.

CAUCE was signed by the Argentinean and Uruguayan governments on August 20, 1974. PEC was signed by the Brazilian and Uruguayan governments on August 1975, together with a treaty of friendship, a pact on sea transport and a pact on fluvial and lacustrine transport, a credit pact between the Bank of Brazil and the Central Bank of Uruguay and various reversal notes.

CAUCE and PEC implied the granting of unilateral concessions by each of the signing countries for the exports of their counterparts. These concessions had a character of exclusivity, not being extended to the rest of the ALALC member countries. For Uruguay, it meant entering with tariff zero in Argentina and Brazil, with those products for which concessions were given. For each of these, quotas were established - in physical volume or in value - restrictive of the quantities that could enter in preferential conditions.

in 1980, the substitution of ALALC by ALADI supposed the renegotiation of CAUCE and PEC. It was so disputed by the Resolution 400 (XX-E) dated December 19,1980, approved by the Conference of the Contracting Parts of ALADI. As per this resolution, on December 20, 1982 the Protocol of Suitability of CAUCE was signed, which text suffered adjustments through various protocols, to consolidate itself, finally, into a unique instrument which text forms part of the protocol signed by the plenipotentiaries of Argentina and Uruguay on November 27, 1989. This was inscribed in ALADI as Economic Complementation Agreement #1.

In virtue of the protocol, the complete duty-free process was confirmed by Argentina for its industrial tariff range for the import of products originating and coming from Uruguay, in quantities equivalent to 5% of the respective Argentinean production registered for each product the previous year.

PEC followed a similar process to CAUCE's. It's adequacy to ALADI supposed the signing of a protocol on MAY 27, 1982 and, then, an economic complementation agreement on December 20, 1982. Finally, on August 13, 1986 a new text for PEC was agreed in the economic cooperation agreement signed in Brasilia by Presidents Sarney and Sanguinetti. This was inscribed in ALADI as Economic Complementation Agreement #2.

Uruguay's trade with its neighbours multiplied since CAUCE and PEC came into force. The bilateral pacts assured the access to the neighbouring markets in preferential conditions and the promotion policies - subsidies, fiscal exemptions, credit with preferential interest rates, real salary reduction - warranted the exportations' profitability. In 1973 Uruguay exported to Argentina US$ 100 million. CAUCE channelled more than 90% of this trade. In the same way, imports of Argentinean origin were triplicated and CAUCE channelled up to 40% of that commercial flow.

As far as its trade with Brazil is concerned, Uruguay sold US$ 16 million in 1973 and by the end of the eighties exported already more than US$ 200 million. 80% of this commerce was channelled through the PEC. In the same period, the Uruguayan imports with Brazilian origins were six times higher.

It's important to highlight that the concessions Uruguay gave to Brazil and Argentina were, basically, in products which were non-competitive to national production. Argentina and Brazil tended to supply Uruguay with raw materials originating in the chemical industry, rubber, plastic and steel industry as well as with machinery and transport means, relatively displacing other extraregional suppliers.

In this way, Uruguay's international trade relationships started to redirect towards the subregion. Exports to Argentina that represented only 1-2% of Uruguay's total external sales on the eve of CAUCE, resulting between 8-10% at the end of the eighties. Exports to Brazil evolved from 5% to 16-17% in a similar period, including years in which Brazil bought up to the fourth of Uruguayan sales abroad. This redirecting process was intensified during the decade of the eighties and Uruguayan imports with Argentinean and Brazilian origin represented more than 40% of the total external sales (before the agreements came into these imports were 25%).

For some authors, this redirecting of the commercial trends did not mean any substantial modification in the productive specialisation pattern. The production would have simply obtained an amplified Subregional market, in which the protection would be as high or higher than the local market. For others, instead, a restructuring of the organisation of the local enterprises would have been produced, adapting them to compete with the Argentinean and Brazilian enterprises. In certain sectors, moreover, exports to the subregion would have been a first stage, continued with the regular and growing access to other markets where the commercial advantages of CAUCE and PEC did not operate.

Concluding, bilateral pacts with Argentina and Brazil generated the expansion of the subregional trade and produce a new insertion of Uruguay in the international division labour. The production means previously obtained in developed countries, were now obtained in the subregion. At the same time, food and raw materials of primary origin, which were traditionally placed in developed countries, were channelled in a growing proportion - through non-dominant - in the regional markets. Industrial accounts oriented towards the internal market were reconverted in export industries. The intraindustrial trade and productive interconnections of industrial type were specially developed.

Asunción Treaty

In 1990, with the new governments in Argentina and Brazil, neoliberal policies were adopted. The orientation towards the cooperation through industrial complementation was substituted by one that stressed the liberalisation of commercial flows. the attraction of external investments, the deregulation of the economy, the privatisation and the reduction of the State economic intervention. In the frame of such reorientation of the bilateral Argentinean - Brazilian agenda, both countries invited Paraguay and Uruguay to form the MERCOSUR

In MERCOSUR, in comparison with previous integration processes, the differences of size and of situation of the incorporated countries were taken into account, prejudicing the perspectives of the smallest countries. Paraguay and Uruguay were invited to the process without having real opportunities to negotiate their participation. For Uruguay, at least, because of its great commercial and economic dependence on the region, there were no alternatives: either to join or to suffer the potential loss of a market which had been conquered with effort since the sixties.

The Asunción Treaty is composed of a preamble and six chapters. In the preamble there is a list of the signing parties and an explanation of the aims and principles. The two first chapters express the purposes, principles, instruments and a detail of the organic structure. The other four chapters contain general disposition.

The annexes have no interest today because they have been substituted by later rules. Three of the annexes were referred to the intermercosur commerce Commercial Liberalisation Programmés (Annex I, General Origin Regime (Annex II) and Salvagaurdia Clauses (Annex IV). The third annex established a procedure for the solution of controversies. The fifth created the sub-groups of work of the GMC.

Annex III of the Asunción Treaty foresaw that, within the 120 days of the treaty coming into force, the Common Market Group would take to the governments of the party States a proposal of a controversies solution system to be into force during the transition period.

The Common Market Group proposed a project that was approved by the Common Market Council through Decision #1, on December 17, 1991, in Brasilia city, known as "Protocol of Brasilia for the Solution of Controversies." The controversies solution system contained in the Protocol of Brasilia, suffered some modifications and some additions in the Protocol of Ouro Preto.

After the transition process between 1991 and 1994 and an intense process of diplomatic and technical negotiations, and numerous difficulties that seemed to endanger the MERCOSUR future, the four countries reached an agreement that left the bases of a future union established.

The Protocol of Ouro Preto was signed in the VII Meeting of the CMC, on December 17, 1994, in Ouro Preto. It is formed by a preamble - where the Asunción treaty is confirmed - the MERCOSUR aims are re-established and the differential treatment principal is accepted. In its main apart, the Ouro Preto protocol deals with the institutional aspects, the normative aspects and, once again, with the solution of controversies.

In spite of having been the main aim established by the Treaty of Asunción, the Ouro Preto protocol did not create a common market. In virtue of this last agreement, from January 1995 on, the MERCOSUR started functioning, from a point of view, as an imperfect customs union, and from another, as an imperfect free trade zone. The referred "imperfections" will have to be corrected in virtue of the establishment of an adequate regime and a list of exceptions.

The adequation regime and the list of exceptions must be reduced in an automatic and linear manner. The customs union's completion, according to what was negotiated in the MERCOSUR, will occur on January 1st, 2006. Argentina, Brazil and Uruguay, will be able to maintain a maximum of 300 tariff items from the common nomenclature of the

MERCOSUR until January 1st, 2001. Paraguay will be able to maintain a maximum of 399 tariff items until the year 2006.

Besides, Uruguay could provisionally maintain the benefits provided by PEC and CAUCE. The Uruguayan products included in these bilateral pacts will maintain its access conditions to the Brazilian and Argentinean markets until the year 2001. The list of products included will be reduced in a gradual, lineal and automatic way until it reaches zero in 2001.

In spite of these exceptions the present stage of integration means a drastic change in the Uruguayan commercial relationships with its neighbours. First and foremost, Uruguay can now enter Argentinean and Brazilian markets - and also Paraguayan - with tariff zero in all headings of the tariff universe, without quantitative quota restrictions. Secondly, the bilateral preferences that Uruguay had in Argentinean and Brazilian markets were quatrilateralized. Finally, the Uruguayan market was opened for all products of Argentinean, Brazilian or Paraguayan origin.

Conclusions

Possible future developments

As has been the case a few times throughout Uruguayan history, in the next years the country will be faced with the need to take important decisions which will have a deep impact for the welfare of its inhabitants. Many of these decisions are closely related to the MERCOSUR. This agreement undoubtedly represents opportunities, challenges and threats with respect to Uruguay, which has generated a wide range of criticism.

The main criticism may be summarised as follows. On the one side, there are some who argue that Uruguay should unilaterally open to the world in the same way as Chile did. On the other side, it is considered that the MERCOSUR will produce economic and social disintegration of all the region, that Uruguay will disappear as a country and that the only benefited by MERCOSUR will be a handful of big transnational enterprises. There is a real risk of weakening and loss of the industrial base due to lack of competitiveness with Argentina and Brazil. Uruguay would see its eventual advantages restricted only to industries where economies of scale do not exist or are small or insignificant.

This criticism has the support of a popular perception of the process of change. The supporters of such view hold the MERCOSUR responsible for the increase in unemployment and informal employment. It is difficult, in actual fact, to determine to what extent the regional integration is to blame and in what ways the liberalisation process of the national economy initiated by the government of Lacalle in 1990 may have played a role in this. The predominance of a liberal economic policy and of subsidiary intervention of the State empower the strongest enterprise groups, settled mainly in Argentina and Brazil, to impose strategic decisions.

The Uruguayan situation is made worse by the profound asymmetry existing between Argentina and Brazil, on one side, and Paraguay and Uruguay, on the other, as well as the growing dependency of the Uruguayan economy on the subregional trade. Although formally the four member States of the MERCOSUR have the same power in its decision organs, periodically and in a surprising way, at impulses of the aims of national macroeconomic policy or by pressure of national interest groups, the governments of the "bigger partners". The regional integration, sometimes seems to conduct at the compass of the cojunctural national situations of Argentina and Brazil.

The levels of productive activity, of employment and consumption, as well as the evolution of the main macroeconomic variables, have followed the regional demand shocks. Then, for example, between 1991 and 1994, the Argentinean economic expansion was the key factor to induce the expansion of services in Uruguay as well as building industry and some other industrial sectors. This shock had its impact on employment, income, internal consumption and even the evolution of inflation. However, in 1994 the Argentinean economy turned recessive and deflationary, due to the crises experienced by that country.

Simultaneously, the implementation of the Real Plan in Brazil gave origin to a positive shock that gave dynamism to the agroindustrial sectors and made the anti-inflationary control difficult. The reversion of the Brazilian situation, since 1995, coupled with the Argentinean recession, have generated a new impact: productive recession, unemployment increase, stagnation of consumption and better conditions for the inflation control.

Finally a series of weaknesses exist. These seem to apply solely to Uruguay having a very reduced internal market, a financial system that has not yet reached an adequately modernised level, a technological research web that is not sufficiently structured , predominance of family type enterprises, high energy, labour and fiscal charges costs. The labour and social costs, specially, have a greater effect on the enterprises' economic-financial equation, making their regional competitiveness difficult.

On the other hand, MERCOSUR represents a great opportunity of specialise its production, developing the advantages that Uruguay presently has or can generate. Among these advantages its economic and political stability have been highlighted. Also, the free movement of capitals, its strategic position within MERCOSUR and a comparatively high level of education of Uruguay's population, living standard and social integration.

In the meantime, negotiations to deepen and enlarge MERCOSUR continue. As per the international tendency, services will be the area from which the MERCOSUR agreements will be expanded. On financial services Argentina, Paraguay and Uruguay show a quite important unilateral openness, in international terms. The negotiation has already been initiated by Argentina, with Uruguay's support. Brazil has been reluctant to accept this proposal.

The debate in the insurance and stock exchange areas has given the opportunity to reconsider national reality. The liberalisation of the insurance market has implied a adequation of MERCOSUR and, in the same sense, a new law exists on the stock market which, it is expected, will offer better perspectives to the capitals market in Uruguay.

The reduction of the economical weight of the State and its social security reform complement the Uruguayan effort to adapting to new conditions of subregional and international competitiveness.

Bibliography

A.L.A.D.I., Division de Información y Estadistica. A.L.A.D.I. en Cifras. Montevideo: A.L.A.D.I., 1993 31pp

ABREU BONILLA, Sergio. Mercosur e Integración. 2 ed. Montevideo, Fundacion de Cultura Universitaria, 1991. 189 pp

ALEXANDER, Robert. Montevideo. The 1996 Grolier Multimedia Encyclopedia. Version 8.01.s.1. Grolier Electronic Publishing Inc. 1996.

ALONSO, José. La problemática social en el proceso de integración, Economia y particapacion en el Mercosur, p. 23-34. Montevideo: Red de Apoyo a Organizaciones Sociales del Mercosur, 1996.

BUSQUEDA. El gobierno planteó al FMI firmar un "stand-by" con una duración sin precedentes: hasta 1999. Búsqueda, v. 17, n. 879, p 1. Montevideo: 23 de enero de 1997.

-----, Los buenos, los malos y los tontos. Búsqueda, v. 26, n 878, p. 2. Montevideo: 16 de enero de 1997.

-----, En 1996 la economia uruguaya creció mas de lo previsto por el gobierno; el desempleo se convirtió en su principal problema, Búsqueda, v. 26, n. 876, p16/17. Montideo: 2 de enero de 1997.

-----, El ex ministro Alejandro Végh Villegas dijo que la posición de Brazil no permite hacer augurios positivos sobre el Mercosur, Búsqueda, p. 15. Montevideo: 21 de marzo de 1996.

CAETANO, Gerardo, & Rilla, José. Historia Contemporánea del Uruguay - de la Colonia al Mercosur. Colección Claeh. Montevideo: Fin de Siglo, 1994. 396 pp.

CARLEVARO TORRES, Héctor. Acuerdos excluidos del Programa de Liberación Comercial del Tratado de Asunción y de las normas del Acuerdo de Complementación Económica no. 18. Enfoques, v. 1, n. 2, p. 52-56. Montevideo: COMI.SEC., 1994.

COMI.SEC. Lo que queremos saber, nesesitamos preguntar y debemos aprender. Montevideo: COMI.SEC., 1995. 62 pp.

EKMEKDJIAN, Miguel Ángel. Introduccio\ón al Derecho Comunitario Latinoamericano. Buenos Aires: Depalma, 1994. 551 pp.

MAGARIÑOS, Gustavo. Uruguay en el Mercosur. Reimpresion de la 1 ed. Montevideo: Fundacion de Cultura Universitaria, 1991. 103 pp.

MANNISE, Efrain. La negociación comercial importa más que la estabilidad cambiara. Búsqueda, p. 22. Montevideo: 21 de marzo de 1996.

MINDSCAPE. Mindscape World Atlas MPC. Mindscape Inc., 1995. Electromap Inc., 1995.

REYES ABADIE, Washington, & VÁZQUEZ ROMERO, Andrés. Crónica General del Uruguay, v. 2: La emancipación. Montevideo: Banda Oriental, s.f.

SALA, Lucia. La persectiva histórica y teórica de la integración. Mercosur - Claroscuro de una Integración. Ciclo de cinferencias realizado en la Facultad de Ciencias Económicas y Administración. p. 11-14. Montevideo: Fin de Siglo, 1991

SANTO, Michele. Entrando en razones. Búsqueda, v. 26, n. 880, p. 2. Montevideo: 30 de enero de febrero de 1997.

SEMINO, Miguel Angel. Fundamentos de la reforma, in: Constitución de la República Oriental del Uruguay. Montevideo: Idea, 1997. 151 pp.

STOLOVICH, Luis. Un pequeño pais ante el desafio de la integración económica regional: el Uruguay en el Mercosur. Economia y Participación Social en el Mercosur. Montevideo: Red de Apoyo a Organizaciones Sociales de Mercosur, 1996. p. 143-165.

VACCHINO, Juan Mario. Integración Latinoamericana de la ALALC A LA ALADI. Buenos Aires: Depalma, 1983. 250 pp.

VAZ, Daniel. Mercosur: una visión panorámica de la situación del Uruguay. Cuadernos de Negocios Internacionales e Integración, v. 1, n. 2, p. 12-22. Montevideo: Licenciatura en Negocios Internacionales e Integración de la Falcultad de Ciencias Empressariales de la Universidad Católica del Uruguay Dámaso Antonio Larrañaga, 1995.

WEINSTEIN, Martin. Uruguay. The 1996 Grolier Multimedia Encyclopedia. Version 8.01.s.1 Grolier Electronic Publishing Inc. 1996.

WILKIE, Richard. Buenos Aires, The 1996 Grolier Multimedia Encyclopedia. Version 8.01.s.1 Grolier Electronic Publishing Inc. 1996.

Chapter 5
CHILE

Dario Menanteau-Horta

INTRODUCTION

On June 25, 1996, after long and skillful negotiations, Chile signed a trade agreement with the MERCOSUR founding countries - Argentina, Brazil, Uruguay, and Paraguay. The Common Market of the Southern Cone nations, initially established as a customs-union to increase trade among these countries, also has long-term objectives of promoting economic development and the integration of all Latin America.

Chilean President Eduardo Frei Ruiz-Tagle emphasized the socio-political importance of this trade agreement for the region, declaring that "all the presidents that joined together in San Luis [Argentinian province where the treaty signing ceremony took place] confirmed that we are not only talking about economic issues here, but also about a regional integration project of the largest proportions."

The five MERCOSUR countries represent a potential single market of 200 million people, nearly 45% of the Latin American population, over 60% of its geographical area, and more than half of its industrial production with a total GNP of about US$800 billion dollars.

Chile's associate status with MERCOSUR provides an important mechanism expected to stimulate the economies of all five members of this agreement. Chile will be able to expand international markets, increase exports of value-added products to these southern cone countries, and have better access to their diverse products at lower prices for Chilean consumers. Recent estimates suggest that there will be a 30 to 40% drop in prices in local markets for 70% of the products Chile currently buys from Mercosur countries.

Additional perceived benefits for Chile with this agreement include (1) opportunities for manufacturing and service industries to generate an estimated 150,000 new jobs, (2) development and improvement of the national infrastructure such as roads, railroads, and harbor facilities, as well as (3) opportunities to explore new areas of investment, trade, and scientific and technological cooperation among the five nations of MERCOSUR.

The Chilean Congress declared their support for the treaty as a whole, despite some concerns that certain sectors of the economy, especially agriculture, may be vulnerable and have negative effects with the trade accord. The Chamber of Deputies approved the agreement on August 14, 1996, approving also by a large majority of 76 to 26 votes, the complementary measures which include the Protocol of Physical Integration and the Declaration of Democratic Commitments in MERCOSUR. On September 11, 1996, the Senate, in an overwhelming vote of 36 senators in favor and only 3 opposed, approved the agreement that allows Chile to become an associate member of MERCOSUR.

The implementation of the treaty began on October 1, 1996, with the immediate tariff reduction to 19% for all Chilean exports and 15% for imports from the Mercosur common market.
According to the treaty, the products were classified in four major categories for the purpose of lowering tariffs gradually and avoiding harmful consequences for certain areas of the economy. Those products

included in the "general" list category had a 40% tariff reduction and were scheduled to become 0% over the next eight years. Tariffs for products classified as "sensitive" were reduced by 30%, but allowing a gradual process of three to six years for lowering and eliminating tariffs. Items considered "special sensitive" will maintain their current tariffs during the first four years of the agreement, and at that time a tariff reduction plan will take place for the following six years. The fourth category of products, "exceptions" includes some agricultural items with a waiting period of fifteen and up to eighteen years (as is the case of wheat and flour) to start a process of gradual trade liberalization.

Chile's association with MERCOSUR countries constitutes an important trade alliance moving towards a more sustainable common market and economic integration in Latin America. The agreement, according to government officials, fits the overall international trade strategy model of "Open Regionalism," characterized by legal and economic flexibility to negotiate and advance in developing a regional economy, attaining physical integration with neighboring countries, and continuing honoring bilateral trade agreements.

This trade strategy also responds to Chile's new challenges derived from the increasing globalization of social and economic problems; the end of the cold war and consequent adjustments in the international balance of power; and the rapid expansion of market economies during the last decade.

SOME CONCEPTS ABOUT INTEGRATION

"Integration" has been broadly defined as a process by which various parts become unified in order to establish a whole. Myrdal (1956), referring to the interaction between social and economic factors, suggests that integration may well represent a goal for social change rather than a situation of static equilibrium.

The concept of "integration" that emerged in Europe after WWII and enjoyed acceptance among some Latin American economists in later years emphasized the classical definition of market integration of national economies in a region. As early as 1949, the Ministers of the European Organization for Economic Cooperation, defined the concept of integration as the development of a single large market in which quantitative restrictions affecting the exchange of products (i.e., import and export quotas), monetary obstacles, tariffs, and other economic barriers are eliminated permanently.

The European Community for Coal and Steel refers to "integration" as a process of cooperation among nations conducive to define common goals and mechanisms for a better utilization of natural resources by a national organization of production and changes to increase living levels, the main objective of all economic activity.

Pinto (1966) also provides an economic definition of the concept, indicating that integration is a process which has an immediate or final objective of organizing and common area where members of two or more national economies could participate in an exchange of individuals as well as other productions and consumption factors.

In Latin America, particularly during the 1960's, regional integration was conceived as a fundamental requirement to secure and accelerate economic development. It is during this time that the idea of integration gained new followers and acceptance among government officials, political leaders, and business interests. Together, they gave impulse to the creation of new institutions to foster Latin American integration as a key factor for economic and social progress in all countries of the region.

A general perspective of integration as a process of economic and social change as well as the formulation of practical goals for Latin America development was suggested by the Inter-American Development Bank in its early activities with governments and institutions in the region. According to this, integration, as a process, could evolve from a simple form of commercial alliances to the most advanced type of social, economic, cultural, and political structure characterized by an Economic Community in Latin America. Intermediate forms and mechanisms of integration are, among others, "Free Trade Areas," which include reduction or elimination of tariffs and other trade restrictions; "Custom Unions," which involve elimination of commercial barriers and trade duties among the members as well as a system of common tariffs when dealing with third parties; and "Common Markets," which, in addition to economic measures fostering trade and commerce also introduce other 'supranational' and integration arrangements among countries (IDB, 1966).

A HISTORICAL SYNOPSIS

The idea of regional integration emerged almost simultaneously with the political independence of Latin America from Spain in the early 1800's. In fact, Bolivar's aspirations to establish a united Latin America preceded the independence of Peru and Bolivia. First references to his integration plans are found in an article published in the Morning Chronicle of London, September 5,1810, in which he proclaimed his first call to unity of the new countries in Latin America, saying that if Venezuelans become forced to declare war against Spain, that would be the moment that all the people of Latin America should unite in a confederation for their freedom and independence. (Menanteau-Horta, 1973)

In the "Manifesto of Cartagena of 1812," and also as liberator and president of Venezuela in 1814, Bolivar insisted on the idea that real independence of the new nations was to be achieved and maintained only within a union of all Latin American countries. In 1818 he suggested the signing of a Regional American Pact to reduce nationalism and eliminate frontiers.

In Chile, on May 6, 1818, Bernardo O'Higgins, liberator and first president of the country, called for the celebration of a congress for the purpose of establishing "a great Confederation of American countries" (Barros, 1970). This idea, also expressed by Bolivar, was followed by the organization of the Panama Congress in 1826, where a treaty was signed with the following objectives: 1) establishment of a League of Latin American countries for the defense of its members; 2) organization of a regional army of 60,000 soldiers; 3) opportunity for Latin Americans to freely choose and change citizenship in other League's nation; 4) declaration against slavery; and 5) basis for mediation in inter-American conflicts. (De Galindez, 1954.p. 165)

Despite these positive steps to articulate a regional structure in Latin America, the Panama Congress had limited attendance with only eight delegates from Mexico, Central America, Colombia, and Peru. Bolivia, Brazil, and Chile did not participate, and Argentina declined the invitation. Internal conflicts and territorial wars between the new countries stopped those early integration efforts in Latin America.

For over a century (1830's to 1950's), the political will and administrative arrangements of Latin American governments to facilitate regional integration remained dormant. The most visible group which maintained the ideas and even a romantic notion of a united Latin American community was the active network of intellectuals and writers of the region. Individuals such as José Marti, from Cuba; Andres Bello, a Venezuelan with a long and distinguished list of work in Chile; Alfonso Reyes, from Mexico; Domingo F. Sarmiento, from Argentina, and others expressed their strong voices in favor of Latin American cooperation and unity. (Ripoll, 1966)

Andres Bello writes about these ideas and the importance of regional trade, saying: "Just a glance over the map of America is enough to perceive how God has wanted to facilitate trade among its people and make of them a society of brothers." (Bello, 1848) Sarmiento, making specific reference to South American countries, suggests that if these nations do not achieve unity, then the entire region will remain behind in its growth and progress. Henriquez Urena, a writer from Dominican Republic who lived in Cuba and Mexico, proclaims that the unity of history, purpose, political experiences, and intellectual life made Latin America a single entity, a "Magna Patria," a people whose destiny was to become more united. (Henriquez Urena, 1925)

Although the lessons shared by these teachers, writers, and intellectuals were instrumental to expanding education and creating some Latin American awareness about the perils of cultural dependency, particularly from Europe and the United States, their message failed to be articulated in policies and practical programs leading toward regional integration.

It was not until the post-second-war period during the late 1950's and 1960's that Latin American governments reopened the chapter of integration as a necessary road to achieve social and economic development. New leadership inspired in the notion that democratic principles need to be based on firm economic grounds and improved social conditions for most Latin Americans sought the opening of inter-regional market alliances, increased trade, and the development of an institutional framework for economic integration. During this period, the following institutions and agreements were achieved:

- The Inter American Development Bank, founded in 1959;
- The Central American Common Market, created also in 1959;
- The Latin American Free Trade Association (LAFTA), originated in 1960 with the initial participation of Argentina, Brazil, Chile, Mexico, Paraguay, Peru, and Uruguay, and joined later by Bolivia, Colombia, Ecuador, and Venezuela. LAFTA represented one of the most serious regional integration efforts as it involved nearly 90% of the land and population of Latin America and about 90% of the region's Gross National Product.
- The Andean Group established in 1964 by Bolivia, Chile, Colombia, Ecuador, Peru, and Venezuela in order to accelerate the integration process.
- Punta del Este Conference held in 1967, in which the presidents of the Americas called for the creation of a single, region-wide Latin American Common Market.

Over the years, Chile has been an active member in most of these organizations and a strong supporter of the regional integration process.

Table 5-1 Chile: Social and Economic Indicators

	Year	
Land Area (Km2)	1996	756,629
Population (thousands)	1996	14,462
Population (Avg. Annual Growth Rate)	1987-96	1.6
Rural Population (Percent)	1996	12.2
Density (Pop. Per Km2)	1996	19.1
Fertility Rate (per woman)	1993	2.5
Crude Birth (Per 1,000 Live Births)	1992	22.5
Crude Death (Per 1,000 pop.)	1992	6.5
Infant Mortality (Per 1,000 Live Births)	1993	15.6
Life Expectancy at Birth (Years)	1993	74
Labour Force	1994	5,099
Unemployment Rate (Percent)	1996	7.1
Illiteracy (Percent)	1995	4.8
Avg. Years of Schooling (Pop. >25 yrs.)	1995	6.7
GDP (Avg. Annual Growth rate)	1987-96	7.1
Gross Domestic Investment (% of GDP)	1996	27.7
Gross Domestic Savings (% of GDP)	1996	25.5
Exports (US$ Million FOB)	1995	16,446
Imports (US$ Million CIF)	1995	15,348
Trade Balance (US$ Million)	1996	1,098
Foreign Debt (US$ Million)	1996	27,517

Source: Inter-American Development Bank (1997). Chile: Statistics and Quantitative Analysis

CHILE'S ECONOMIC DEVELOPMENT

The history of economic development in Chile is closely related to the country's ability to export natural resources to world markets and to major political and social changes in the nation. The importance of international trade and a dynamic foreign policy, therefore, becomes a fundamental priority for fostering good relations and new markets.

Throughout the years, the state's role in economic and industrial planning, international relations, and social policies has been strong in leadership and control. Under the military regime, however, government functions in economic and social issues were drastically reduced. The international image of Chile was tarnished because of human rights violations, and the relative isolation imposed by the authoritarian administration of General Pinochet embodied some degree of nationalism and curtailed the development of more vigorous international and Latin American policies. Also, the presence of military governments in neighboring countries during the 1970's and 1980's put a hold on some of the regional integration ideas.

Today the country moves toward the consolidation of democracy, although many social and economic problems left unattended during the dictatorship still remain (Collins and Lear, 1995). Chile has returned in full force to a more balanced strategy of internal development with a dynamic international trade agenda.

During the 19th century and the early years of this century, the Chilean economy was externally driven by international demands for agricultural and mining products. Inside the country, however, social problems emerged as a consequence of this narrowly defined export economy. Poor labour conditions became a central issue for the majority of workers required to work long days for low wages and without contracts, accident prevention, or indemnity for work-related accidents. During the last decade of the 19th century, Chile experienced no less than 200 labour strikes which, in absence of appropriate legislation, were all considered illegal and resulted in their leaders being prosecuted.

Chile's dependency on its nitrate industry at the beginning of this century was severely affected by the collapse of European markets during World War I and by the production of synthetic nitrates by Germany in 1919. The economic recession brought high unemployment and massive migration of miners and other workers to Santiago, the capital city, and other urban centers. The growing social and economic disparities between the rich and the poor became more visible, and the labor movement turned more militant. Rapid industrialization and growing urban populations during the last half-century enhanced the rise of the middle class composed primarily of professional and technical groups, merchants, and small business owners.

After the economic crisis of the late 1920's and early 1930's, the Chilean government applied the import substitution model, accelerating industrialization and legitimizing the State's economic and public policy roles.

The decades of 1940's and 50's were characterized by some additional gains in social and economic benefits for the middle class, urban, and industrial workers. In addition, political participation of the middle and working classes in Chile legitimized the State's role as an active agent in policy creation, implementation of government programs, and public investments for industrial growth and economic development.

These changes facilitated the election of two important governments representing different ideologies for economic and social reforms but with a common interest to improve and expand Chile's capabilities in international trade and Latin American affairs: The Christian Democratic administration of Eduardo Frei Montalva (1964-1970) and the Socialist government of Salvador Allende (1970-1973).

The Frei Administration: (1964-1970)

The Christian Democratic government under Eduardo Frei Montalva offered a rapid but peaceful transformation of the political and socio-economic structure of Chile. Key ideas for this "revolution in freedom" were economic growth with 'popular promotion' as basic processes for development.

Major accomplishments of Frei's administration with profound effects on economic and social development were the "Chileanization" of the copper industry, by which the government purchased 51 percent of the stocks from U.S. mining companies; the 1967 agrarian reform law which placed limits on farm size; and government increases of the public budget allocated to all social programmés, reaching 20% of the country's GNP between 1965 and 1970 and the highest level of 25.8% in 1972. During those years, Europe, U.S.A., and Japan spent about 22% of their GNP in social programmés.

Expansion of social benefits moved parallel to a growing democracy expressed by increased participation in the electoral process from 1915 to 1970. In 1925, voters represented only 7.4% of the total population, increasing to 20.5% in 1949 and reaching 36% in 1970.

President Frei Montalva was a vigorous leader and defender of the basic principles guiding national development and Latin American integration.

He was actively involved in many of the key meetings and a vocal supporter of government decisions, resolutions, and declarations calling for cooperation and unity of Latin America.

Felipe Herrera (1969), former President of the Inter-American Development Bank, recognizes Frei's leadership in this process when he states: "A decisive progress towards an ideological enlightenment about Latin American integration took place at the beginning of 1965, when the President of Chile, Eduardo Frei, requested a report on this issue to (economists) Jose Antonio Mayobre, Raul Prebish, Carlos Sanz de Santa Maria, and Felipe Herrera. Our response originated the first public debate on the topic of regional integration and constituted the most important analysis elaborated until then about the directions to be followed if the integration process were to be effectively promoted" (p.133).

Perhaps one of the most important events in which President Frei participated and helped to set up favourable conditions for future developments of regional integration, including MERCOSUR today, was the meeting of the American Presidents in Punta del Este, Uruguay, in April, 1967. The Punta del Este Declaration established, for the first time, the public commitment of all presidents of the Americas to create, progressively, a Latin American Common Market. President Frei and other Latin American presidents who signed the Punta del Este Declaration conceived economic integration as a collective instrument to accelerate the development of their countries and the entire region.

The Allende Government: (1970-1973)

Salvador Allende in 1970 attempted a transition to socialism by improving government functioning and implementing social and economic reforms within democratic boundaries. In the process, however, hostility and conflict between the government led by Allende and the forces of the opposition increased.

Another major obstacle confronted by Allende's government were the economic and political pressures of U.S. companies with investments in Chile and the covert operations launched by the CIA with the approval of the Nixon administration.

Industrial and commercial interests from U.S. multinational companies such as ITT, Kennecott, Braden Copper, and others were highly instrumental in sponsoring conspiracy and facilitating subversive activities in Chile. Time magazine on November 6, 1972, reported the efforts of Kennecott in organizing an international blockade of Chilean copper shipments to European and other harbors in the world. Also, in May 1973, the Foreign Relations Sub-committee of the U.S. Senate confirmed the type of relations between the CIA and ITT. According to this report, ITT offered the CIA one million dollars to support a plan against Allende (Cordova-Claure, 1974, p.76).

Trade between Chile and the United States dropped dramatically during the short three years of Allende's government. Exports to the United States in 1970 represented 14.7% of all exports from Chile. This proportion fell to 8.8% in 1971 and to 5.7% in 1972. Imports of U.S. products also diminished from 25.8% of total Chilean imports in 1970 to 11.8% in 1972.

The U.S. hostility towards Chile is also illustrated by the rapid decline in credits and other financial assistance provided to Chile between 1970 and 1973. Short-term financing from US sources also plummeted from 74.8% of the total in 1970 to 6.6% during the first half of 1972.

Credit to Chile from all U.S. government agencies collapsed from US$80.3 million in 1969, before Allende, to less than US$10 million in 1973, at the time of the military coup. Private U.S. banks which in 1970 carried loans to Chile for US$220 million allocated less than US$20 million for similar credits by the end of 1972. International institutions such as the World Bank and the Inter-American Development Bank cut their credits and financial flow to Chile from US$32.3 million in 1970 to zero in 1972 (Bitar, 1986).

By 1973 the economic crisis of Chile was fueled by inflation, debt, instability, lack of foreign investments, and shrinking international trade.

<u>The Military Regime</u>: (1973-1990)

Chile's long-standing tradition of over 150 years of political democracy was abruptly interrupted by the military coup of September 11, 1973. The dictatorship brought rampant violations of human rights together with the establishment of a free-market, conservative economic model. The consolidation of Pinochet's regime was achieved by a self-proclaimed condition of "internal war" in an effort to justify political persecution, exile, and torture (Menanteau, 1995).

Former Swedish Ambassador to Chile, Harald Edelstam, estimated at about 15,000 the number of people killed during the days following the 1973 coup. In addition, 35,000 were made political prisoners, 7,000 were arrested, nearly 30,000 students were expelled from universities, and more than 100,000 workers lost their jobs (Taufic, 1974).

The 1991 National Commission for Truth and Reconciliation reported the findings concerning a total of 2,279 verified cases of people who were detained-disappeared, executed, tortured, and killed by agents of the State from September 11, 1973, to March 11, 1990.

Terrazas (1992) suggests that the number of victims is likely much larger. He reports that the categories of human rights violations are more diverse, and the number of victims is staggering for a small country like Chile. The high numbers of individuals who were detained (356,000), tortured (146,000), and exiled (842,000) reveal the intensity of the conflict.

The consolidation of a free-market economy introduced major reforms characterized by a limited role of the State on economic development followed by a major privatization plan.

Government budget cuts in health, housing, and education were made during the military regime. Public health programmés lost over 51 percent of their budgets during the first 15 years. On a per capita basis, health expenditures dropped from US$29 in 1973 to nearly US$10 in 1988. In public housing, budgets reduced from US$225 million to about US$77 million during the same period. Budget cuts in education were made at all levels; by 1988 social investment in public education had shrunk to 2.73% of the GNP, compared to 4.29 of the GNP during the last year of Allende's government in 1973.

Privatization of large government industries coupled with tax incentives to foreign investment and deregulation of major industrial activities are additional elements of the legacy of the military regime.

In 1973, the State had control over 600 major industries in the country with mixed results in terms of their efficiency, productivity, and capacity to be self-supporting. Some of these enterprises have been organized by CORFO -Production Promotion Corporation- a government agency that had played a key role in the industrialization process of Chile for decades. Other industries, however, were under State control because of intervention and nationalization plans of Allende's government.

During the first year of the military regime, a total of 350 enterprises were returned to their owners. Later, in 1983, CORFO designed a comprehensive privatization program to transfer state- owned businesses and industries to the private sector by 1987. This plan also included attempts to attract foreign credit and capital investment, as well as to stimulate production increases for domestic and international markets.

The orientation of the Chilean economy to exports rapidly paid off with diversification of production and the expansion of the economy into new development areas. For instance, while in 1973 copper constituted 82% of total exports, in 1988 it was about 40% of total international sales. Also, in 1971, Chile used to export a total of about 400 products to only 60 countries. In 1988, international trade linked Chile with 112 nations around the world, buying over 1,340 products.

Chile's transition from a predominantly monoexport economy highly dependent on copper to one more highly diversified in terms of products

Table 5-2 Chilean Foreign Trade (in US $ Millions)

Year	Exports	Imports	Total	Balance
1990	8,372.7	7,036.8	15,409.5	1,335.9
1991	8,941.5	7,353.5	16,295.0	1,588.0
1992	10,007	9,236.9	19,244.3	770.5
1993	9,198.7	10,180.8	19,379.5	(982.1)
1994	11,604.1	10,879.0	22,483.1	725.1
1995	16,038.6	14,653.2	30,691.8	1,385.4

and international markets was largely achieved with major structural adjustments of the economy over several years of tight military control.

Chile's Open Economy, International Trade, and Mercosur

The return to representative democracy in 1990 opened new possibilities for fostering trade and commerce with countries and with emerging trade blocks such as the European Union, the Asia-Pacific Economic Cooperation (APEC), the North American Free Trade Agreement (NAFTA), and MERCOSUR.

The elections of President Patricio Aylwin in 1990 and President Eduardo Frei Ruiz-Tagle in 1994 demonstrated that the country was ready to move on in the direction of sustained economic growth with social equity and democratic participation.

The Chilean economy has continued experiencing a rapid growth of exports to an expanding world market. Trade sources affirm that "Chile has one of the world's most open economies." In less than a decade, the total export values more than double. In 1988, Chilean exports had a value of US$7 billion compared to US$16 billion in 1996.

Total Chilean trade including exports and imports represents over 45% of the national Gross Domestic Product, which has been considered the

Table 5-3 Chile—MERCOSUR Trade, 1990-1995 (in US $ 1,000's)

Country	Year	Exports	Imports	Trade Balance	Total Trade
Argentina	1990	113,515	505,098	-389,583	616,613
	1991	257,417	553,790	-296,373	811,207
	1992	461,557	633,603	-172,046	1,095,160
	1993	588,965	580,855	8,110	1,169,820
	1994	637,100	954,736	-317,636	1,591,836
	1995	585,611	954,736	-798,913	1,970,135
Brazil	1990	487,431	1,384,524	-76,751	1,051,613
	1991	447,622	697,560	-249,938	1,145,182
	1992	450,944	996,158	-545,214	1,447,102
	1993	407,080	1,060,207	-653,127	1,467,287
	1994	604,669	999,777	-395,108	1,604,446
	1995	1,056,808	1,194,691	-137,883	2,251,499
Paraguay	1990	24,014	40,373	-16,359	64,387
	1991	37,838	59,434	-21,596	97,272
	1992	42,672	61,378	-18,706	104,050
	1993	48,579	68,107	-19,528	116,686
	1994	57,682	55,593	2,035	113,221
	1995	75,965	57,997	17,968	133,962
Uruguay	1990	27,061	16,273	10,788	43,334
	1991	27,106	20,966	6,140	48,072
	1992	35,302	49,312	-14,010	84,614
	1993	44,451	51,782	-7211	96,353
	1994	52,927	43,994	8,933	96,921
	1995	56,295	39,941	16,354	96,236

Total MERCOSUR	1990	652,021	1,123,926	-471,905	1,775,947
	1991	769,983	1,123,926	-561,767	2,101,733
	1992	990,475	1,331,750	-749,976	2,730,926
	1993	1,089,195	1,760,451	-671,756	2,850,146
	1994	1,352,324	2,054,100	-701,776	3,406,424
	1995	1,774.679	2,677,153	-902,474	4,451,832

Source: DIRECONMULTI (ACCESO A LOS MERCADOS). Data from Banco Central de Chile.

highest in Latin America and one of the highest in the world economy.

Between 1990 and 1994, exports of goods and services grew by 41.7% with a more diversified composition of exported items than in previous years. In the 1980's, for example, nearly 50% of all Chilean exports were mining products, and industrial exports represented less than one-third of all exports. Today, these two sectors have reached a more balanced output representing about 44% of the country's total exports.

Trade liberalization and reduction of import duties have been important additional efforts of Chile to expand the country's presence in the world market. Import duties have been reduced from a rate of 100% in 1974, 25.8% in 1985, and to a rate of 11% for most products today. Lower duties are applied to products from countries with which Chile has negotiated trade agreements, as in the case of LAFTA and MERCOSUR. According to the Association Agreement with MERCOSUR, it is expected that by the year 2014 zero tariffs will be reached for all products.

From 1990 to 1995, commerce and trade between Chile and MERCOSUR increased from US$1.7 billion to over US$4.4 billion, about 150% growth. During this period, imports from MERCOSUR doubled from US$1.2 billion to US$2.6 billion, but Chilean exports to this common market nearly tripled.

MERCOSUR represents nearly 15% of Chile's total international trade, and this proportion is expected to increase in future years, especially due to the industrial sector. In 1995, over one-third (34%) of all Chilean exports to MERCOSUR valued at about US$700 million were manufactured goods and industrial products. This represents a more diversified list of export items with higher value added than raw materials. This list of products includes wines, furniture, canned food, appliances, clothes, and tires.

The business climate in Chile and public policies oriented to maintain an open and liberalized economy have continued to attract new investments from a variety of international companies from around the world. Foreign investment laws, and particularly the Decree Law 600 which regulates entry and conditions of investments from international sources, offer ample guarantees and a non-discriminatory treatment for national and international investors. Foreign investment in Chile under D.L. 600 rose from about US$165 million in 1985 to US$1.3 billion in 1990 and to over US$3.02 billion in 1995.

While foreign investment still remains concentrated on mining (56.8%) with nearly US$1.72 billion in 1995, the industrial and service sectors are becoming highly competitive in attracting foreign capital. Investments in services such as communications, banking, insurance, and others increased 176% in 1995 with respect to 1994. This trend has continued, and from January to November, 1996, total foreign investment in Chile increased 70% compared to the same period a year earlier.

Diversification and sustained economic growth combined with a new entrepreneurial vision and adaptation to larger block markets have contributed to an expansion of Chilean investment abroad. Total Chilean investments abroad reached US$4.8 billion or 9.2% of GDP in 1995. Geographical and cultural proximity in addition to trade agreements for economic cooperation make MERCOSUR countries in general, and particularly Argentina, the favorite places for Chilean investors.

Table 5-4 Chilean Investment in MERCOSUR (in US # Millions, 1990-March 1996)

Country	Materialized Investment	Participation %	Value of project $US Millions
Argentina	3,132.8	93.4	6,805.0
Brazil	187.2	5.6	227.0
Paraguay	12.6	0.4	27.4
Uruguay	22.6	0.7	22.6
Total	3355.2	100	7082.2

Source: Ministry of Foreign Relations

Chilean investment in MERCOSUR amounted to almost US$3.4 billion in 1995, Argentina being the principal recipient with over 90% of the capital invested during the 1990-1995 period. In addition, the Chilean presence as a major investor continues to expand in other Latin American countries with recent acquisitions in Brazil, Paraguay, and Peru. According to the Santiago Chamber of Commerce, Chilean foreign investment from 1990 through the first quarter of 1997 totals almost US$16 billion.

CONCLUSION

Today's general economic environment of Chile is one characterized by an active business climate, sustained economic growth, competitive markets, stable government, competent decision makers, and a skillful and hard-working labor force. As a recent news report states, "Chile's stable political system, free market economy, and transparent investment regulations have made it the most dynamic market in Latin America. According to Central Bank estimates, 1996 GDP growth was 7.2%, the highest in South America. Per capita annual income rose to US$5,200, well above the South American average. This sustained growth has created a breeding ground for an entrepreneurial spirit, and modern business practices that is unparalleled in Latin America."

The Chilean economic performance and the association with MERCOSUR have not been exempt from difficulties and criticism.
Social and economic inequalities still remain deeply rooted in Chilean society, and marginalization emerges when the poor do not have access to basic public services.

Larrain (1997) questions the social and environmental sustainability of the Chilean economy driven by deregulation, privatization, and exploitation of natural resources. The result has been a condition of social unsustainability which is described from a social perspective as follows: "Almost 30% of the country's population live in a situation of poverty--that is 4 million Chileans, of whom 1 million are completely indigent. Unjust distribution of income, which began during the military dictatorship, has continued without change."

The well-publicized success story of Chile's economy is open to question in a system where most of the wealth is highly concentrated in the hands of a few. In fact, the top 20% of the Chilean rich earn twelve times more than the 20% of those in poverty. Despite economic growth, the gap between the rich and the poor remains, and a large proportion of the working poor are not fully covered by a comprehensive social service system to provide them with health care, sickness leave, or some protection for unfair dismissal.

The extent to which Chile (and the MERCOSUR members if they follow the same economic growth model as Chile) could maintain the same rate of economic expansion of the last few years using the present production conditions has also been questioned. Larrain (1997) remarks: "The environmental unsustainability of Chile's current export model is reflected in the collapse of species, the loss of ecosystems and agricultural land, the proliferation of zones which are saturated by pollution and the generalized deterioration of the health of the population."

Despite these problems, in a recent United Nations' ranking of countries around the world according to their human development programs, Chile achieved fourth place in Latin America behind Costa Rica, Argentina, and

Uruguay.

Also, a study conducted by CEPAL entitled "Preliminary Balance of the Economies of Latin America and the Caribbean" ranked Chile in second place in terms of overall economic growth in Latin America during 1996. CEPAL's Secretary General Gert Rosenthal, discussing the results of this study, concluded:

"From all perspectives, Chile's performance is good and it once more finds itself among the region's leaders." In reference to Chile's international trade agreements, including MERCOSUR, he suggests that these new integration strategies "will strengthen its foreign trade in coming years."

These positive comments may also be interpreted in light of the spirit and principles of Latin American integration, according to which MERCOSUR and regional trade are, indeed, key components of economic growth with the challenges and responsibilities to achieve development of a more equitable society in all Latin America.

REFERENCES

Barros, Mario (1970). Historia Diplomatica de Chile. Ediciones Ariel, Barcelona, Spain.

Bello, Andres (1848). "Modo de Escribir la Historia," El Araucano, Santiago de Chile.

Bitar, Sergio (1986). Chile Experiment in Democracy. Institute for the Study of Human Issues, Philadelphia.

Collins, J. and Lear, J. (1995). Chile's Free Market Miracle: A Second Look. Institute for Food and Development Policy, Oakland, California.

Cordova-Claure, Ted (1974). Chile No. Grupo Editor de Buenos Aires, Buenos Aires, Argentina.

De GAlindez, Jesus (1954). Iberoamerica, Las Americas Publishing Co., New York. (pp. 164-165).

Henriquez Urena, Pedro (1925). "La Utopia de America," Patria de la

Justicia, La Plata, Argentina.

Herrera, Felipe (1969). Chile en America Latina. Editorial Zig-Zag, Santiago, Chile.

Larrain, Sara (1997). "Chile Advances in the Global Adventure: Who Benefits?", CHIP Environmental Report,(May), Santiago, Chile.

Menanteau-Horta, Dario (1996). "Internal War and Political Genocide in Chile." Midwest Sociological Association Meetings, Chicago, Illinois.

Menanteau-Horta, Dario (1973). "Alguna Observaciones Sobre la Integracion de America latina." Revista de la Integracion, No. 13, May. BancoInter-Americano para el Desarrollo - Instituto para la Integracion de America Latina (BID -INTAL).

Muchnik E., Errazuriz L. y Dominguez J. (1996) "Impacto de la Associacion de Chile al Mercosur en el Sector Agricola y Agroindustrial." Centro de Estudios Publicos #253, Santiago, Chile.

Myrdal, Gunnar (1956). Solidaridad o desintegracion. Fondo de Cultura, Mexico.

Pinto, Francisco A. (1966). "Necesidad de un Sistema Institucional y Juridico para la Integracion Latinoamericana," in Factores para la Integracion Latinoamericana, BID, Fondo de Cultura, Mexico.

Taufic, Camilo (1974). Chile en la Hoguera. Ediciones Corregidor Buenos Aires, Argentina.

Terrazas-Guzman, Mario (1992). Quien se Acuerda de Sheila Cassidy? Alfabeta Impresores, Santiago, Chile.

Media Sources: El Mercurio, 5/8, 1970; Ercilla, 1974; Time,1972; CHIP News,1996-1997.

Ministerio de Relaciones Exteriores, Chile. (1996) Acuerdo de Complementacion Economica Chile-Mercosur.

Various Reports from: Central Bank of Chile, Ministry of Finance, Banco de Chile, Inter-American Development Bank.

Chapter 6

NAFTA and the MERCOSUR: Prospects for Cooperation

By Robert Riley

INTRODUCTION

Since 1990, when then-President George Bush of the United States called for a Western Hemisphere free trade area in his Enterprise for the Americas Initiative, considerable attention has been devoted to the study of current and prospective integration efforts for North and South America. This was heightened in 1994 when U.S. President Clinton convened the Summit of the Americas in Miami, and the 34 participating countries (excluding only Cuba) agreed in principle to the formation of a hemisphere-wide free trade zone by the year 2005. Since that time, despite lack of progress in laying the groundwork for such an agreement and despite opposition in Congress to granting fast track approval to the accession of Chile to the North American Free Trade Agreement (NAFTA), discussion of such a possibility has only widened. When the Summit of the Americas reconvened in Bello Horizonte, Brazil in May 1997 the issue was once again in the spotlight.

Two primary developments - the formation of the NAFTA between the U.S., Canada, and Mexico in late 1992 (effective in 1994) as well as the establishment of the customs union known as Mercado Común del Sur (MERCOSUR) between Argentina, Brazil, Paraguay, and Uruguay in 1994 (effective in 1995) - have delineated the path of future trade integration in the hemisphere. What are the prospects for cooperation between these two blocs? How likely is it that they will be effectively combined into a single free trade area, and under what conditions will such a move be more likely? This chapter intends to explore the prospects for the integration of these two areas into one larger free trade area, or for conflict between them. It will also attempt to assess the prospects for deeper integration within either bloc beyond current levels.

Other recent events have energized the debate over the possible path of further integration in the Western Hemisphere. Bolivia will become an associate member of the MERCOSUR in 1997, while Chile entered as an associate member in 1996. Further, Chile has eagerly sought to become a member of the NAFTA and has discussed the possibility of full ascension to the MERCOSUR.[1] Also, the Mexican peso crisis of late 1994 into 1995 reopened some of the acrimonious debate that had surrounded the formation of the NAFTA originally; conflicts between Brazil and its partners in the MERCOSUR have generated uncertainty about any deepening of that agreement for the time being.

These and other events have also reinvigorated the academic research into a wide range of issues surrounding economic integration. These research efforts have explored the proper design of a Western Hemisphere trade agreement, the relationship between regional trade agreements and broader multilateral arrangements such as the World Trade Organization, the impact of existing arrangements on both member and non-member countries alike, and the political changes that have provided impetus to integration efforts. While each of these topics is interesting and certainly relevant to the broad discussion of Western Hemisphere integration, the focus of this essay will be the much narrower one listed above, namely the prospects that the NAFTA and the MERCOSUR as now constituted will be merged into a single larger arrangement as opposed to two (perhaps in conflict) independent blocs, and that either of these will be deepened in further stages of economic integration..

The next section summarizes briefly the history of economic policy in Latin America as well as the history of the two trade pacts as background for examining the prospects of future "supra integration" between the two trading blocs and for further intrabloc integration. The third section explores a basic model of free trade negotiations and provides a framework for understanding the prospects for cooperation between the NAFTA and the MERCOSUR. The fourth section examines some of the general economic and social data that might provide some clues as to the actual possibilities for a single hemisphere-wide trade area in the foreseeable future. The fifth and final section will then summarize the primary findings and offer a few concluding remarks.

Perhaps the single most important idea to emerge in this discussion is that the *degree of similarity* between members needs to be more carefully considered in any discussion of the likelihood of initial or further economic integration. This factor can be added to the list of more standard conditions under which such efforts are more likely to occur, and to provide a fuller framework for assessing the likelihood of any future outcomes. While the analysis is at an admittedly crude level it helps both review and broaden current thinking on the issue.

A BIT OF HISTORY

In order to better understand the prospects for future developments in Western

Hemisphere integration it is, in this author's estimation, essential to review the broad path of economic development and policy in Latin America over the twentieth century. While it is not the case that development and policy have been uniform across the region it is possible to identify at least some common trends. A discussion of these helps in our understanding of the genesis and continued existence of current trade arrangements in Latin America, as well as the conditions under which broader or deeper cooperation might take place.

In the most general terms, Latin America experienced rapid growth and integration into the world economy in the latter half of the nineteenth century until the start of World War I. Much of this was due to the expansion of overseas markets with the Industrial Revolution, significant immigration into Latin America, and a decline in global transportation costs, so that Latin American could join the general (if not steady) economic prosperity of the times. While some writers, most noticeably Raul Prebisch, argued that this export-led growth actually immiserized Latin American economies by fostering their dependency on more advanced economies, most economists have concluded that this period was one of remarkable growth in per capita GDP and a narrowing of income inequality across most countries in the region.

Throughout this period, Latin American countries pursued liberal, open trade policies and sought to achieve greater integration with the rest of the world. While trade arrangements were not necessarily formalized in this period, the political interests of exporters coupled with successful economic conditions helped generate a movement to free trade both within and outside of Latin America. Unlike more recent decades, however, much of the increased trade was not intraregional (among Latin American economies themselves), but rather interregional.[2]

While there is some debate over when this "golden era" ended (with the First World War or the global depression of the 1920s and 1930s),[3] there is no doubt that by the 1930s economic conditions had deteriorated dramatically in Latin America. Declining terms of trade meant that export-led growth no longer served as an engine for development, and growth slowed dramatically (as it did in the rest of the world). At the same time, war and economic depression meant that the rest of the world could no longer afford to finance development in Latin America and capital flows to the region dried up. One consequence was nearly a one hundred percent delinquency on international debt by several economies in the region and general default by nearly all.

This experience of the 1930s, which lasted into the 1940s, was one of the primary contributing factors to the development by the 1950s of what are commonly referred to as import-substitution policies. These policies typically involved dramatic increases in tariffs and other trade barriers in an attempt to develop successful local industries that could replace overseas producers as the primary source of manufactured items. These barriers were typically accompanied by looser fiscal and monetary policies as well as overvalued exchange rates. All were pursued as a means of reducing the dependency of the "peripheral economies" of Latin America on the "core economies" of the developed world through the development of an industrial base in the region.

One of the outcomes of import substitution strategies was a tariff and overall protection structure that was highly variable both across countries as well as within countries. As the framework below suggests, this would make negotiation of any preferential trading areas much more difficult. As documented by Sebastian Edwards, Chile had the highest standard deviation of tariff rates in the world (equal to 634%) while Brazil, Columbia, and Uruguay were also near the top of the dispersion list.[4] Not only do highly dispersed tariffs create uncertainty and distortions in decision-making, they make it more difficult to negotiate common tariff structures as part of, say, a preferential trade agreement.

This import-substitution strategy, of course, did not work as planned. By the 1960s, with the region still lagging far behind the rest of the less-developed world in terms of growth and development, some nations began to experiment with subregional trading arrangements while many more turned to increased international borrowing.[5] The latter development took full force by the 1970s as developed countries sought to recycle petrodollars into increased lending, and developing countries in Latin America and elsewhere sought to enhance improved commodity export earnings with international borrowing. From 1973 to 1980, developing countries' long-term external debt grew at annual average rates of over 20%, reflecting increases in both private and public debt levels.[6] As is well known, this dramatic increase in debt levels, a sudden drop in the terms of trade that substantially reduced the export revenues of Latin American countries, as well as a dramatic increase in world interest rates resulted in the debt crisis of the 1980s, initiated by Mexico's default on external debt in 1982. This once again threw most Latin American economies into disarray, and led to recession, unemployment, and greater income inequality.

The initial response of Latin America was again a reversion to more restrictive trade policies as a means of securing a net financial inflow that could be used to at least partially meet debt-servicing requirements. This approach changed within a few years, however, as many Latin American economies began to more aggressively pursue general market reforms and trade liberalization. Mexico, for example, joined the General Agreement on Tariffs and Trade (GATT) in 1985 and began a process of general privatization and deregulation aimed at improving efficiency and productivity. At the same time, many of these governments began to explore at least informally not just general multilateral trade liberalization but also preferential trading arrangements (which had surged in popularity worldwide after the formation of the European Economic Community). The latter development was due, at least in part, to the frustration felt by many countries at the pace of multilateral trade liberalization under the auspices of the GATT but primarily to skepticism about the old inward-oriented policies of previous decades.

The two major arrangements that emerged as a result of the shift in economic philosophy in Latin America by the mid-1990s were the NAFTA and the MERCOSUR. In 1991, the countries of Brazil, Argentina, Paraguay, and Uruguay began discussions to form a customs union (eliminating barriers between them and adopting a common external tariff) after Brazil and Argentina had first agreed to such a move in 1988. Final agreement was made in 1994, with an effective date of January 1, 1995, creating the MERCOSUR. The NAFTA, which became effective in 1994, was agreed upon by the three "North American" economies and followed a series of free trade initiatives between Canada and the U.S. over the previous 25 years. As a means to try understand the subsequent discussion it is useful to briefly review the events that led up to each of these agreements as well as the general provisions of each.

The MERCOSUR member countries account for roughly one-half of GDP in Latin America and about three-fourths of its population. Leading up to the formation of this significant trading arrangement was a series of bilateral agreements between Argentina and Brazil throughout the 1980s, following changes in the political environment of the two countries. It was not until Carlos Menem was elected president of Argentina in 1989 and Fernando Collor as president of Brazil in 1990 that the necessary convergence of economic philosophies allowed each to significantly consolidate earlier moves to replace managed trade and industrial targeting with market-oriented programs more generally.

The bilateral arrangements between the two preceding the formation involved a wide range of issues, from cooperation in nuclear development and military exchange, to cooperation in communications and trade relations. Each of these helped lay the groundwork for (not conflict-free) attempts at deeper integration, and reflected what below will be named "co-similarization" necessary for a more substantial effort at integration to succeed.

The MERCOSUR arrangement, however, has been regarded as unusual in that it involves two quite large economies and two quite small economies (Paraguay and Uruguay). Further, it involves four countries whose general trade policies had diverged in the years prior to the agreement. As Sebastian Edwards puts it:

> *What is particularly interesting about MERCOSUR is that it groups the two largest countries in South America ... with two of the smallest .... While Argentina recently embraced a significant free trade stance....Brazil is aiming at a higher and more variable tariff structure....*[7]

In the same vein, a recent article about the U.S. trade policy for Latin America, one author states that

> *....U.S. trade policy with Latin America fluctuates from (a) a sincere*

> *desire to pursue further integration schemes as a way to secure preferential access to a fast growing market and (b) to one of historical misgivings, apprehension, concerns and dislikes about integrating the United States with a region some consider to be still unstable and to be so different from their own.*[8]

These comments seem to suggest that in general a greater degree of dissimilarity makes a free trade agreement or a general move to deeper integration less likely. This, of course, does not imply that the degree of similarity between potential members is the only factor in determining the likelihood of cooperation between (otherwise no MERCOSUR would likely exist), only that it is one of several that needs to be considered.

The MERCOSUR as presently constituted leaves much room for deeper integration, as it intends to eliminate all intra regional tariffs on even the most sensitive items by 2000 and, by one year later, harmonize all external tariffs applied against nonmembers. It makes, however, no provisions for trade in services or protection of intellectual property rights, two key features of the NAFTA. Further, no agreement has been reached on the free movement of labour between members and, at this writing, that seems a remote possibility. While there has been discussion of broader policy coordination, this is nowhere near the European-style "macro-harmonization" that is thought needed for monetary union.

In many regards the Mercosur has been successful in promoting intra regional trade.

Trade between the primary four members totaled $4 billion in 1991. By 1996 that figure had risen to about $16.1 billion.[9] At this point in time, it would not appear that this has been due to trade diversion (as trade with nonmembers has grown at historical standards, among other factors) but rather efficient trade creation.

Just as surprising to many analysts was the rapid formation of the NAFTA as it again involved countries that in many respects had divergent policies, institutions, and conditions. It can be argued, however, that the general economic reforms that Mexico began to pursue in the mid-1980s represented a convergence to U.S. and Canadian policies or institutions in a broad sense. This would, ceteris paribus, then increase the probability of an agreement among the three nations. Even though non-trade matters did not include specific provisions for harmonization it does appear that there is at least greater recognition of the desire to move in that direction.

The NAFTA, signed by the three participants in 1992, followed a free trade agreement between the U.S. and Canada that became effective in 1988 and which served as a template for the wider agreement. The basic provisions of the NAFTA include elimination of trade barriers over 15 years, starting in 1994, according to a schedule of phaseouts determined on a product-by-product basis. Rules of origin remain quite stringent, particularly in textiles and apparel. The agreement also seeks to promote direct foreign investment through the establishment of national treatment and most favoured nation (MFN) rules and the allowance for foreign investment in key Mexican sectors such as petrochemicals. Commitment to the protection of intellectual property rights is also a cornerstone of the agreement, requiring the

Mexican government to enforce "Northern-style" rights.

Alongside the NAFTA itself are two important side agreements, one on environmental policy and one on labour standards. While many feel that these do not adequately address issues of minimum safeguards in the two areas, each was implemented with the objective of preventing further divergence in standards between countries and ideally seek convergence of them when possible. It can be argued that as Mexico enjoys the economic growth predicted as a result of the NAFTA it will be able to afford more of, and thus "buy" more of, the sorts of labour or environmental conditions critics of the treaty hope for.

As with the MERCOSUR, the agreement required political changes on both sides of the North-South border. In Mexico, the election of Carlos Salinas brought not just a philosophical shift in favour of market reforms but also a willingness to risk political capital in a move to free trade. In the U.S. it required the joint efforts of a Republican President and a Democratic Congress and the agreement to discuss environmental and labor issues alongside the broader negotiations. Ironically, the agreement took effect with a Democratic President and a (soon-to-be) Republican Congress! The role played by export interests was crucial in generating the political momentum needed for ratification of the agreement by the U.S.

As with the MERCOSUR, no steps toward deeper attempts at integration have been achieved beyond these provisions. In fact, not even an attempt at harmonizing common external tariffs was made (though it could be argued that the rules of origin are at least a partial substitute for these). It would appear that integration in the hemisphere is more likely to proceed first in a general widening of the NAFTA with the inclusion, possibly, of countries such as Chile or in a widening of the MERCOSUR with the ascension of Bolivia and Venezuela in the MERCOSUR, rather than in a deepening of the existing agreements. Before either a widening or deepening of existing agreements takes place some effort will be required to stabilize them as neither has been conflict-free.

Conflicts among members of either bloc have not been uncommon. In the MERCOSUR, for example, a Brazilian move to provide incentives to a Korean auto company to build a plant in Brazil has brought vociferous complaints from Argentina. In the NAFTA, efforts to allow international trucking have hit snags as the U.S. trucking industry have halted such transportation under safety concerns. Ongoing tariff disputes with one nation imposing tariffs on another (tariffs by the U.S. on corn straw brooms from Mexico) and subsequent retaliation (by Mexico on American wine and spirits) threaten to slow further attempts at integration and reflect the tensions and differences that still exist despite already-negotiated agreements.

As of this writing, the impact of the NAFTA has been thought to be minimal. As reported in *The New York Times*, researchers at the University of California at Los Angeles concluded that "the impact on trade-related employment during the first three years after NAFTA is estimated to be, at the very least, a near zero net impact and, more likely, a moderately positive number."[10] This is despite a change from a U.S. trade surplus with Mexico of about $3 billion in 1993 to a U.S. trade deficit with

Mexico of about $14 billion in 1995. The study has also concluded that the export jobs created because of NAFTA are of higher pay than those lost in import-competing sectors due to import expansion from existing Mexican plants or to relocation of U.S. facilities to the south. If so, this could be a significant factor in the possible expansion of the NAFTA in the intermediate term.

Several notable free trade agreements beyond the NAFTA and the MERCOSUR exist in Latin America in what some have called the "spaghetti bowl" of free trade agreements or others have labeled the (often inefficient) "hub and spoke system" of preferential trading areas.[11] Perhaps the most important of these is the Andean Pact between Bolivia, Columbia, Ecuador, Venezuela, and Peru which became effective in 1995 and establishes a customs union as well as a supranational parliament. Also important is the Caribbean Community and Common Market (CARICOM) between fourteen Caribbean states and which became effective in 1973 as a customs union with unevenly applied but commonly established external tariffs. Important to the evolution of hemisphere-wide integration will be the fashion in which these and other subregional agreements are linked together, as well as how they are connected to the two primary agreements in the hemisphere, the NAFTA and the MERCOSUR. If the general theory developed below is correct, then the prospects for an expanded NAFTA and MERCOSUR to work cooperatively could well depend on which primary bloc that a country such as Chile or a sub-bloc like the CARICOM happens to join first.

An interesting development are recent efforts at greater economic cooperation between Mexico and Chile. With Chile now an associate member of the MERCOSUR and Mexico a member of NAFTA, an incipient (or more substantial) relationship between the two could make them a "hub" between the two larger trade blocs and in turn influence the path of integration between the two blocs. The efforts to develop trade relations between the Mexico and Chile include greater access to agricultural and manufacturing markets for each, tightened rules of origin for products, and harmonization of at least some safety and technical standards. It could well be that any agreements in this area are simply the first step in bringing Chile closer to Mexican standards under the NAFTA and thus enhance the prospects for Chile's membership in the NAFTA. This too would make sense in the framework developed below.

A MODEL OF NEGOTIATED TRADE AGREEMENTS

In standard trade theory it is differences between countries that help explain patterns of trade across national borders. In the traditional theory, comparative (and absolute) advantages arise from differences in technologies, relative resource endowments, and preferences. These in turn allow countries to improve welfare by taking advantage of their differences through the exchange of goods and services.

In the newer trade theory, emerging in the early 1980s, the role of economies of scale and "historical accident" have been further developed after a long hiatus. In this theory, comparative advantages can be established by a head start (that can be due to sheer historical accident or perhaps, in theory, deliberate government policy) in an industry that allows a country to achieve economies of scale against potential competitors and thus maintain a cost-advantage over them. Once again, however, it is differences between firms across countries that will make trade mutually beneficial, even if those countries are in many ways similar to one another.

Despite economists' arguments in favour of free trade, trade barriers have been the norm rather than the exception. This is likely due to political realities and institutions that induce policy makers to efficiently and rationally (in a political sense) restrict trade. In the same vein, it may be argued that attempts at trade liberalization historically - either in the multilateral fashion favored in the few decades after World War II, or the regionally preferential fashion favoured more recently - reflect changes in the political environment that give greater weight to export interests over import-competing interests.

In general, economists have identified several factors beyond this that work in favour of market reforms, including trade liberalization. According to Sebastian Edwards these include:

1. An expansion of exports above the historical rate.
2. High productivity growth rate.
3. Positive trade balances, or reasonably low trade deficits.
4. Relatively low unemployment.
5. Increasing real wages.[12]

We might add to this list as other factors that tend to favor trade liberalization in the form of regional agreements geographical proximity and stability. An interesting question that has not been explored in any meaningful sense is to what degree broad similarities - economic, social, or political - help explain patterns of trade as well as trade policy changes toward regional or broader free trade arrangements. In general, a higher degree of similarity in conditions and institutions can be expected to reduce the costs associated with adjustment to a new trade regime for each country as well as help ameliorate frictions between members of a trade agreement.

The depth of integration will depend on each of these factors, and how much further countries may move beyond initial integration depends on the evolution of these factors over time. The first stage of integration, the removal of trade barriers between members, is not automatic but certainly requires a much lower threshold of convergence of conditions. If barriers are lowered but not eliminated, a preferential trade arrangement is created, whereas a free trade area is created if barriers are (eventually) eliminated. The later stages of integration include the adoption of common external trade barriers against outside countries, creating a customs union; the free movement of labour and capital, usually requiring some exchange rate coordination, in addition to a customs union creates a common market; in an economic union, the coordination of macroeconomic and microeconomic policy; and ultimately the adoption of a common currency to the previous moves creates an economic union. In most discussions of Western Hemisphere integration it is assumed that in the foreseeable future only the formation of a free trade area (with some features to encourage direct foreign investment) is likely. This seems reasonable; however, it is also instructive to explore the possibility of deeper integration over a longer period of time.

In this case, the noncooperative Nash equilibrium is at point E and represents the point at which the two countries end up without a free trade agreement.

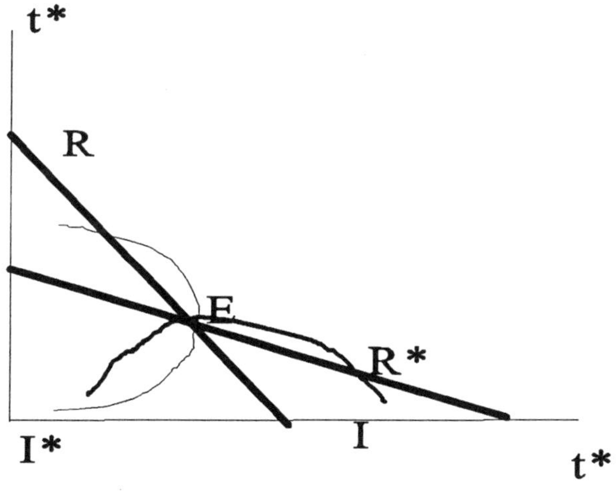

The curves labeled by the letter I denote trade indifference curves for each country and show the combinations of North and South tariff rates that yield the same level of social utility to each country. For North, tariff indifference model, two countries – North and South- produce two products, sevices (S) and manufacturing (M). Each considers imposing a tariff (I) on its imports of products from the other. Assume that the North exports services to the South while the South exports manufactured goods to the North. An asterisk will be used to denote a variable for the South. Each country is assumed to behave in Nash fashion by selecting its tariff level to maximize its social utility, given the tariff level implemented by the other country. In the standard Mayer-type model it is possible to derive each country's reaction curve that shows its optimal tariff rate for any tariff rate that might be imposed by the other country from a standard production possibility-social indifference curve diagram. These reaction curves are labeled with the letter R in the diagram above.

In this case, the noncooperative nash equilibrium is at point E and represents the point at which the two countries end up without a free trade agreement. The curves labeled by the letter I denote trade indifference curves for each country and show the combination of North and South tariff rates that yield the same level of social utility to each country. For North, tariff indifference curves further to the "west" represent higher levels of social utility while for South, curves further to the "south" in the diagram represent higher levels of social utility.[15] The reaction curve for either country is the locus of the "peaks" of the trade indifference curves.

A free trade agreement that eliminates tariffs and other trade barriers between the two countries is represented by the origin (zero tariffs for each country) and can be the outcome of a cooperative negotiation process. The essential point is that a move to free trade under such an agreement from the noncooperative equilibrium at point E is possible in that it provides each country with a higher level of social utility under the standard assumptions regarding tariff indifference curves, and given that the indifference curves depicted for the two countries intersect each other at right angles.[16]

While Mayer (1981) discusses the possibility of reaching free trade under different tariff-cutting formula and given differences in market power of the parties involved, no mention is made of the role played by the degree of similarity between the two countries (or set of countries) or the position of the noncooperative equilibrium (point E in the diagram above). In the formation of trade areas, customs unions, or other integration agreements, it is useful to consider the importance of economic, political, and social similarity of the countries involved. Most typically these arrangements have taken place between countries that are in many key respects similar to one another (with Mexico as a partner to the U.S. and Canada being a notable exception!) For the European Community early on, for example, there was considerable discussion of the inclusion of countries such as Portugal, Greece, and Spain, all of which had lagged the rest of Western Europe in economic and broader social development. Further, differences in political systems, particularly in Spain, remained a stumbling bloc for the entry of these countries into broader European economic integration. The first countries to join the original six signatories to the Treaty of Rome were those with relatively similar economic and political conditions (countries such as Ireland, the United Kingdom, and Denmark). The application of Spain was first rejected on grounds of that the authoritarian regime of Franco was inconsistent with the political ideals of the Community. Even after Franco's death and Spain's return to democracy, Spain's admittance was delayed until after the democratic reforms could be consolidated so that negotiations for admittance lasted from at least 1979 into

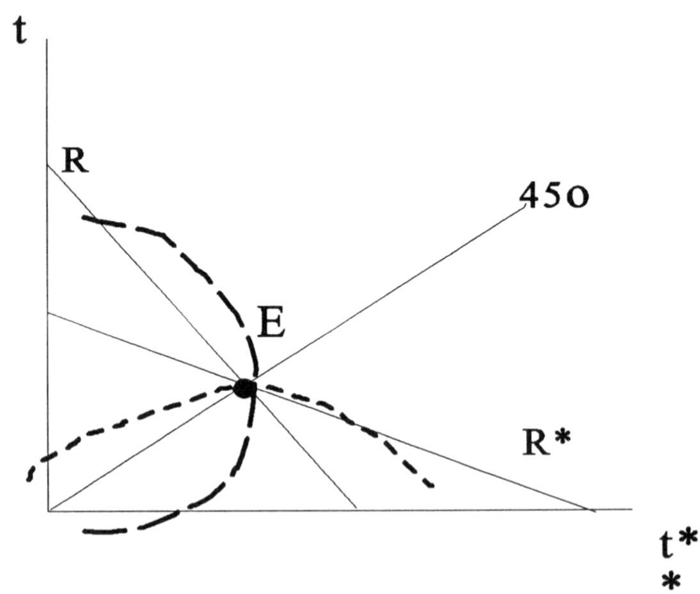

1985, with Spain joining in 1986.

In order to think about this more clearly, suppose that in the previous model North and South have identical or symmetric trade indifference curves which reflects identical preferences regarding tariffs or trade policy more generally.

This would require a similarity of general tastes as well as a similarity of economic and political. Of course, the two cannot be alike in every conceivable way (with identical factor endowments, technology, and tastes) as the two would then have no incentive to trade whatsoever. In the case of "sufficient similarity" beyond the differences needed for trade, though no formal proof is provided here, it should be the case that the reaction curves for the two countries are symmetric to one another: the distance between the origin and the vertical intercept of one will equal the distance between the origin and the horizontal intercept for the other, and vice-versa. In this case, the intersection of the two reaction curves will lie on a 45-degree line out of the origin.

Further, the indifference curves for the two countries will then be mirror images of one another (if we rotated the horizontal axis 90 degrees and placed it on the vertical axis, the two indifference curve maps would coincide with one another). Assuming that a free trade agreement is possible in the first place (i.e., that it would be a Pareto-improvement from the noncooperative equilibrium at point E) we would have the situation depicted in the diagram above in which the noncooperative trade indifference curves "embrace" the origin representing the free trade, cooperative outcome. The curvature of the trade indifference curves given the noncooperative point, as before, plays an important role in the feasibility of free trade.

Now consider the impact that an emergent difference between the two countries - be it economic, social, or political - arises so that the reaction curve for the South shifts outward. This could be due to, say, a change in political structure that results in greater influence by import-competing firms or groups in the South, resulting in higher levels of protection by the South as an optimal response to any level of tariffs or protection pursued by the North. It could be due to a change in attitudes that raise concerns about the role played by international trade in income distribution or other economic conditions. No matter the source of the change it is described in the graph below.

Here the noncooperative equilibrium moves from point E to point F.[17] As it is the change in perspective for the South that matters here only its trade indifference curves are depicted. The interesting point is that while free trade (again represented by the origin point) was possible originally, it is no longer feasible given this emergent difference between the two countries as the South will no longer find a move from the noncooperative equilibrium at point F to the free trade point at the origin a Pareto improvement. It appears that for the North, however, such a move would be even more welfare-improving than initially, as the noncooperative point at F is even further to the east than before.

This helps to clearly illustrate the role that is generally played by international similarities in the formation of preferential trade areas or deeper levels of integration, and to elucidate why it is that many such agreements have traditionally been between countries that are, in significant ways, more alike than they are different. Of course, as the NAFTA or even the MERCOSUR demonstrate, it is possible that other factors such as geographical proximity can outweigh any at least apparent differences between the participants.[18]

These general observations are not new to this chapter. Other authors have examined the degree of similarity between countries that have formed free trade agreements, though without the sort of formalization provided above. As Hufbauer and Schott put it:

> *Per capita GDP serves as a proxy for many variables that reflect the "tilt" of business playing fields, such as wage costs, health and safety conditions, and environmental controls. The greater the difference in these background conditions between any two countries, the larger the scope for disagreement as they enter a free trade arrangement.*[19]

In order to assess this for existing free trade agreements they calculate a "diversity index" for per capita real GDP given by:

$$d = \left(\sqrt{\sum_{j=1}^{n} w_j \ x \ (p_j - p_A)^2} \right) / \ p_A$$

where n denotes the number of countries in the arrangement, w the ratio of each country's population to population of the trade region, and p the per capita real GDP of the country (j) or the entire trade area (A). The index value for some arrangements is reported in table 6-1:

Table 6-1 "Diversity Index"

North America	.38
European Union	.31
EFTA	.13
Australia-New Zealand	.09
ASEAN	.48
Other East Asia	.41
West Asia	.34
MERCOSUR	.08
Andean Group	.32
CACM	.36
CARICOM	.61
Other Latin America	.45
Western Hemisphere	.73

Source: Hufbauer and Schott, *Western Hemisphere Economic Integration*, 1994, p. 49.

While one might reasonably dispute the appropriateness of this measure as a proxy for broader diversity between countries, it is at least a clear example of the importance that has been attached, albeit less formally, to the degree of similarity between members of an integration arrangement in other writings. If we do believe that this measure is a good proxy for more general diversity, it would indicate that attempts at broader Western Hemisphere integration, ceteris paribus, will be rather difficult as the countries that would be involved are much more diverse than those grouped in the MERCOSUR or the NAFTA alone.

As another illustration, consider the last macroeconomic crisis for Latin America as a whole, namely the debt crisis of the 1980s. Throughout this period average external debt levels increased significantly for the region as a whole. It can be argued that the variance of debt performance measures also rose over this period since countries were affected differently by the crisis and the problems they faced were not homogeneous: for some, the rise in interest rates was the primary source of default, while for others changes in commodity prices played a more decisive role.[20] For some, it was the combination of all

Table 6-2 Levels of External Debt

	1985	1986	1987	1988	1989	1990	1991	1992
Argentina	491	610	717	525	538	412	443	454
Brazil	362	452	431	314	290	321	327	311
Paraguay	252	249	282	192	143	107	124	114
Uruguay	295	245	253	201	191	181	195	196
std. Dev.	90	153	184	134	152	119	123	128

Source: Hufbauer and Schott, op. cit., p. 88.

three of these that precipitated the crisis. Table 2 reports the level of external debt for the MERCOSUR countries as a percent of exports of products for various years, as well as the standard deviation for each year.

For the years 1985-1989, the average standard deviation was equal to 152%, while from the years 1990-1992 it equaled 123%. In this sense, there was convergence of this particular macro variable in the years preceding the substantive discussions for the formation of the MERCOSUR which, ceteris paribus, would make such an agreement more likely.

How might this analysis be of general use as we consider the possibility of integration of two existing trading blocs such as the NAFTA and MERCOSUR? In fact, how might this model be of use in thinking about any level of economic integration, including monetary union? It clearly suggests that in making any prognostication about the possible path of future development at least some consideration should be given to the degree of similarity or dissimilarity between the prospective participants. This would include an examination of the degree of macroconvergence taking place between the countries involved as well as the broader socioconvergence and microconvergence occurring between them. The remainder of this paper is devoted to a general discussion of the economic conditions of the current members of the MERCOSUR and the NAFTA, and a brief commentary on the broader political or social conditions that might nurture or impinge on an integration of the two blocs.

MACROECONOMIC FACTORS

It is well known that deeper economic integration in the form of macroeconomic policy coordination or monetary union such as that sought in Europe requires a considerable degree of macro harmonization in the participating countries. The European Union has agreed upon clear (though perhaps not achievable!) convergence criteria regarding inflation, budget deficits, interest rates, government debt, and exchange rate stability. Perhaps not as obvious, nor as widely accepted, is the proposition that (less strict) macroharmonization is needed for initial integration efforts as well. It is much easier for two or more countries that are experiencing similar macroeconomic conditions - usually positive, though perhaps negative - to arrive at agreement on international trade policy. This is due to the political realities generated by economic conditions, though it might also be due to broader economic or social considerations.

Most would agree that in general Latin America as a region has experienced marked improvement in macroeconomic conditions in the 1990s, though of course substantial concerns remain. For most countries in the region, debt indicators have improved, inflation rates have been reduced, and growth has been more consistently positive than in the 1980s. An interesting question for our purposes here is to what degree macro variables for the existing MERCOSUR and NAFTA members have converged and what the prospects for further convergence might be in the foreseeable future.

Table 3 reports, subject to availability, real GDP growth rates for the MERCOSUR members, the NAFTA countries, and Chile for the years 1991 through 1995. According to this author's calculations, the average growth rate over this period for the MERCOSUR members was approximately equal to 4.7%; the comparable figure for the NAFTA members was about 1.4%. Further, the standard deviation of returns of growth rates for the MERCOSUR as a whole was 2.9 percentage points and for the NAFTA as a whole it was about 2.7 percentage points. By this latter measure, the variability of growth rates over this latest period was remarkably similar between the two areas. It can be reasonably argued that the variability of growth of potential signatories to an integration agreement is important in the prospect of arriving at an actual agreement. On the other hand, it is at least as reasonable to expect that average growth rates are an important factor in the successful negotiation of an integration agreement, both in absolute as well as relative terms. For the U.S. and Canada, whose economic growth has been weak by historical standards (though the U.S. did experience solid growth in 1996 according to the latest data) it might be difficult to muster the necessary political support for either a broadening or a deepening of the NAFTA. Further, in line with the general thesis of this essay, it will generally be more difficult for two sides to reach an agreement if there is a sufficiently wide disparity in growth rates between them. In the U.S., for example, it might not be surprising to see opponents of a hemisphere-wide agreement to point at substantially higher or lower growth in Latin America as a threat to the economic security of the U.S. This has not been unusual, in this author's view, in U.S. economic relations more generally. If on the other hand, "they" are more like "us" it will be more difficult to muster opposition on this count.

Over the past five years, the U.S. has enjoyed a period of sustained economic growth with low inflation not exceeding, by nearly any measure, about 3% per year. As is well known, Latin American countries experienced significant inflation over the 1980's. Even in 1990, Argentina had an inflation rate (as measured by the percentage change in the GDP price deflator) of about 2023%.

Table 6-3 Real Growth in GDP in Percentage Terms

	1991	1992	1993	1994	1995
Argentina	8.9	8.7	5.0	7.4	---
Brazil	.9	-.9	4.5	5.6	---
Paraguay	2.5	1.8	3.7	3.1	4.7
Uruguay	2.9	7.4	1.7	6.8	9.8
U.S.	-1.0	2.7	2.2	3.5	2.0
Canada	-1.8	.1	2.1	4.1	2.3
Mexico	3.6	2.6	.6	4.5	-6.2
Chile	6.0	10.4	6.0	4.6	---

Source: International Monetary Fund, *International Financial Statistics*, March 1997, and author's calculations.

In the same year Brazil had an inflation rate of 2591%, Paraguay a rate of 38%, and Uruguay 100%. These rates have, however, fallen dramatically over the years since then, though they might still be considered high by OECD standards. Table 4 provides inflation rates as measured by percent changes in consumer price indices again for years from 1991 through 1995.

The average MERCOSUR inflation rate over the period was approximately equal to 723%, though obviously the surge in inflation in Brazil in 1993-1994

Table 6-4 Inflation Rates

	1991	1992	1993	1994	1995
Argentina	172	25	11	4	3
Brazil	425	991	2100	2686	84
Paraguay	25	16	18	18	21
Uruguay	102	69	54	59	45
U.S.	4	3	3	2.5	2.8
Canada	5.6	1.5	1.9	.2	2.2
Mexico	18.8	11.9	8.0	6.9	35.0
Chile	21.8	15.4	11.9	12.0	7.9

Source: International Monetary Fund, *International Financial Statistics*, various issues, and author's calculations.

substantially raised this figure. The average for these countries in 1995 was about 38%, a substantial reduction by any standards. The average inflation rate for the NAFTA countries was approximately equal to 7% over the same period, though this is also biased by the rise in inflation in Mexico in 1995 due to the dramatic fall of the peso over that year. The standard deviation of inflation rates for the MERCOSUR members was 346% over the entire period, and only 8.8% for NAFTA.

Experience suggests, and this data would generally confirm, that high inflation is usually associated with highly volatile inflation rates which are arguably a more serious problem for economic development and readiness for cooperation with other countries. Not only does variable inflation confuse price signals to both firms and to consumers, but also tends to destabilize both nominal and real exchange rates. This latter problem is particularly relevant to the likelihood of economic integration, even at the most basic level. For the western Hemisphere, inflationary episodes in Latin America and inflationary reform in the U.S. have in the 1980s resulted in sharp increases in the value of the U.S. dollar vis-a-vis the southern currencies. It can reasonably be argued that this has generally increased pressures for protectionism in the United States and considerably diminished the prospects for broader economic cooperation in the Hemisphere. Indeed, U.S. Congressional opposition to fast-track approval for Chilean accession to the NAFTA could stem at least partially from the Mexican peso crisis in late 1994 and early 1995 that lead to a dramatic fall in the U.S. trade balance with Mexico.

Another consideration in assessing the prospects for economic integration, particularly at the initial stage of a preferential trading arrangement would be the trend in export performance across countries involved in the formation of the trade agreement. The performance of export markets, as it can affect the ability or desire of export interests in lobbying for expanded sales opportunities through trade liberalization, can certainly influence the outcome. It might be reasonably argued that the more similar the position of export interests across potential members of a trade agreement the more likely they will be able to negotiate a favorable outcome. Table 5 reports for the Mercosur and the NAFTA countries the per capita export levels (in U.S. dollars) as well as an "export diversity index" calculated by this author in a fashion similar to the per capita real GDP diversity index described above.[21]

Table 6-5 Per Capita Export Levels

Country	1990	1991	1992	1993	1994	1995
Argentina	379.5	363.3	366.1	387.3	456.3	603.0
Brazil	217.1	215.0	239.6	254.7	283.3	298.5
Paraguay	227.2	170.2	147.6	164.6	173.8	167.7
Uruguay	547.9	516.0	543.9	512.7	603.6	660.1
U.S.	1574.9	1669.3	1754.6	1800.5	1966.6	2223.1
Canada	4824.8	4462.4	4499.4	4889.4	5505.7	6523.3
Mexico	301.9	306.0	307.7	332.0	235.7	438.8
Chile	639.2	671.3	739.1	668.0	829.4	1129.5
NAFTA index	.58	.55	.54	.55	.58	.57
Mercosur index	.31	.27	.24	.20	.22	.24

Source: International Monetary Fund, *International Financial Statistics*, March 1997, and author's calculations.

Some interesting points are to be made about the diversity indices. First, there

Some interesting points are to be made about the diversity indices. First, there remains a substantial difference between the intra regional homogeneity of the two blocs. This could well suggest that by this measure the two groups of countries are still significantly different, and would perhaps encounter difficulties in negotiating broader integration. In general, however, with both the U.S. and Canada at the top of the exports per capita list they might very well be interested in broader trade liberalization

and overcome any frictions associated with a much higher level of intra regional diversity. Second, by this measure, the MERCOSUR has become a more homogeneous region with a significant decline in its diversity index, while the NAFTA countries have experienced no substantial difference in their index. This has led to a broadening of the diversity levels between the two regions, which according to the model described above, might indicate a lower probability of wider cooperation in the hemisphere (by this measure.)

While growth, export, and inflation measures are only two of the many that need to be considered in a more comprehensive study of the convergence of conditions between the two trade blocs and the prospects for cooperation between them, the discussion above helps illustrate the ways in which changes have enhanced the prospects for such cooperation, but also highlight the amount of work required before deeper efforts can be undertaken. In many ways, the early successes in Latin America over the past several years- in reducing inflation, easing the external debt burden, and sustaining positive economic growth - have to be strengthened and sustained before broader efforts at integration in the hemisphere are likely to succeed. A recent edition of Business Latin America put it in the following way:

> *...(Mercosur) officials (are) feeling more circumspect than expansive. Mercosur members have responsibly decided that it is time to resolve the myriad problems that plague the integration process before the group spreads itself too thin....All six partners have committed...to solving the many problems that plague integration efforts. Some goals, such as common social-security rules and compatible education programmes represent reforms that are daunting enough at the national level.*[22]

What are the general prospects for Latin America in consolidating the reforms of the past decade that enhance the prospects for broader integration?

While the region has made great strides over the last decade it is not clear that economic reforms, including the integration efforts mentioned above, have been consolidated and that economic stability will be the norm rather than the exception. In order for further successful market reforms to occur, not only is a necessary level of interregional convergence needed but also a sufficient level of intra regional harmonization is required in order to sustain the concerted efforts of the members of each region in that direction. According to two economists:

> *It must be borne in mind, however, that stability (in Latin America) is far from having been consolidated. Some structural factors of macroeconomic instability are still intact, the debt crisis has left sequels which have not yet been overcome, and fresh macroeconomic tensions have appeared as a by-product of the faster implementation of structural reform.*[23]

It will be difficult for MERCOSUR or Latin America as a whole to work cooperatively on broadening existing arrangements without sufficient stable harmonization of internal conditions and policies. As has already been suggested in this essay, it is not clear that this condition has been met. The recent dispute between Argentina and Brazil in the automobile industry has, it could be argued, arisen because of differences of opinion regarding industrial and developmental policy between the two countries. The Brazilian government argued strenuously that its decision to subsidize the Korean plant in Bahia is only part of an attempt to develop the greatly underdeveloped northeastern and western regions of its country. Until these sorts of internal issues can be adequately sorted out, as the MERCOSUR governments themselves realize, there is little hope of broadening external economic relations.

SOCIAL AND POLITICAL FACTORS

Broader or deeper efforts at economic integration will require both a firm political commitment by the governments of Latin America as well as a minimum level of social stability that has been in many ways lacking in its history. Political instability is, as experience demonstrates, typically tied to economic policy volatility. In order to initiate and then consolidate economic reforms, then, Latin American governments must have a sufficient level of political flexibility. While the compatibility of an open, market-oriented economy with either democratic or autocratic political structures has been the subject of much debate, it has often been the case in Latin America that economic policy change has coincided with political change.

Over the past decade, economic liberalization in the region has coincided with political, democratic liberalization as well. While by no means a settled matter it can be reasonably argued that the sustainability of market reforms will depend on the sustainability of current political institutions that have accompanied them over the past decade. Abrupt political changes in any direction could quite well result in abrupt changes in economic policy as well. It would seem that gradual political change, typically toward more pluralistic government, tends to follow economic reform in Latin America.

In order to broaden integration to the North, MERCOSUR countries will not only need to convince the U.S. and Canada that recurring costs and frictions will be avoided through smoothly operating political and economic systems but also demonstrate that they are converging at a sufficient pace to Northern notions of democracy. Without arguing the rightness or the fairness of this, it will be hard to achieve hemisphere-wide integration at any level without adequate political reforms in Latin America. [24] Thus, a smooth, stable transition to more pluralistic forms of government will certainly enhance the prospects for at least wider economic integration.

To what degree is this already happening? In general, the process has begun, though reversals certainly are not uncommon. In the case of Mexico, for example, it appeared that at least by 1990 the ruling PRI Party, which has dominated Mexican politics since the revolution, had started to open the political process. Indeed, municipal elections around Mexico City in 1996 gave opposition parties significant increases in representation in Congress. Despite progress, however, the Chiapas uprising in 1994 represented a sharp reminder that the Mexican political system is still subject to serious setbacks that could, if sustained, diminish the prospects for internal consolidation as well as external cooperative efforts.

In Argentina and Brazil, functioning democracies have been in place for at least a decade. In Argentina, military coups and semi-functioning democracy since 1940 was replaced in 1983 with a return to a fledgling but full democracy. While severely tested at the start of the 1990s, the democracy managed to survive. Perhaps a sign of the democratic times, current President

Carlos Menem, whose second term expires in 1999, has slowed reforms in response to low approval ratings (under 20% recently) that threaten his ruling Peronista party in the fall Congressional elections. This is well in the spirit of U.S.-style democracy!

Brazil had its first direct elections for President in 1989, though the transition from the authoritarian to democratic regimes had begun earlier. A civilian government took over in 1985, following an economic recovery in 1984 from what were arguably the worst few years for the Brazilian economy since 1945. The years from 1985 to 1989 were a severe test of the move toward democratic government in that it was a period of economic difficulties. However, despite several changes in the leadership of the civilian government, reversion to the former military state was avoided, providing what appears to now be a solid foundation for a democratic government. It is much less likely that either the Brazilian or the Argentinean governments would face a "democratic coup" as occurred in Peru in 1991 when Alberto Fujimori suspended Congress and imposed certain police-state practices, albeit with wide popular support.

Like Argentina, the issue seems to be less the democratic foundations of the Brazilian government but rather the susceptibility of elected officials to popular sentiment in a degree that exceeds the role of popular opinion in the United States. Current President Fernando Henrique Cardoso has recently criticized former President Collor de Mello for opening the Brazilian economy too rapidly. This, as well as the decision to subsidize the Korean auto facility, can very well be interpreted as responses to internal political pressures and are among the factors that worry Brazil's partners in the MERCOSUR

The degree to which democratic reforms and stable, democratically based market reforms can be harmonized in the MERCOSUR nations depends to a

Table 6-6 Disparities – Quality of Life

	GDP per capita (1988)	Life Expectancy (at birth - 1993)	Adult illiteracy (% - 1990)	Birth rate (per 1000 – 1993)
Argentina	4363	72	5	20
Brazil	4621	67	19	24
Paraguay	2590	70	10	32
Uruguay	5787	73	4	17
Canada	17681	78	<5	15
Mexico	5323	71	13	27
U.S.	19851	76	<5	16

Sources: Per capita GDP figures are from Robert Summers and Alan Heston, "The Penn World Table: An Expanded Set of International Comparisons," *Quarterly Journal of Economics*, May 1991. The remaining figures are from the 1995 *World Development Report* by the World Bank.

large degree on the broader level of social and economic development that takes place over the next several years. In the European Union model, collective decision making across national governments was thought to depend, it would appear, on at least some harmonization of social and economic conditions through transfers between countries. While the Mercosur members have not committed themselves to an intragroup subsidy program, deliberate efforts have been made to identify differences in microeconomic and macroeconomic policy in the hopes of achieving substantial harmonization in them. This in turn could lead to convergence of broader social or economic conditions, enhancing the prospects for deeper or broader integration.

Current disparities within MERCOSUR and between Mercosur and the U.S. or Canada remain quite wide, indicating that substantial progress needs to be made if hemisphere-wide effort are to make much progress. Consider Table 6, which provides some basic summary demographic data for the NAFTA and the MERCOSUR nations.

The GDP figures by Summer and Heston are widely quoted as they attempt to measure per capita amounts in terms of purchasing power. By this measure as well as the others reported above it appears that the MERCOSUR nations in many ways lag behind the NAFTA countries. Considerable progress will be needed before broader integration steps are likely.

Over the 1970s, most observers agree, the income distribution has widened substantially in most Latin American countries so that the lowest quintile of the population in the region earned the lowest percent of GDP in the world. If broader or even deeper integration is to succeed, substantial progress will be needed in the efforts to alleviate poverty. In part this is to help alleviate the social unrest and political turmoil that has set Latin America apart from its Northern neighbors and provide the internal stability and convergence needed for international negotiations. Table 8 below provides some of the summary statistics for health and education that illustrate the wide disparities in the hemisphere. In general, it seems that the region made strides from 1960 to 1980 though still lagged much of the rest of the world.

Table 6-7

	Under five mortality rate per 1000 births 1993	Infant mortality (per 1000 births - 1993)	Primary pupil -teacher ratio (1993)	% age group enrolled tertiary ed (1992)
Argentina	27	24	---	43
Brazil	63	57	23	12
Paraguay	46	37	23	8
Uruguay	21	19	21	32
Canada	8	7	17	99
Mexico	43	35	30	14
U.S.	10	9	---	76

Source: World Bank, *World Development Report*, 1996.

The debt crisis of the 1980s and the subsequent slowdown in growth rates was a setback for the countries as social spending was dramatically reduced, and at least trimmed some of the rates of improvement, though by many of the standard indicators they were better off in 1993 than in 1983. This by no means implies that all individuals within a country continued to enjoy improvements in living standards, or that past improvements will not be eroded by continued sluggish growth. In fact, the uprising in Chiapas (Mexico), the hostage crisis at the Japanese embassy in Peru in late 1996, labour protests in Venezuela and Colombia reflect broad underlying social discontent among significant groups of the populations. It remains clear at least that Latin American countries significantly lag the U.S. and Canada in terms of broad living standards, which will remain an obstacle to broadening integration across the North-South divide.

An issue that is perhaps often overlooked in discussions of hemisphere-wide integration is the apparent deterioration of infrastructure in much of Latin America. Investment in this was also reduced in the 1980s in response to the debt crisis, and has likely curtailed the sustainable rate of growth for most nations in the region. This trend continued into the early 1990s as the percent of GDP spent on investment continued to fall. Even Chile, which has committed to increased spending on infrastructure, has been unable to find no more than about a quarter of the funds needed to meet its spending target. This has been exacerbated by the experience of the peso crisis in which international lending was again threatened by changes in borrower's conditions. Table 9 below shows that gross capital formation as a percent of GDP has decline dramatically for most countries since 1988.

Table 6-8 Capital Formation as a percentage or gap

	1980	1988	1991
Argentina	22.4	13.8	10.3
Brazil	21.9	23.6	19.4
Paraguay	22.9	23.2	23.6
Uruguay	16.9	12.4	12.3
Mexico	28.0	20.0	20.0
U.S.	20.0	18.0	15.3

Source: *Statistical Abstract of Latin America*, UCLA, 1995.

It is important to point out, that even though the U.S. has experienced a drop in GDP devoted to capital formation and has recently begun to discuss more earnestly the need for increased infrastructure spending, the issue is thought to be much more serious for Latin America as it lags in absolute terms in infrastructure needs.[25]

In all areas though to be vital for economic growth and development - education, infrastructure, and broad health investment - the region has made marked strides since 1960, though the rate of improvement was slowed by economic crises in the last decade. Prospects for integration efforts will be enhanced by a return to previous rate of progress.

CONCLUDING REMARKS

This chapter has first attempted to develop a more formal framework for understanding the role played by broad economic or social similarity across countries in the pursuit of economic integration. While previous research has made at least allusion to the importance of convergence or harmonization of standards, conditions, and policies in cooperative economic efforts, no systematic attempt has been made at clearly analyzing the role it plays in those efforts. Second, this chapter has attempted to informally explore the conditions within as well as across the MERCOSUR and NAFTA countries as a means of assessing the prospects for cooperation between the two blocs in the form of a hemisphere-wide preferential trading area or deeper level of integration.

While this analysis is admittedly superficial it at least helps us frame the discussion regarding the future path of hemispheric integration efforts. Recent events have raised some doubts that individual countries or subregions will in the near-term be able to sufficiently consolidate previous efforts at harmonization. That in turn will make further efforts at wider or deeper integration more difficult. The discussion also suggests that the disparate conditions between North and South remain quite wide and will remain an obstacle to broader efforts as well.

On one level, at least according to some observers, this could actually work to promote broader trade liberalization than would piecemeal expansion of the existing two trade blocs in the hemisphere. In a recent *Wall Street Journal* piece, Sebastian Edwards wrote that

> *...in many countries two misguided notions have taken place. First, that maintaining protection at home would enhance these countries' negotiating position with the U.S., and second, that by forming regional trade blocs - irrespective of the trade diversion they may generate - the grand goal of achieving hemispheric integration would, in the end, be advanced.*

This chapter has remained agnostic on this point and has rather simply attempted to assess the prospects for cooperation between the two blocs in a move toward a hemisphere-wide bloc.

It could well be however, that other factors such as proximity or external-to-the-hemisphere developments will be sufficient to revive discussions about and efforts toward a Free Trade Area of the Americas (FTAA). Prognosticators ten years ago would not have predicted the rapidity of the formation of the NAFTA nor the MERCOSUR. The same might be true for a FTAA.

[1] The signals from Chile, however, have been mixed. When Chilean President Frei visited Washington in March 1997 to meet with U.S. President Clinton both Presidents expressed the desire for fast-track approval by Congress for Chilean accession to the NAFTA. Only one month earlier Chilean Foreign Minister Insulza said his country would not push the issue (*Minneapolis Star and Tribune*, January 9, 1997, p. 3).

[2] For a good summary of these and more recent trends in Latin American economies see Angus Maddison, *Unorthodox Policies But Rapid Growth*, pp.129-140 in Richard Salvucci, *Latin America and the World Economy: Dependency and Beyond*, D.C. Heath and Company, 1996.

[3] For a good review of these issues again see Salvucci, *op. cit.*

[4] Sebastian Edwards, *Crisis and Reform in Latin America: From Despair to Hope*, Oxford University Press, 1995, p. 127.

[5] The Latin American Free Trade Area was established by the Montevideo Treaty and became effective in 1961. This involved, however, not a general liberalization of trade as a means of export promotion but rather bilateral barrier reductions intended to help develop import-substituting local industries.

[6] For more details on these developments as well as the debt crisis, see Anne

O. Krueger, *Origins of the Debt Crisis: 1970-1982*, pp. 166-72, in Salvucci, *op. cit.*

[7] Edwards, *op. cit.*

[8] Patricia Gray Rich, "Latin America and Present U.S. Trade Policy," *The World Economy*, January 1997, pp. 87-101.

[9] Source: *Business Latin America*, January 27, 1997, p. 5.

[10] See "NAFTA's Impact on Jobs Has Been Slight, Study Shows," *The New York Times*, December 19, 1996. A draft of the entire study may be found on the Web page of the North American Integration and Development Center of UCLA at *WWW.Naid.*

[11] For a good discussion of these, see Jagdish Bhagwati and Arvind Panagariya, *The Economics of Preferential Trade Agreements*, Washington, D.C., The AEI Press, 1996.

[12] Edwards, *op. cit.*, p. 124.

[13] Johnson, H.G. (1953-4), "Optimum Tariffs and Retaliation," *Review of Economic Studies*, v. 21, 142-53.

[14] Mayer, Wolfgang (1981), "Theoretical Considerations on Negotiated Tariff Adjustments," *Oxford Economic Papers*, v. 3, 135-53.

[15] See Johnson (1953-4) for a formal derivation of these tariff indifference curves.

[16] In fact, the set of Pareto-efficient tariff combinations include not only free trade but many others along a locus through the origin and between the two indifference curves depicted. See Mayer (1981).

[17] While the indifference curves for the South do not appear to have changed much in shape, it is quite likely that they would under these circumstances. In fact, they might rotate counterclockwise so that a given reduction in the South tariff rate requires a larger reduction in the North tariff if South social utility is to remain constant.

[18] In fact, many academics noted that the NAFTA was the first agreement reached by countries at such disparate levels of development, which might validate this argument if we think that differences in development proxy more general dissimilarity.

[19] Gary C. Hufbauer and Jeffrey J. Schott, *Western Hemisphere Economic Integration*, Institute for International Economics, 1994, p. 48.

[20] For a good discussion of this, see Krueger, op. cit.

[21] The squared difference between each country's per capita exports and the region's average per capita exports is multiplied by that country's share of the

region's population. These weighted squared differences are added up, the square root is taken, and that number is divided by average per capita exports for the region. Data for exports and population is taken from the IMF's Source: International Monetary Fund, *International Financial Statistics*, March 1997.

[22] "Mercosur: Regrouping," *Business Latin America*, January 27, 1997, p.4

[23] Jose Maria Fanelli and Roberto Frenkel, "Stability and Structure: Interactions in Economic Growth", *CEPAL Review*, August 1995, pp. 25-41.

[24] As an extreme example, the continued economic embargo by the U.S. of Cuba, and the enactment of the recent Helms-Burton law in the U.S., demonstrates the role that political differences can have in the formation of (North) American economic policy.

[25] As one example, the number of telephone mainlines in the U.S. and Canada, respectively, per 1000 people equaled 565 and 592 in 1992. The figures for Argentina and Brazil were 123 and 71, respectively. These data are from the World Bank's *World Development Report*, 1995.

Conclusions

The Future: Relations between the EU and MERCOSUR

Rightly or wrongly, the countries of MERCOSUR have seen the European Union (EU) as their example or model. In turn, the EU has, from its earliest days, encouraged the integration process among these countries. In fact, probably unknown to many experts, the EU, using a financial grant from the European Parliament (which has been recently renewed), has, for some years now, been training MERCOSUR administrators.

MERCOSUR has come a long way in a very short period of time. In fact, one could suggest that in the few years in which it has been in existence, MERCOSUR has made more progress in its moves toward integration than the Founder Member States of the old EEC had made in the first years of its existence. This is certainly the case in the area of the coordination of economic and monetary policies.

Despite and because of this progress, MERCOSUR now finds itself at a crossroads. It faces problems in the fields of economic and monetary policy coordination. Here, the slower progress of Brazil (when compared with Argentina) in reducing its public sector and in privatization is a cause for concern. Similarly, that country's occasional unilateral action in imposing trade controls is worrying. This does lead the author to raise the issue of the creation by the MERCOSUR countries of institutions similar to the Commission of the European Communities and the European Court of Justice.

A number of observers also believe that these countries now face infrastructure problems—notably in the field of transport. Similarly, questions are being raised about consumer rights and the environmental standards.

As the MERCOSUR countries stand at a crossroads, they will pay closer attention to the freeing of trade in services. This is an area where great progress can be made and benefits gained.

In the international sphere, while the call made by the United States for the creation of a Free Trade Area of the Americas (FTAA) by 2005, will, to some degree, occupy the attention of the MERCOSUR countries, their main interests are likely to be focused elsewhere. As with the EU, MERCOSUR, pushed very much by Brazil, sees a deepening of the integration process within MERCOSUR as the number one priority. Thus, membership of NAFTA or the FTAAs is out of the question for the immediate future. In contrast, MERCOSUR is perfectly willing to admit new members from Latin America—either as full or associate members. But, MERCOSUR strongly desires to deepen relations with the EU. It is to those relations which we shall now turn.

Relations between the EU and MERCOSUR

For many years now, the EU has been both the principal trading partner and source of foreign capital investment for the MERCOSUR countries.

In a report prepared by the commission for the EU General Affairs Council, in November 1994 (this document is reproduced in Appendix No. 4), the existing strong relations between the two parties were emphasized. In particular, it was noted that following an informal political dialogue, already in 1992, the Commission and representatives of MERCOSUR concluded an inter-institutional arrangement, which led to the flow of expertise, assistance in training, and finance from the EU to MERCOSUR. It was therefore logical that a more far reaching agreement be made between the two parties. However, the agreement made is not a free trade agreement—it is, in fact, an Interregional Framework Cooperation Agreement (see Appendix No. 3). This agreement therefore covers other areas as well as trade, and, interestingly enough, includes an article on a Political Dialogue. In Title 1, article 2, the Agreement "covers trade and economic matters, cooperation regarding integration and other fields of mutual interest in order to bring about closer relations between the parties and their respective institutions." Thus, while it is not a free trade agreement, to the author, the long-term aim is the preparation of such an agreement. However, cooperation is taking place in a number of areas which are not generally covered by free trade agreements.

At an institutional level, while the supreme body is the Cooperation Council, the real working bodies are the Joint Cooperation Committee, and, especially the Join Trade Sub-Committee. This sub-committee has created three working groups which are responsible for goods, services, and commercial standards and disciplines. Between now (May 1997) and the meeting in Uruguay at the end of this year, they will provide a so-called "photograph" of trade and commercial practices in the sectors relating to competition, anti-dumping, veterinary and plant health standards, rules of origin, systems import licenses and consumer policy.

To the author, the aim of all this work is to prepare the ground for the conclusion of a very far-reaching free trade area. According to Community sources, it is likely that these negotiations could begin by early next year. They would then probably last until 2002 or 2003, making the implementation of the agreement by 2005 a distinct possibility. By then, the EU should have completed its second round of reforms of the Common Agricultural Policy (CAP) which could otherwise be a major problem area between the EU and MERCOSUR. Another area of controversy between the two parties is Brazil's car import regime. Following EU complaints, Brazil has retorted that it is a perfectly legitimate regime, intended to deepen the integration process within MERCOSUR, and which will only last until 1999.

Final Observations

As has already been observed, MERCOSUR has come a long way in a relatively short time. It now stands at a crossroads as it tries to deepen its integration process. More attention will have to be paid to trade in services and to the infrastructure.

In the specific case of Brazil there is the problem of the slower pace of reform of public sector finances and privatization than is the case in Argentina. Here, President Cardoso's recent success in obtaining a change in the Constitution allowing him a second term of office bodes well for reform.

On a particularly positive note, it should be stressed that the countries of MERCOSUR do have a great advantage when compared with the EU. This is the fact that they, with the exception of Brazil, share a common language, Spanish--but then Portuguese and Spanish speakers do understand each other.

At an institutional level, to the author it seems that, sooner or later, the MERCOSUR countries, in their integration process, will need to create organs like the Commission and the European Court of Justice.

Finally, the EU's diplomatic and political recognition of the present and future importance of MERCOSUR is critical. In turn, the MERCOSUR countries welcome the Joint Framework Cooperative Treaty as a counterweight to the insensitive influence of the United States in Latin America. Then, the growing importance of MERCOSUR will enable it to strengthen its negotiating position vis-à-vis both the EU and the USA. Here, the experience of the EU provides a successful pioneering example. Lastly, to the author, a future free trade agreement between MERCOSUR and the EU could become a powerful international trading bloc.

Notes

1. José Frederico Alvarez and Alexandre A. Tombini, "The Road Towards Hemispheric Integration: the FTAA Initiative," Brazil File, June 1997, George Washington University, Washington, D.C.

Index

List of Appendices

ASUNCIÓN TREATY

The Argentine Republic, the Federative Republic of Brazil, the Republic of Paraguay and the Eastern Republic of Uruguay, hereinafter referred to as the "States Parties",

CONSIDERING that the expansion of their domestic markets, through integration, is a vital prerequisite for accelerating their processes of economic development with social justice,

BELIEVING that this objective must be achieved by making optimum use of available resources, preserving the environment, improving physical links, co-ordinating macroeconomic policies and ensuring complementarity between the different sectors of the economy, based on the principles of gradualism, flexibility and balance,

BEARING IN MIND international trends, particularly the integration of large economic areas, and the importance of securing their countries a proper place in the international economy,

BELIEVING that this integration process is an appropriate response to such trends,

AWARE that this Treaty must be viewed as a further step in efforts gradually to bring about Latin American integration, in keeping with the objectives of the Montevideo Treaty of 1980,

CONVINCED of the need to promote the scientific and technological development of the States Parties and to modernize their economies in order to expand the supply and improve the quality of available goods and services, with a view to enhancing the living conditions of their populations,

REAFFIRMING their political will to lay the bases for increasingly close ties between their peoples, with a view to achieving the above-mentioned objectives.

HEREBY AGREE AS FOLLOWS:

CHAPTER I
PURPOSES, PRINCIPLES AND INSTRUMENTS

Article 1

The States Parties hereby decide to establish a common market, which shall be in place by 31 December 1994 and shall be called the "common market of the southern cone" (MERCOSUL).

This common market shall involve:

The free movement of goods, services and factors of production between countries through, inter alia, the elimination of customs duties and non-tariff restrictions on the movement of goods, and any other equivalent measures;

The establishment of a common external tariff and the adoption of a common trade policy in relation to third States or groups of States, and the co-ordination of positions in regional and international economic and commercial forums;

The co-ordination of macroeconomic and sectorial policies between the States Parties in the areas of foreign trade, agriculture, industry, fiscal and monetary matters, foreign exchange and capital, services, customs, transport and communications and any other areas that may be agreed upon, in order to ensure proper competition between the States Parties;

The commitment by States Parties to harmonise their legislation in the relevant areas in order to strengthen the integration process.

Article 2

The common market shall be based on reciprocity of rights and obligations between the States Parties.

Article 3

During the transition period, which shall last from the entry into force of this Treaty until 31 December 1994, and in order to facilitate the formation of the common market, the States Parties shall adopt general rules of origin, a system for the settlement of disputes and safeguard clauses, as contained in annexes II, III and IV respectively to this Treaty.

Article 4

The States Parties shall ensure equitable trade terms in their relations with third countries. To that end, they shall apply their domestic legislation to restrict imports whose prices are influenced by subsidies, dumping or any other unfair practice. At the same time, States Parties shall co-ordinate their respective domestic policies with a view to drafting common rules for trade competition.

Article 5

During the transition period, the main instruments for putting in place the common market shall be:

(a) A trade liberalisation programme, which shall consist of progressive, linear and automatic tariff reductions accompanied by the elimination of non-tariff restrictions or equivalent measures, as well as any other restrictions on trade between the States Parties, with a view to arriving at a zero tariff and no non-tariff restrictions for the entire tariff area by 31 December 1994 (annex I);

(b) The co-ordination of macroeconomic policies, which shall be carried out gradually and in parallel with the programmes for the reduction of tariffs and the elimination of non-tariff restrictions referred to in the preceding paragraph;

(c) A common external tariff which encourages the foreign competitiveness of the States Parties;

(d) The adoption of sectorial agreements in order to optimise the use and mobility of factors of production and to achieve efficient scales of operation.

Article 6

The States Parties recognise certain differentials in the rate at which the Republic of Paraguay and the Eastern Republic of Uruguay will make the transition. These differentials are indicated in the trade liberalisation programme (annex I).

Article 7

In the area of taxes, charges and other internal duties, products originating in the territory of one State Party shall enjoy, in the other States Parties, the same treatment as domestically produced products.

Article 8

The States Parties undertake to abide by commitments made prior to the date of signing of this Treaty, including agreements signed in the framework of the Latin American Integration Association (ALADI), and to co-ordinate the positions in any external trade negotiations they may undertake during the transition period. To that end:

(a) They shall avoid affecting the interests of the States Parties in any trade negotiations they may conduct among themselves up to 31 December 1994;

(b) They shall avoid affecting the interests of the other States Parties or the aims of the common market in any agreements they may conclude with other countries members of the Latin American Integration Association during the transition period;

(c) They shall consult among themselves whenever negotiating comprehensive tariff reduction schemes for the formation of free trade areas with other countries members of the Latin American Integration Association;

(d) They shall extend automatically to the other States Parties any advantage, favour, exemption, immunity or privilege granted to a product originating in or destined for third countries which are not members of the Latin American Integration Association.

CHAPTER II
ORGANISATIONAL STRUCTURE

Article 9

The administration and implementation of this Treaty, and of any specific agreements or decisions adopted during the transition period within the legal framework established thereby, shall be entrusted to the following organs:

(a) The Council of the Common Market

(b) The Common Market Group

Article 10

The Council shall be the highest organ of the common market, with responsibility for its political leadership and for decision-making to ensure compliance with the objectives and time-limits set for the final establishment. of the common market.

Article 11

The Council shall consist of the Ministers for Foreign Affairs and the Ministers of the Economy of the States Parties.

It shall meet whenever its members deem appropriate, and at least once year with the participation of the Presidents of the States Parties

Article 12

The presidency of the Council shall rotate among the States Parties, in alphabetical order, for periods of six months.

Meetings of the Council shall be co-ordinated by the Ministers for Foreign Affairs, and other ministers or ministerial authorities may be invited to participate in them.

Article 13

The Common Market Group shall be the executive organ of the common market and shall be co-ordinated by the Ministries of Foreign Affairs.

The Common Market Group shall have powers of initiative. Its duties shall be the following:

- to monitor compliance with the Treaty;
- to take the necessary steps to enforce decisions adopted by the Council;
- to propose specific measures for applying the trade liberalisation programme, co-ordinating macroeconomic policies and negotiating agreements with third parties;
- to draw up programmes of work to ensure progress towards the formation of the common market.

The Common Market Group may set up whatever working groups are needed for it to perform its duties. To start with, it shall have the working groups mentioned in annex V.

The Common Market Group shall draw up its own rules of procedure within 60 days of its establishment

Article 14

The Common Market Group shall consist of four members and four alternates for each country, representing the following public bodies:

- Ministry of Foreign Affairs;
- Ministry of the Economy or its equivalent (areas of industry, foreign trade and/or economic co-ordination);
- Central Bank.

In drafting and proposing specific measures as part of its work up to 31 December 1994, the Common Market Group may, whenever it deems appropriate, call on representatives of other government agencies or the private sector.

Article 15

The Common Market Group shall have an administrative secretariat whose main functions shall be to keep the Group's documents and report on its activities. It shall be headquartered in the city of Montevideo.

Article 16

During the transition period, decisions of the Council of the common market and the common Market Group shall be taken by consensus, with all States Parties present.

Article 17

The official languages of the common market shall be Spanish and Portuguese, and the official version of its working documents shall be that drafted in the language of the country in which each meeting takes place.

Article 18

Prior to the establishment of the common market on 31 December 1994, the States Parties shall convene a special meeting to determine the final institutional structure of the administrative organs of the common market, as well as the specific powers of each organ and its decision-making procedures.

CHAPTER III
PERIOD OF APPLICATION

Article 19

This Treaty shall be of unlimited duration and shall enter into force 30 days after the date of deposit of the third instrument of ratification. The instruments of ratification shall be deposited with the Government of the Republic of Paraguay, which shall notify the Governments of the other States Parties of the date of deposit.

The Government of the Republic of Paraguay shall notify the Governments of each of the other States Parties of the date of entry into force of this Treaty.

CHAPTER IV
ACCESSION

Article 20

This Treaty shall be open to accession, through negotiation, by other countries members of the Latin American Integration Association their applications may be considered by the States Parties once this Treaty has been in force for five years.

Notwithstanding the above, applications made by countries members of the Latin American Integration Association who do not belong to sub-regional integration schemes or an extraregional association may be considered before the date specified.

Approval of applications shall require the unanimous decision of the States Parties.

CHAPTER V
DENUNCIATION

Article 21

Any State Party wishing to withdraw from this Treaty shall inform the other States Parties of its intention expressly and formally and shall submit the document of denunciation within 60 days to the Ministry of Foreign Affairs of the Republic of Paraguay, which shall distribute it to the other States Parties.

Article 22

Once the denunciation has been formalised, those rights and obligations of the denouncing State deriving from its status as a State Party shall cease, while those relating to the liberalisation programme under this Treaty and any other aspects to which the States Parties, together with the denouncing State, may agree within the 60 days following the normalisation of the denunciation shall continue. The latter rights and obligations of the denouncing Party shall remain in force for a period of two years from the date of the above-mentioned normalisation.

CHAPTER VI
GENERAL PROVISIONS

Article 23

This Treaty shall be called the "Treaty of Asunción".

Article 24

In order to facilitate progress towards the formation of the common market, a Joint Parliamentary Commission of MERCOSUL shall be established. The executive branches of the States Parties shall keep their respective legislative branches informed of the progress of the common market established by this Treaty.

DONE at the city of Asunción, on 26 March 1991, in one original in the Spanish. and Portuguese languages, both texts being equally authentic. The Government of the Republic of Paraguay shall be the depositary of this Treaty and shall send a duly authenticated copy thereof to the Governments of signatory and acceding States Parties.

Argentine Republic:
Carlos Saul Menem Guido di Tella
Federative Republic of Brazil:
Fernando Collor Francisco Rezek
Republic of Paraguay.
Andrés Rodríguez Alexis Frutos Vaesken
Eastern Republic of Uruguay:
Luis Alberto Lacalle Herrera H. Gros Espiell

ANNEX I
TRADE LIBERALISATION PROGRAMME

Article 1

The States Parties hereby agree to eliminate, by 31 December 1994 at the latest, any duties, charges and other restrictions applied in their reciprocal trade.

With regard to the schedules of exceptions submitted by the Republic of Paraguay and the Eastern Republic of Uruguay, the period for their elimination shall extend to 31 December 1995, on the terms of Article 7 of this annex.

Article 2

For the purposes of the preceding Article:

(a) "Duties and charges" shall mean customs duties and any other charges of equivalent effect, whether related to fiscal, monetary, foreign exchange or other matters, levied on foreign trade. This concept does not cover fees and similar charges corresponding to the approximate cost of services rendered; and

(b) "Restrictions" shall mean any administrative, financial, foreign exchange or other measures by which a State Party unilaterally prevents or impedes reciprocal trade. This concept does not cover measures taken in the situations envisaged in Article 50 of the Montevideo Treaty of 1980.

Article 3

As of the date of entry into force of the Treaty, the States Parties shall begin a programme of gradual, linear and automatic tariff reductions, which shall benefit products classified according to the tariff nomenclature used by the Latin American Integration Association, observing the following timetable:

DATE / PERCENTAGE TARIFF REDUCTION

30 June 1991	31 Dec. 1991	30 June 1992	31 Dec. 1992	30 June 1993	31 Dec. 1993	30 June 1994	31 Dec 1994
47	54	61	68	75	82	89	100

Preferences shall apply to the tariff in force at the time of their application and shall consist of a percentage reduction in the most favourable duties and charges applied to imports of products coming from third countries not members of the Latin American Integration Association.

If one of the States Parties increases this tariff for imports from third countries, the established timetable shall continue to apply at the tariff level in force on 1 January 1991.

If tariffs are reduced, the corresponding preference shall apply automatically to the new tariff on the date on which that new tariff enters into force.

For the above purposes, the States Parties shall exchange among themselves and shall transmit to the Latin American Integration Association, within 30 days of the entry into force of the Treaty, updated copies of their customs tariffs and of those in force on 1 January 1991.

Article 4

Preferences agreed to in partial scope agreements concluded by the State Parties among themselves in the framework of the Latin American Integration Association shall be expanded, under the present tariff reduction programme, according to the following timetable:

DATE / PERCENTAGE TARIFF REDUCTION

31 Dec. 1990	30 June 1991	31 Dec. 1991	30 June 1992	31 Dec. 1992	30 June 1993	31 Dec. 1993	30 June 1994	31 Dec. 1995
00 - 40	47	54	61	68	75	82	89	100
41 - 45	52	59	66	73	80	87	94	100
46 - 50	57	64	71	78	85	92	100	
51 - 55	61	67	73	79	86	93	100	
56 - 60	67	74	81	88	95	100		
61 - 65	71	77	83	89	96	100		
66 - 70	75	80	85	90	95	100		
71 - 75	80	85	90	95	100			
76 - 80	85	90	95	100				
81 - 85	89	93	97	100				
86 - 90	95	100						
91 - 95	100							
96-100								

These reductions shall apply only in the context of the corresponding partial scope agreements and shall not benefit other members of the common market; nor shall they apply to products included in the respective schedules of exceptions.

Article 5

Without prejudice to the mechanism described in Articles 3 and 4, States Parties may also expand preferences by means of negotiations conducted in the framework of the agreements envisaged in the Montevideo Treaty of 1980.

Article 6

The tariff reduction timetable referred to in Articles 3 and 4 of this annex shall not apply to products included in the schedules of exceptions submitted by each of the States Parties with the following quantities of ALADI nomenclature items:

Argentine Republic:	394
Federative Republic of Brazil:	324
Republic of Paraguay:	439
Eastern Republic of Uruguay:	960

Article 7

The schedules of exceptions shall be reduced at the end of each calendar year in accordance with the following timetable:

(a) For the Argentine Republic and the Federative Republic of Brazil, by 20 per cent per year of the component items; this reduction applies from 31 December 1990;

(b) For the Republic of Paraguay and the Eastern Republic of Uruguay, the reduction shall be at the following rates:

10 per cent on the date of entry into force of the Treaty
10 per cent on 31 December 1991
20 per cent on 31 December 1992
20 per cent on 31 December 1993
20 per cent on 31 December 1994
20 per cent on 31 December 1995

Article 8

The schedules of exceptions contained in appendices I, II, III and IV include the first reduction envisaged in the preceding Article.

Article 9

Products which are removed from schedules of exceptions on the terms set forth in Article 7 shall automatically benefit from the preferences resulting from the tariff reduction programme established in Article 3 of this annex. They shall benefit, at the least, from the minimum percentage reduction provided on the date on which they are removed from the schedules.

Article 10

States Parties may apply up to 31 December 1994, to products included in the tariff reduction programme, only the non-tariff restrictions expressly mentioned in the notes supplementing the complementarity agreement to be concluded by the States Parties in the framework of the Montevideo Treaty of 1980.

As of 31 December 1994, all non-tariff restrictions shall be eliminated from the common market area.

Article 11

In order to ensure observance of the tariff reduction timetable established in Articles 3 and 4, and also the formation of the common market, the States Parties shall co-ordinate any macroeconomic and sectorial policies which may be agreed upon and to which the Treaty establishing the common market refers, beginning with those connected with trade flows and the composition of the States Parties' productive sectors.

Article 12

The provisions of this annex shall not apply to the partial scope agreements, economic complementarity agreements Nos. 1, 2, 13 and 14 or trade and agricultural agreements signed in the framework of the Montevideo Treaty of 1980, such agreements being governed exclusively by their own provisions.

ANNEX II
GENERAL RULES OF ORIGIN

CHAPTER I
GENERAL RULES FOR CLASSIFICATION OF ORIGIN

Article 1

The following shall be classified as originating in the States Parties:

(a) Products manufactured wholly in the territory of any of the Parties, when only materials originating in the States Parties are used in their manufacture;

(b) Products included in the chapters or headings of the tariff nomenclature of the Latin American Integration Association referred to in annex 1 of resolution 78 of the Committee of Representatives of that Association, simply by virtue of the fact that they are produced in their respective territories.

The following shall be classified as produced in the territory of a State Party:

(i) Mineral, plant and animal products, including hunting and fishing products, extracted, harvested or gathered, born and raised in its territory or in its territorial waters or exclusive economic zone;

(ii) Marine products extracted outside its territorial waters and exclusive economic zone by vessels flying its flag or leased by companies established in its territory; and

(iii) Products resulting from operations or processes carried out in its territory by which they acquire the final form in which they will be marketed, except when such processes or operations simply involve assembly, packaging, division into lots or volumes, selection and classification, marking, the putting together of assortments of goods or other equivalent operations or processes:

(c) Products in whose manufacture materials not originating in the States Parties are used, when such products are changed by a process carried out in the territory of one of the States Parties which results in their reclassification in the tariff nomenclature of the Latin American Integration Association under a heading different from that of such materials, except in eases where the States Parties determine that the requirement of Article 2 of this annex must also be met.

However, products resulting from operations or processes carried out in the territory of a State Party, by which they acquire the final form in which they will be marketed, shall not be classified as originating in the States Parties when such operations or processes use only materials or inputs not originating in their respective countries and simply involve assembly, division into lots or volumes, selection, classification, marking, the putting together of assortments of goods or other similar operations or processes;

(d) Until 31 December 1994, products resulting from assembly operations carried out in the territory of a State Party using materials originating in the States Parties and third countries, when the value of those materials is not less than 40 per cent of the f.o.b. export value of the final product; and

(e) Products which, in addition to being produced in their territory, meet the specific requirements established in annex 2 of resolution 78 of the Committee of Representatives of the Latin American Integration Association.

Article 2

In cases where the requirements of Article 1 (c) cannot be met because the process carried out does not involve a change in nomenclature heading, it shall suffice that the c.i.f. value of the third country materials at the port of destination or the maritime port does not exceed 50 per cent of the f.o.b. export value of the goods in question.

In considering materials originating in third countries for States Parties with no outlet to the sea, warehouses and free zones granted by the other States Parties when the materials arrive by sea shall be treated as the port of destination.

Article 3

The States Parties may establish, by mutual consent, specific requirements of origin which shall prevail over general classification criteria.

Article 4

In determining the specific requirements of origin referred to in Article 3 and in reviewing those already established, State Parties shall take the following elements, individually or jointly, as a basis:

I. Materials and other inputs used in production:

(a) Raw materials:

(i) Preponderant raw material or that which essentially characterises the product; and

(ii) Main raw materials.

(b) Parts or components:

(i) Part or component which essentially characterises the product;

(ii) Main parts or components; and

(iii) Percentage of parts or components in relation to total weight.

(c) Other inputs.

II. Type of processing used.

III. Maximum proportion of the value of materials imported from third countries in relation to the total value of the product arrived at using the valuation procedure agreed to in each case.

Article 5

In exceptional cases, where specific requirements cannot be met because of circumstantial supply problems: availability, technical specifications, delivery date and price, taking into account the provisions of Article 4 of the Treaty, materials not originating in the States Parties may be used.

In the situation envisaged in the preceding paragraph, the exporting country shall issue the corresponding certificate informing the importing State Party and the Common Market Group, together with any background information and evidence justifying the issue of that document.

If such cases occur repeatedly, the exporting State Party or the import State Party shall inform the Common Market Group of the situation so that the specific requirement can be reviewed.

This Article does not cover products resulting from assembly operations and shall apply pending the entry into force of the common external tariff for products subject to specific requirements of origin and their materials or inputs.

Article 6

Any State Party may request that requirements of origin established pursuant to Article 1 above be reviewed. Such requests shall propose and justify the requirements applicable to the product or products in question.

Article 7

For the purpose of meeting requirements of origin, materials and other inputs originating in the territory of any State Party and used by a State Party in the manufacture of a given product shall be classified as originating in the territory of this latter State Party.

Article 8

The criterion of maximum use of materials or other inputs originating in States Parties may not be taken into account in establishing requirements which involve the imposition of materials or other inputs of those States Parties when, in their view, such materials or inputs do not meet adequate supply, quality or price standards or are not adapted to the industrial processes or technologies used.

Article 9

In order for originating goods to benefit from preferential treatment, they must have been shipped directly from the exporting country to the importing country. For these purposes, the following shall be deemed direct shipment:

(a) Goods not shipped through the territory of a country that is not a party to the Treaty;

(b) Goods shipped in transit through one or more countries that are not parties to the Treaty, with or without transhipment or temporary storage, under the supervision of the competent customs authority in such countries, provided that;

(i) Transit is justified by geographical reasons or transport considerations;

(ii) The goods are not intended for trade or use in the country of transit; and

(iii) The goods are not subjected, during shipment and storage, to any operation other than loading, unloading or handling to keep them in good condition or ensure their conservation.

Article 10

For the purposes of these general rules, it shall be understood that:

(a) Products coming from free zones located within the geographical boundaries of any of the States Parties shall meet the requirements envisage in these general rules;

(b) The term "materials" shall include raw materials, intermediate products and parts and components used in the manufacture of goods.

CHAPTER II
DECLARATION, CERTIFICATION AND VERIFICATION

Article 11

In order for imports of products originating in the States Parties to benefit from the reductions in duties, charges and restrictions they have granted each other, the export documentation for such products must include a declaration certifying that they meet the requirements of origin established in accordance with the preceding chapter.

Article 12

The declaration referred to in the preceding Article shall be issued by the final producer or the exporter of the goods and certified by an official department or professional association with legal personality, authorised by the Government of the exporting State Party.

In authorising professional associations, States Parties shall make sure that they are organisations which have national jurisdiction and can delegate authority to regional or local associations while remaining directly responsible for the veracity of the certifications issued.

The States Parties undertake to establish, within a period of 90 days from the entry into force of the Treaty, a harmonised regime of administrative penalties for cases of false certification, without prejudice to the corresponding criminal proceedings.

Article 13

Certificates of origin issued for the purposes of this Treaty shall be valid for 180 days from the date of their issue.

Article 14

In all cases, the standard form annexed to agreement No. 25 of the Committee of Representatives of the Latin American Integration Association shall be used until such time as another form approved by the States Parties comes into effect.

Article 15

States Parties shall transmit to the Latin American Integration Association the list of official departments and professional associations authorised to issue the certification referred to in the preceding Article, with a record and exact copy of the authorised signatures.

Article 16

If a State Party considers that the certificates issued by an official department or professional association authorised by another State Party are not in compliance with the provisions of these general rules, it shall inform that State Party accordingly so that the latter can take whatever steps it deems necessary to solve the problems that have arisen

In no case may the importing country hold up import procedures for products covered by the certificates referred to in the preceding paragraph. It may, however, in addition to requesting the corresponding additional information from the governmental authorities of the exporting country, take whatever measures it deems necessary to safeguard fiscal interests.

Article 17

For the purposes of subsequent verification, copies of certificates and the corresponding documents shall be kept for two years from the date of their issue.

Article 18

The provisions of these general rules and any amendments thereto shall not affect goods already loaded for shipment on the date of their adoption.

Article 19

The provisions of this annex shall not apply to the partial scope agreements, economic complementarity agreements Nos. 1, 2, 13 and 14 or trade and agricultural agreements signed in the framework of the Montevideo Treaty of 1980, such agreements being governed exclusively by their own provisions.

ANNEX III
SETTLEMENT OF DISPUTES

1. Any disputes arising between the States Parties as a result of the application of the Treaty shall be settled by means of direct negotiations.

If no solution can be found, the States Parties shall refer the dispute to the Common Market Group which, after evaluating the situation, shall within a period of 60 days make the relevant recommendations to the Parties for settling the dispute. To that end, the Common Market Group may establish or convene panels of experts or groups of specialists in order to obtain the necessary technical advice.

If the Common Market Group also fails to find a solution, the dispute shall be referred to the Council of the common market to adopt the relevant recommendations.

2. Within 120 days of the entry into force of the Treaty, the Common Market Group shall propose to the Governments of States Parties a system for the settlement of disputes which shall apply during the transition period.

3. Before 31 December 1994, the States Parties shall adopt a permanent disputes settlement system for the common market.

ANNEX IV
SAFEGUARD CLAUSES

Article 1

Each State Party may, up to 31 December 1994, apply safeguard clauses to imports of products benefiting from the trade liberalisation programme established under the Treaty.

The States Parties hereby agree that they shall use these rules only in exceptional cases.

Article 2

If imports of a given product damage or threaten serious damage to its market as a result of a significant increase in imports of that product from the other States Parties over a short period of time, the importing country shall request the Common Market Group to hold consultations with a view to ending such a situation.

The importing country shall accompany its request with a detailed statement of the supporting facts, reasons and justifications.

The Common Market Group shall begin consultations within a maximum of 10 calendar days from the submission of the request by the importing country and shall conclude them, having taken a decision thereon, within 20 calendar days from the start of consultations.

Article 3

The existence or otherwise of damage or the threat of serious damage within the meaning of these rules shall be determined by each country, taking into account trends, inter alia, in the following aspects related to the product in question.

(a) Production level and capacity used;
(b) Employment level;
(c) Share of the market;
(d) Level of trade between the parties concerned or participating in the consultations;
(e) Performance of imports and exports in relation to third countries.

None of the above-mentioned factors shall, on its own, be decisive for determining the existence of damage or the threat of serious damage.

In determining the existence of damage or the threat of serious damage, factors such as technological changes or shifts in consumer preferences towards similar and/or directly competitive products in the same sector shall not be taken into account.

Application of the safeguard clause shall be subject, in each country, to the final approval of the national section of the Common Market Group.

Article 4

In order not to interrupt any trade flows which may have been generated, the importing country shall negotiate a quota for imports of the product in respect of which the safeguard clause has been invoked. This quota shall be governed by the same preferences and other conditions established in the trade liberalisation programme.

The above-mentioned quota shall be negotiated with the State Party in which the imports originate, during the period of consultation referred to in Article 2. If the period of consultation ends without an agreement being reached, the importing country which considers itself affected may fix a quota which shall be maintained for one year.

In no event may a quota fixed unilaterally by the importing country be less than the average physical volume imported in the last three calendar years.

Article 5

Safeguard clauses shall apply for a year and may be extended for a further consecutive year on the terms established in this annex. Such measures may be adopted only once for each product.

In no event may the application of safeguard clauses extend beyond 31 December 1994.

Article 6

The application of safeguard clauses shall not affect goods already loaded for shipment on the date of their adoption. Such goods shall be computed into the quota provided for in Article 4.

Article 7

During the transition period, any State Party which considers itself affected by serious difficulties in its economic activities shall request the Common Market Group to hold consultations so that the necessary corrective measures can be taken.

Within the periods established in Article 2 of this annex, the Common Market Group shall evaluate the situation and decide on the measures to be taken, according to the circumstances.

ANNEX V

WORKING GROUPS OF THE COMMON MARKET GROUP

For the purposes of co-ordinating macroeconomic and sectorial policies, the Common Market Group shall establish, within 30 days of its formation, the following working groups:

Subgroup 1: Commercial issues
Subgroup 2: Customs issues
Subgroup 3: Technical standards
Subgroup 4: Fiscal and monetary policies relating to trade
Subgroup 5: Inland transport
Subgroup 6: Maritime transport
Subgroup 7: Industrial and technological policy
Subgroup 8: Agricultural policy
Subgroup 9: Energy policy
Subgroup 10: Co-ordination of macroeconomic policies

PROTOCOL OF OURO PRETO

The Argentine Republic, the Federative Republic of Brazil, the Republic of Paraguay and the Eastern Republic of Uruguay, hereinafter referred to as the "States Parties",

In compliance with the provisions of Article 18 of the Treaty of Asuncion of 26 March 1991,

Aware of the importance of the progress made and of the introduction of the customs union as a stage in the establishment of a common market,

Reaffirming the principles and objectives of the Treaty of Asuncion and mindful of the need to give special consideration to the less developed countries and regions of Mercosul,

Mindful of the forces for change inherent in any integration process and the consequent need to adapt the institutional structure of Mercosul to the transformations that have taken place,

Recognising the outstanding achievements of the existing bodies during the transition period,

Hereby agree as follows:

CHAPTER I
STRUCTURE OF MERCOSUL

Article 1

The institutional structure of Mercosul shall comprise the following organs:

I. The Council of the Common Market (CCM);

II. The Common Market Group (CMG);

III. The Mercosul Trade Commission (MTC);

IV. The Joint Parliamentary Commission (JPC);

V. The Economic-Social Consultative Forum (ESCF);

VI. The Mercosul Administrative Secretariat (MAS).

Sole paragraph - Auxiliary organs necessary to attain the objectives of the integration process may be established, under the terms of this Protocol.

Article 2

The following are inter-governmental organs with decision-making powers: the Council of the Common Market, the Common Market Group and the Mercosul Trade Commission.

Section I
Council of the Common Market

Article 3

The Council of the Common Market is the highest organ of Mercosul, with responsibility for the political leadership of the integration process and for making the decisions necessary to ensure the achievement of the objectives defined by the Treaty of Asuncion and the final establishment of the common market.

Article 4

The Council of the Common Market shall consist of the Ministers for Foreign Affairs and the Ministers of the Economy of the States Parties, or their equivalents.

Article 5

The Presidency of the Council of the Common Market shall be rotated among the States Parties, in alphabetical order, for periods of six months.

Article 6

The Council of the Common Market shall meet whenever it deems appropriate, and at least once every six months, with the participation of the Presidents of the States Parties.

Article 7

The meetings of the Council of the Common Market shall be co-ordinated by the Ministers for Foreign Affairs, and other ministers or ministerial authorities may be invited to participate.

Article 8

The following are duties and functions of the Council of the Common Market:

I. To supervise the implementation of the Treaty of Asuncion, its protocols, and agreements signed within its context;

II. To formulate policies and promote the measures necessary to build the common market;

III. To assume the legal personality of Mercosul;

IV. To negotiate and sign agreements, on behalf of Mercosul, with third countries, groups of countries and international organisations. These functions may be delegated, by express mandate, to the Common Market Group under the conditions laid down in paragraph VII of Article 14;

V. To rule on proposals submitted to it by the Common Market Group;

VI. To arrange meetings of ministers and rule on agreements which those meetings refer to it;

VII. To establish the organs it considers appropriate, and to modify or abolish them;

VIII. To clarify, when it considers necessary, the substance and scope of its decisions;

IX. To appoint the Director of the Mercosul Administrative Secretariat;

X. To adopt financial and budgetary decisions;

XI. To approve the rules of procedure of the Common Market Group.

Article 9

The rulings of the Council of the Common Market shall take the form of Decisions which shall be binding upon the States Parties.

Section II

The Common Market Group

Article 10

The Common Market Group is the executive organ of Mercosul.

Article 11

The Common Market Group shall consist of four members and four alternates for each country, appointed by their respective governments, who must include representatives of the Ministries of Foreign Affairs, the Ministries of the Economy (or their equivalents) and the Central Banks. The Common Market Group shall be co-ordinated by the Ministries of Foreign Affairs.

Article 12

When drafting and proposing specific measures in the course of doing its work, the Common Market Group may, whenever it deems appropriate, call on representatives of other organs of government or of the institutional structure of Mercosul.

Article 13

The Common Market Group shall hold ordinary or extraordinary meetings, as often as necessary, in accordance with the terms of its rules of procedure.

Article 14

The following are duties and functions of the Common Market Group:

I. To monitor, within the limits of its competence, compliance with the Treaty of Asuncion, its Protocols, and agreements signed within its framework;

II. To propose draft Decisions to the Council of the Common Market;

III. To take the measures necessary to enforce the Decisions adopted by the Council of the Common Market;

IV. To draw up programmes of work to ensure progress towards the establishment of the common market;

V. To establish, modify or abolish organs such as working groups and special meetings for the purpose of achieving its objectives;

VI. To express its views on any proposals or recommendations submitted to it by other Mercosul organs within their sphere of competence;

VII. To negotiate, with the participation of representatives of all the States Parties, when expressly so delegated by the Council of the Common Market and within the limits laid down in special mandates granted for that purpose, agreements on behalf of Mercosul with third countries, groups of countries and international organisations. When so mandated, the Common Market Group shall sign the aforementioned agreements. When so authorised by the Council of the Common Market, the Common Market Group may delegate these powers to the Mercosul Trade Commission;

VIII. To approve the budget and the annual statement of accounts presented by the Mercosul Administrative Secretariat;

IX. To adopt financial and budgetary Resolutions based on the guidelines laid down by the Council;

X. To submit its rules of procedure to the Council of the Common Market;

XI. To organise the meetings of the Council of the Common Market and to prepare the reports and studies requested by the latter;

XII. To choose the Director of the Mercosul Administrative Secretariat;

XIII. To supervise the activities of the Mercosul Administrative Secretariat;

XIV. To approve the rules of procedure of the Trade Commission and the Economic-Social Consultative Forum.

Article 15

The decisions of the Common Market Group shall take the form of Resolutions which shall be binding upon the States Parties.

Section III
The Mercosul Trade Commission

Article 16

It shall be the task of the Mercosul Trade Commission, a body responsible for assisting the Common Market Group, to monitor the application of the common trade policy instruments agreed by the States Parties in connection with the operation of the customs union, as well as to follow up and review questions and issues relating to common trade policies, intra-Mercosul trade and third countries.

Article 17

The Mercosul Trade Commission shall consist of four members and four alternates for each State Party and shall be co-ordinated by the Ministries of Foreign Affairs.

Article 18

The Mercosul Trade Commission shall meet at least once a month, or whenever requested to do so by the Common Market Group or any of the States Parties.

Article 19

The following are duties and functions of the Mercosul Trade Commission:

I. To monitor the application of the common trade policy instruments both within Mercosul and with respect to third countries, international organisations and trade agreements;

II. To consider and rule upon the requests submitted by the States Parties in connection with the application of and compliance with the common external tariff and other instruments of common trade policy;

III. To follow up the application of the common trade policy instruments in the States Parties;

IV. To analyse the development of the common trade policy instruments relating to the operation of the customs union and to submit Proposals in this respect to the Common Market Group;

V. To take decisions connected with the administration and application of the common external tariff and the common trade policy instruments agreed by the States Parties;

VI. To report to the Common Market Group on the development and application of the common trade policy instruments, on the consideration of requests received and on the decisions taken with respect to such requests;

VII. To propose to the Common Market Group new Mercosul trade and customs regulations or changes in the existing regulations;

VIII. To propose the revision of the tariff rates for specific items of the common external tariff, inter alia, in order to deal with cases relating to new production activities within Mercosul;

IX. To set up the technical committees needed for it to perform its duties properly, and to direct and supervise their activities;

X. To perform tasks connected with the common trade policy requested by the Common Market Group;

XI. To adopt rules of procedure to be submitted to the Common Market Group for approval.

Article 20

The decisions of the Mercosul Trade Commission shall take the form of Directives or Proposals. The Directives shall be binding upon the States Parties.

Article 21

In addition to the duties and functions described in Articles 16 and 19 of this Protocol, the Mercosul Trade Commission shall be responsible for considering complaints referred to it by the National Sections of the Mercosul Trade Commission and originated by States Parties or individuals, whether natural or legal persons, relating to the situations provided for in Article 1 or 25 of the Brasilia Protocol, when they fall within its sphere of competence.

Paragraph 1. The examination of the aforesaid complaints within the Mercosul Trade Commission shall not prevent the complainant State Party taking action under the Brasilia Protocol for the Settlement of Disputes.

Paragraph 2. Complaints arising in the circumstances described in this Article shall be dealt with in accordance with the procedure laid down in the Annex to this Protocol.

Section IV
The Joint Parliamentary Commission

Article 22

The Joint Parliamentary Commission is the organ representing the parliaments of the States Parties within Mercosul.

Article 23

The Joint Parliamentary Commission shall consist of equal numbers of members of parliament representing the States Parties.

Article 24

The members of the Joint Parliamentary Commission shall be appointed by the respective national parliaments, in accordance with their internal procedures.

Article 25

The Joint Parliamentary Commission shall endeavour to speed up the corresponding internal procedures in the States Parties in order to ensure the prompt entry into force of the decisions taken by the Mercosul organs provided for in Article 2 of this Protocol. Similarly, it shall assist with the harmonisation of legislations, as required to advance the integration process. When necessary, the Council shall request the Joint Parliamentary Commission to examine priority issues.

Article 26

The Joint Parliamentary Commission shall submit Recommendations to the Council of the Common Market through the Common Market Group.

Article 27

The Joint Parliamentary Commission shall adopt its rules of procedure.

Section V
The Economic-Social Consultative Forum

Article 28

The Economic-Social Consultative Forum is the organ representing the economic and social sectors and shall consist of equal numbers of representatives from each State Party.

Article 29

The Economic-Social Consultative Forum shall have a consultative function and shall express its views in the form of Recommendations to the Common Market Group.

Article 30

The Economic-Social Consultative Forum shall submit its rules of procedure to the Common Market Group, for approval.

Section VI
The Mercosul Administrative Secretariat

Article 31

Mercosul shall have an Administrative Secretariat to provide operational support. The Mercosul Administrative Secretariat shall be responsible for providing services to the other Mercosul organs and shall be headquartered in the city of Montevideo.

Article 32

The Mercosul Administrative Secretariat shall carry out the following activities:

I. Serve as the official archive for Mercosul documentation;

II. Publish and circulate the decisions adopted within the framework of Mercosul. In this context, it shall;

(i) Make, in co-ordination with the States Parties, authentic translations in Spanish and Portuguese of all the decisions adopted by the organs of the Mercosul institutional structure, in accordance with the provisions of Article 39;

(ii) Publish the Mercosul official journal.

III. Organise the logistical aspects of the meetings of the Council of the Common Market, the Common Market Group and the Mercosul Trade Commission and, as far as possible, the other Mercosul organs, when those meetings are held at its headquarters. In the case of meetings held outside its headquarters, the Mercosul Administrative Secretariat shall provide support for the State in which the meeting is held;

IV. Regularly inform the States Parties about the measures taken by each country to incorporate in its legal system the decisions adopted by the Mercosul organs provided for in Article 2 of this Protocol;

V. Compile national lists of arbitrators and experts, and perform other tasks defined in the Brasilia Protocol of 17 December 1991;

VI. Perform tasks requested by the Council of the Common Market, the Common Market Group and the Mercosul Trade Commission;

VII. Draw up its draft budget and, once this has been approved by the Common Market Group, do everything necessary to ensure its proper implementation;

VIII. Submit its statement of accounts annually to the Common Market Group, together with a report on its activities.

Article 33

The Mercosul Administrative Secretariat shall be headed by a Director who shall be a national of one of the States Parties. He shall be chosen by the Common Market Group, on a rotating basis, after consultation with the States Parties and shall be appointed by the Council of the Common Market. His term of office shall be two years and he may not be re-elected.

CHAPTER II
LEGAL PERSONALITY

Article 34

Mercosul shall possess legal personality of international law.

Article 35

In the exercise of its functions, Mercosul may take whatever action may be necessary to achieve its objectives, in particular sign contracts, buy and sell personal and real property, appear in court, hold funds and make transfers.

Article 36

Mercosul shall make headquarters agreements.

CHAPTER III
DECISION-MAKING SYSTEM

Article 37

The decisions of the Mercosul organs shall be taken by consensus and in the presence of all the States Parties.

CHAPTER IV
INTERNAL APPLICATION OF THE DECISIONS ADOPTED BY MERCOSUL ORGANS

Article 38

The States Parties undertake to take all the measures necessary to ensure, in their respective territories, compliance with the decisions adopted by the Mercosul organs provided for in Article 2 of this Protocol.

Sole paragraph. The States Parties shall inform the Mercosul Administrative Secretariat of the measures taken to this end.

Article 39

The content of the Decisions of the Council of the Common Market, the Resolutions of the Common Market Group, the Directives of the Mercosul Trade Commission and the Dispute Settlement Arbitration Rulings shall be published in full, in Spanish and Portuguese, in the Mercosul official journal, together with any instrument which, in the view of the Council of the Common Market or the Common Market Group requires official publicity.

Article 40

In order to ensure the simultaneous entry into force in the States Parties of the decisions adopted by the Mercosul organs provided for in Article 2 of this Protocol, the following procedure must be followed:

(i) Once the decision has been adopted, the States Parties shall take the necessary measures to incorporate it in their domestic legal system and inform the Mercosul Administrative Secretariat.

(ii) When all the States Parties have reported incorporation in their respective domestic legal systems, the Mercosul Administrative Secretariat shall inform each State Party accordingly.

(iii) The decisions shall enter into force simultaneously in the States Parties 30 days after the date of the communication made by the Mercosul Administrative Secretariat, under the terms of the preceding subparagraph. To this end, the States Parties shall, within the time-limit mentioned, publish the entry into force of the decisions in question in their respective official journals.

CHAPTER V
LEGAL SOURCES OF MERCOSUL

Article 41

The legal sources of Mercosul are:

I. The Treaty of Asuncion, its protocols and the additional or supplementary instruments;

II. The agreements concluded within the framework of the Treaty of Asuncion and its protocols;

III. The Decisions of the Council of the Common Market, the Resolutions of the Common Market Group and the Directives of the Mercosul Trade Commission adopted since the entry into force of the Treaty of Asuncion.

Article 42

The decisions adopted by the Mercosul organs provided for in Article 2 of this Protocol shall be binding and, when necessary, must be incorporated in the domestic legal systems in accordance with the procedures provided for in each country's legislation.

CHAPTER VI
DISPUTE SETTLEMENT SYSTEM

Article 43

Disputes which arise between the States Parties concerning the interpretation, application or non-fulfilment of the provisions of the Treaty of Asuncion and the agreements concluded within its framework or of Decisions of the Council of the Common Market, Resolutions of the Common Market Group and Directives of the Mercosul Trade Commission shall be subject to the settlement procedures laid down in the Brasilia Protocol of 17 December 1991.

Sole paragraph. The Directives of the Mercosul Trade Commission are also incorporated in Articles 19 and 25 of the Brasilia Protocol.

Article 44

Before the Common External Tariff convergence process is complete, the States Parties shall review the present Mercosul dispute settlement system with a view to adopting the permanent system referred to in paragraph 3 of Annex III to the Treaty of Asuncion and Article 34 of the Brasilia Protocol.

CHAPTER VII
BUDGET

Article 45

The Mercosul Administrative Secretariat shall have a budget to cover its operating expenses and the expenses authorised by the Common Market Group. This budget shall be funded by equal contributions from the State Parties.

CHAPTER VIII
LANGUAGES

Article 46

The official languages of Mercosul are Spanish and Portuguese. The official version of the working documents shall be that in the language of the country hosting the meeting.

CHAPTER IX
REVIEW

Article 47

When they consider it opportune, the States Parties shall convene a diplomatic conference for the purpose of reviewing the institutional structure of Mercosul established by the present Protocol and the specific functions of each of its organs.

CHAPTER X
ENTRY INTO FORCE

Article 48

This Protocol, which forms an integral part of the Treaty of Asuncion, shall be of unlimited duration and shall enter into force 30 days after the date of deposit of the third instrument of ratification. The Protocol and its instruments of ratification shall be deposited with the Government of the Republic of Paraguay.

Article 49

The Government of the Republic of Paraguay shall notify the Governments of the other States Parties of the date of deposit of the instruments of ratification and of entry into force of this Protocol.

Article 50

With regard to accession and denunciation, the rules established by the Treaty of Asuncion shall apply to this Protocol in their entirety. Accession to or denunciation of the Treaty of Asuncion or this Protocol shall imply, ipso jure, accession to or denunciation of this Protocol and the Treaty of Asuncion.

CHAPTER XI
TRANSITIONAL PROVISION

Article 51

The institutional structure provided for in the Treaty of Asuncion of 26 March 1991 and the organs it created shall be maintained until this Protocol enters into force.

CHAPTER XII

GENERAL PROVISIONS

Article 52

This Protocol shall be called the "Ouro Preto Protocol".

Article 53

All the provisions of the Treaty of Asuncion of 26 March 1991 which conflict with the terms of this Protocol or with the content of the Decisions adopted by the Council of the Common Market during the transition period are hereby repealed.

Done at the city of Ouro Preto, Federative Republic of Brazil, on 17 December 1994, in one original in the Portuguese and Spanish languages, both texts being equally authentic. The Government of Paraguay shall send an authenticated copy of this Protocol to the Governments of the other States Parties.

Argentine RepublicCarlos Saul Menem Guido Di Tella
Federative Republic of Brazil
Itamar Franco Celso L. N. Amorin
Republic of Paraguay
Juan Carlos Wasmosy Luis Ramirez Boettner
Eastern Republic of Uruguay
Luis Alberto Lacalle Herrera Sergio Abreu

ANNEX TO THE PROTOCOL OF OURO PRETO

General Procedure for Complaints to the Mercosul Trade Commission

Article 1

Complaints submitted by the National Sections of the Mercosul Trade Commission and originated by States Parties or individuals, whether natural or legal persons, in accordance with the provisions of Article 21 of the Protocol of Ouro Preto shall be subject to the procedure laid down in this Annex.

Article 2

The complainant State Party shall submit its complaint to the Pro-Tempore Chairman of the Mercosul Trade Commission who shall take the necessary steps to include the question on the Agenda of the next meeting of the Mercosul Trade Commission at least one week beforehand. If no decision is taken at that meeting, the Mercosul Trade Commission shall, without taking further action, pass on the dossier to a Technical Committee.

Article 3

Within a maximum of thirty (30) calendar days, the Technical Committee shall prepare and submit to the Mercosul Trade Commission a joint opinion on the question. This opinion or the conclusions of the experts making up the Technical Committee, if there is no joint opinion, shall be taken into consideration by the Mercosul Trade Commission when it rules on the complaint.

Article 4

The Mercosul Trade Commission shall rule on the complaint at its first ordinary meeting following receipt of the joint opinion or, should there be none, the conclusions of the experts, although an extraordinary meeting may also be convened for the purpose.

Article 5

If a consensus cannot be reached at the first meeting mentioned in Article 4, the Mercosul Trade Commission shall submit to the Common Market Group the various alternatives proposed, together with the joint opinion or the conclusions of the experts on the Technical Committee, in order that an appropriate decision may be taken. The Common Market Group shall give a ruling within thirty (30) calendar days of the receipt by the Pro-Tempore Chairman of the proposals submitted by the Mercosul Trade Commission.

Article 6

If there is agreement that the complaint is justified, the State Party against which it is made shall adopt the measures approved in the Mercosul Trade Commission or the Common Market Group. In each case, the Mercosul Trade Commission or, subsequently, the Common Market Group shall fix a reasonable period for the implementation of these measures. If this period expires without the State against which the complaint is made having complied with the provisions of the decision adopted, whether by the Mercosul Trade Commission or the Common Market Group, the complainant State may resort directly to the procedure provided for in Chapter IV of the Brasilia Protocol.

Article 7

If a consensus cannot be reached in the Mercosul Trade Commission, or subsequently, in the Common Market Group or if the State against which the complaint is made does not comply within the period provided for in Article 6 with the provisions of the decision adopted, the complainant State may resort directly to the procedure established in Chapter IV of the Brasilia Protocol and shall inform the Mercosul Administrative Secretariat accordingly.

Before giving a ruling, within fifteen (15) days of its being set up, the Arbitration Tribunal must announce the interim measures it considers appropriate under the conditions laid down in Article 18 of the Brasilia Protocol.

ISSN 0378-6978

L 69

Volume 39

19 March 1996

Official Journal
of the European Communities

English edition

Legislation

Contents

1

EN

Acts whose titles are printed in light type are those relating to day-to-day management of agricultural matters, and are generally valid for a limited period.

The titles of all other Acts are printed in bold type and preceded by an asterisk.

II

(Acts whose publication is not obligatory)

COUNCIL

COUNCIL DECISION

of 20 November 1995

concerning the provisional application of certain provisions of the Interregional Framework Cooperation Agreement between the European Community and its Member States, of the one part, and the Southern Common Market and its Party States, of the other part (1)

(96/205/EC)

THE COUNCIL OF THE EUROPEAN UNION,

Having regard to the Treaty establishing the European Community,

Having regard to the proposal from the Commission,

Whereas the Community and the Southern Common Market (Mercosur) have undertaken to adopt procedures for the early application of certain provisions of the Interregional Framework Cooperation Agreement between the European Community and its Member States, of the one part, and the Southern Common Market and its Party States, of the other part, which deal with trade cooperation between the Parties and the institutional framework for such cooperation;

Whereas the provisional application of the provisions in question will contribute to facilitating and promoting closer trade relations between the Community and Mercosur, pending the completion of the procedures required to bring the Agreement into force,

HAS DECIDED AS FOLLOWS:

Article 1

The exchange of letters between the Community and Mercosur, which provides for the provisional application of certain provisions of the Interregional Framework Cooperation Agreement between the European Community and its Member States, of the one part, and the Southern Common Market and its Party States, of the other part, is hereby approved on behalf of the Community.

The text of the exchange of letters is attached to this Decision.

Article 2

The Commission shall represent the Community within the bodies referred to in Articles 27 and 29 of the Agreement.

Article 3

This Decision shall be published in the *Official Journal of the European Communities.*

Done at Brussels, 20 November 1995.

For the Council

The President

J. SOLANA

---

(1) The Interregional Framework Cooperation Agreement between the European Community and its Member States, of the one part, and the Southern Common Market and its Party States, of the other part, was signed, subject to conclusion, at Madrid from 15 to 31 December 1995.

EXCHANGE OF LETTERS

concerning the provisional application of certain provisions of the Interregional Framework Cooperation Agreement between the European Community and its Member States, of the one part, and the Southern Common Market and its Party States, of the other part

A. *Letter No 1*

Brussels, . . .

Sir

I have the honour to refer to the Interregional Framework Cooperation Agreement between the European Community and its Member States, of the one part, and the Southern Common Market and its Party States, of the other part, signed on 15 December 1995 at Madrid.

Pending the entry into force of the said Agreement, I have the honour to propose to you that the European Community and Mercosur provisionally apply the provisions of that Agreement which deal with trade cooperation, as set out in Articles 4 to 8 of Title II of the abovementioned Agreement.

In the interests of ensuring that our cooperation referred to in those provisions is effective, I also have the honour to propose that we provisionally apply the provisions of Articles 27, 29 and 30, which deal with the establishment of the institutions responsible for the implementation of the Agreement.

In conclusion, I have the honour to propose that, if the above is acceptable to Mercosur, this letter and your confirmation shall together constitute an agreement between the European Community and Mercosur.

Please accept, Sir, the assurance of my highest consideration.

On behalf of
the Council of the European Union

B. *Letter No 2*

Brussels, . . .

Sir

I have the honour to acknowledge receipt of your letter of today's date concerning the provisional application of certain provisions of the Interregional Framework Cooperation Agreement between the European Community and its Member States, of the one part, and the Southern Common Market and its Party States, of the other part, signed on 15 December 1995 at Madrid, which reads as follows:

> 'I have the honour to refer to the Interregional Framework Cooperation Agreement between the European Community and its Member States, of the one part, and the Southern Common Market and its Party States, of the other part, signed on 15 December 1995 at Madrid.
>
> Pending the entry into force of the said Agreement, I have the honour to propose to you that the European Community and Mercosur provisionally apply the provisions of that Agreement which deal with trade cooperation, as set out in Articles 4 to 8 of Title II of the abovementioned Agreement.
>
> In the interests of ensuring that our cooperation referred to in those provisions is effective, I also have the honour to propose that we provisionally apply the provisions of Articles 27, 29 and 30, which deal with the establishment of the institutions responsible for the implementation of the Agreement.
>
> In conclusion, I have the honour to propose that, if the above is acceptable to Mercosur, this letter and your confirmation shall together constitute an agreement between the European Community and Mercosur.'

I am able to confirm that Mercosur is in agreement with the contents of your letter.

Please accept, Sir, the assurance of my highest consideration.

On behalf of Mercosur

INTERREGIONAL FRAMEWORK COOPERATION AGREEMENT

between the the European Community and its Member States, of the one part, and the Southern Common Market and its Party States, of the other part

THE KINGDOM OF BELGIUM,

THE KINGDOM OF DENMARK,

THE FEDERAL REPUBLIC OF GERMANY,

THE HELLENIC REPUBLIC,

THE KINGDOM OF SPAIN,

THE FRENCH REPUBLIC,

IRELAND,

THE ITALIAN REPUBLIC,

THE GRAND DUCHY OF LUXEMBOURG,

THE KINGDOM OF THE NETHERLANDS,

THE REPUBLIC OF AUSTRIA,

THE PORTUGUESE REPUBLIC,

THE REPUBLIC OF FINLAND,

THE KINGDOM OF SWEDEN,

THE UNITED KINGDOM OF GREAT BRITAIN AND NORTHERN IRELAND,

Parties to the Treaty establishing the European Community and the Treaty on European Union, hereinafter referred to as the 'European Community Member States', and

THE EUROPEAN COMMUNITY,

hereinafter referred to as 'the Community', of the one part, and

THE ARGENTINE REPUBLIC,

THE FEDERATIVE REPUBLIC OF BRAZIL,

THE REPUBLIC OF PARAGUAY,

THE EASTERN REPUBLIC OF URUGUAY,

Parties to the Treaty of Asunción establishing a Southern Common Market and to the Ouro Preto additional Protocol, hereinafter referred to as the 'Mercosur Party States', and

THE SOUTHERN COMMON MARKET

hereinafter referred to as 'Mercosur', of the other part,

CONSIDERING the deep historical, cultural, political and economic links which unite them, and taking inspiration from the values shared by their peoples;

CONSIDERING their full commitment to the content and principles of the Charter of the United Nations and to democratic values, the rule of law and promoting and respecting human rights;

CONSIDERING the importance which both Parties attach to the principles and values set out in the Final Declaration of the United Nations Conference on Environment and Development held in Rio de Janeiro in June 1992 and those set out in the Final Declaration of the World Summit for Social Development held in Copenhagen in March 1995;

MINDFUL of the fact that both Parties consider the process of regional integration to be an instrument of economic and social development which makes it easier for their economies to become part of the world economy, and, finally, promotes closer relations between peoples and contributes to greater international stability;

REAFFIRMING their desire to uphold and strengthen the tenets of international free trade, in compliance with World Trade Organization rules, with a particular emphasis on the importance of open regionalism;

CONSIDERING that both the Community and Mercosur have specific experience of regional integration which could be of mutual benefit as they forge closer relations determined by their needs;

MINDFUL of the relations of cooperation which have been established by the bilateral agreements between the States of the respective regions and by the Framework Cooperation Agreements which the Mercosur Party States have signed bilaterally with the European Community;

MINDFUL of the results produced by the Interinstitutional Cooperation Agreement of 29 May 1992 between the Southern Common Market Council and the Commission of the European Communities, and emphasizing the need to continue the activities realized by that Agreement;

CONSIDERING the political will of both Parties to achieve what will ultimately be a political and economic interregional association founded on greater political cooperation and progressive and reciprocal liberalization of all trade, taking account of the sensitivity of certain goods and complying with World Trade Organization rules, and founded, finally, on the promotion of investment and closer cooperation;

MINDFUL of the terms of the Joint Solemn Declaration in which both Parties propose to conclude an Interregional Framework Agreement covering commercial and economic cooperation and preparing for gradual and reciprocal liberalization of trade between the two regions as a prelude to the negotiation of an Interregional Association Agreement between them,

HAVE DECIDED to conclude this Agreement and to that end have designated as their Plenipotentiaries:

THE KINGDOM OF BELGIUM:

Erik DERYCKE,

Minister for Foreign Affairs,

THE KINGDOM OF DENMARK:

Niels HELVEG PETERSEN,

Minister for Foreign Affairs,

THE FEDERAL REPUBLIC OF GERMANY:

Klaus KINKEL,

Federal Minister for Foreign Affairs and Vice-Chancellor,

THE HELLENIC REPUBLIC:

Karolos PAPOULIAS,

Minister for Foreign Affairs,

THE KINGDOM OF SPAIN:

Javier SOLANA MADARIAGA,

Minister for Foreign Affairs,

THE FRENCH REPUBLIC:

Hervé de CHARETTE,

Minister for Foreign Affairs,

IRELAND:

Dick SPRING,

Minister for Foreign Affairs,

THE ITALIAN REPUBLIC:

Susanna AGNELLI,

Minister for Foreign Affairs,

THE GRAND DUCHY OF LUXEMBOURG:

Jacques F. POOS,

Minister for Foreign Affairs,

THE KINGDOM OF THE NETHERLANDS:

Hans van MIERLO,

Minister for Foreign Affairs,

THE REPUBLIC OF AUSTRIA:

Wolfgang SCHÜSSEL,

Federal Minister for Foreign Affairs and Vice-Chancellor,

THE PORTUGUESE REPUBLIC:

Jaime GAMA,

Minister for Foreign Affairs,

THE REPUBLIC OF FINLAND:

Tarja HALONEN,

Minister for Foreign Affairs,

THE KINGDOM OF SWEDEN:

Mats HELLSTRÖM,

Minister for European Affairs and Foreign Trade,

THE UNITED KINGDOM OF GREAT BRITAIN AND NORTHERN IRELAND:

Malcolm RIFKIND,

Secretary of State for Foreign and Commonwealth Affairs,

THE EUROPEAN COMMUNITY:

Javier SOLANA MADARIAGA,

Minister for Foreign Affairs,

President-in-Office of the Council of the European Union,

Manuel MARÍN,

Vice-President of the Commission of the European Communities,

THE ARGENTINE REPUBLIC:

Guido di TELLA,

Minister for Foreign Affairs,

THE FEDERATIVE REPUBLIC OF BRAZIL:

Luiz Felipe Palmeira LAMPREIA,

Minister for Foreign Affairs,

THE REPUBLIC OF PARAGUAY:

Luis María Ramírez BOETTENER,

Minister for Foreign Affairs,

THE EASTERN REPUBLIC OF URUGUAY:

Alvaro Ramos TRIGO,

Minister for Foreign Affairs,

THE SOUTHERN COMMON MARKET:

Alvaro Ramos TRIGO,

Minister for Foreign Affairs,

President-in-Office of the Southern Common Market,

WHO, having exchanged their Full Powers, found in good and due form,

HAVE AGREED AS FOLLOWS:

TITLE I

OBJECTIVES, PRINCIPLES AND SCOPE

Article 1

Basis for cooperation

Respect for the democratic principles and fundamental human rights established by the Universal Declaration of Human Rights inspires the domestic and external policies of the Parties and constitutes an essential element of this Agreement.

Article 2

Objectives and scope

1. The objectives of this Agreement shall be to strengthen existing relations between the Parties and to prepare the conditions enabling an interregional association to be created.

2. To those ends, the Agreement covers trade and economic matters, cooperation regarding integration and other fields of mutual interest in order to bring about closer relations between the Parties and their respective institutions.

Article 3

Political dialogue

1. The Parties shall institute regular political dialogue to back up and consolidate closer relations between the European Union and Mercosur. Such dialogue shall be conducted in accordance with the terms contained in the Joint Declaration annexed to the Agreement.

2. The ministerial dialogue provided for in the Joint Declaration shall take place within the Cooperation Council established by Article 25 of this Agreement or within other agreed forums of an equivalent level.

TITLE II

TRADE

Article 4

Objectives

The Parties shall undertake to forge closer relations with the aim of encouraging the increase and diversification of trade, preparing for subsequent gradual and reciprocal liberalization of trade and promoting conditions which are conducive to the establishment of the Interregional Association, taking into account, in conformity with WTO rules, the sensitivity of certain goods.

Article 5

Dialogue on trade and economic matters

1. The Parties shall agree on the scope of cooperation in trade matters without excluding any sector.

2. To those ends, the Parties shall undertake to conduct periodic dialogue on trade and economic matters, within the institutional framework established by Title VIII of this Agreement.

3. In particular, cooperation of this nature shall focus mainly on the following:

(a) market access, trade liberalization (tariff and non-tariff barriers) and trade discipline such as restrictive trade practices, rules of origin, safeguards and special customs arrangements, for example;

(b) the Parties' trade relations with non-member countries;

(c) the compatibility of trade liberalization with GATT and WTO rules;

(d) the identification of goods which the Parties consider to be sensitive or of priority importance;

(e) cooperation and exchanges of information on services, within the Parties' respective spheres of competence.

Article 6

Cooperation on agri-food and industrial standards and certification

1. The Parties agree to cooperate in promoting the approximation of quality standards for agri-food products and industrial goods and certification, in conformity with international criteria.

2. Within the bounds of their spheres of competence, the Parties shall examine the prospects for beginning negotiations for the conclusion of mutual recognition agreements.

3. The primary aim of cooperation shall be to promote any measure which is likely to improve the quality of the Parties' products and businesses.

Article 7

Cooperation in customs matters

1. The Parties shall promote cooperation in customs matters in order to improve and consolidate the legal framework for trade relations between them.

Cooperation in customs matters may also seek to strengthen the customs infrastructure of the Parties and improve their operation within the framework of interinstitutional cooperation.

2. Cooperation may be translated into action by measures including:

(a) exchanges of information;

(b) the development of new training techniques and coordination of activities in the relevant international organizations;

(c) exchanges of officials and senior personnel from customs and tax departments;

(d) simplification of customs procedures;

(e) technical assistance.

3. The Parties hereby signal their interest in giving future consideration, within the institutional framework established by this Agreement, to the conclusion of a Customs Cooperation Protocol.

Article 8

Cooperation in statistical matters

The Parties shall agree to promote an alignment of statistical methods with the aim of achieving mutual recognition and making use of statistics on trade in goods and services and, in general terms, data relating to any field for which statistics can be collected.

Article 9

Cooperation regarding intellectual property

1. The Parties shall agree to cooperate in intellectual property matters in order to encourage investment, the transfer of technology, trade and all associated economic activity, and to prevent distortions of trade.

2. Within the bounds of their respective laws, regulations and policies, and in line with the undertakings made within the TRIPs Agreeement, the arties shall ensure that there is suitable and genuine protection of intellectual property rights, if necessary by arranging for such protection to be stepped up.

3. To the ends described in paragraph 2, intellectual property matters shall encompass copyright and similar rights, trademarks or brands, geographical terms and descriptions of origin, industrial designs and utility models, patents and integrated circuit topography.

TITLE III

ECONOMIC COOPERATION

Article 10

Objectives and principles

1. Guided by their mutual interests and their medium- and long-term economic objectives, the Parties shall promote economic cooperation in such a way as to help to expand their economies, increase their international competitiveness, foster technical and scientific development, improve their standards of living, establish conditions conducive to job creation and job quality and diversify and strengthen economic links between them.

2. The Parties shall encourage the conferring of a regional character on any aspect of cooperation which, by virtue of its scope or economies of scale, results in what they consider to be a more rational and efficient use of available resources and a better outcome.

3. Economic cooperation between the Parties shall have as wide a basis as possible. No sector shall be excluded from the outset, and account shall be taken of the Parties' priorities, mutual interest and areas of competence.

4. In the light of the foregoing, the Parties shall cooperate in all areas which will foster economic and social links and networks between them and which will bring their economies closer together, as well as in all areas in which there is a transfer of specific know-how relating to regional integration.

5. Within the framework of such cooperation, the Parties shall promote the exchange of information on their respective economic indicators.

6. The Parties shall pay attention to protection of the environment and the ecological balance in all their cooperation activities.

7. A regard for social development, particularly the promotion of fundamental social rights, shall motivate the steps taken by the Parties in this field.

Article 11

Cooperation in business

1. The Parties shall promote cooperation in business with the aim of establishing a climate which favours economic development in their mutual interest.

2. Such cooperation shall focus in particular on:

(a) increasing the flow of trade, investment, industrial cooperation projects and the transfer of technology;

(b) encouraging modernization and diversification in industry;

(c) identifying barriers to industrial cooperation between the Parties and eliminating such barriers using measures which promote compliance with competition rules and foster the tailoring of those rules to the needs of the market, giving due attention to the involvement and consultation of operators;

(d) stimulating cooperation between the Parties' economic operators, especially small and medium-sized enterprises;

(e) promoting industrial innovation by developing an integrated and decentralized view of cooperation between operators in the two regions;

(f) ensuring that action seeking to produce a positive influence on cooperation between businesses in the two regions remains a coherent whole.

3. Cooperation shall essentially take the following forms:

(a) more organized contact between the Parties' operators and networks, through conferences, technical seminars, fact-finding missions, attendance at general and specialist fairs and business meetings;

(b) suitable initiatives to back cooperation between small and medium-sized enterprises, such as the promotion of joint ventures, the establishment of information networks, encouraging the opening of trade offices, the transfer of specialist know-how, subcontracting, applied research, licensing and franchising;

(c) promoting initiatives to increase cooperation between Mercosur economic operators and European associations, with the aim of establishing dialogue between networks;

(d) training schemes, encouraging the establishment of networks and backing for research.

Article 12

Promotion of investment

1. Within the bounds of their spheres of competence, the Parties shall promote an attractive and stable climate for greater mutually beneficial investment.

2. Such cooperation shall encompass measures including the following:

(a) promoting regular exchanges of information, the identification and dissemination of information on legislation and investment opportunities;

(b) promoting the development of a legal environment which is conducive to investment between the Parties, particularly, where applicable, through the conclusion between interested Community Member States and Mercosur Party States of bilateral agreements for the promotion and protection of investment and bilateral agreements to prevent double taxation;

(c) promoting joint ventures, particularly between small and medium-sized enterprises.

Article 13

Cooperation regarding energy

1. Cooperation between the Parties shall be directed towards encouraging closer relations between their economies in energy-related industries, taking into consideration the need to use energy rationally and in a manner which respects the environment.

2. Cooperation regarding energy shall essentially take the following forms:

(a) exchanges of information in all appropriate forms, particularly through joint meetings;

(b) transfers of technology;

(c) encouraging the involvement of the Parties' economic operators in joint technological development or infrastructure projects;

(d) technical training programmes;

(e) to the extent that their spheres of competence allow, dialogue regarding energy policy.

3. Where appropriate, the Parties may conclude specific agreements of common interest.

Article 14

Cooperation regarding transport

1. Cooperation between the Parties regarding transport shall seek to back the restructuring and modernization of transport systems and find mutually acceptable solutions for moving people and goods using all modes of transport.

2. Cooperation shall be conducted as a matter of priority by:

(a) exchanges of information on both Parties' transport policies and on matters of mutual interest;

(b) training programmes for transport system operators.

3. Within the framework of the dialogue on trade and economic matters referred to in Article 5, and considering the prospect of interregional association, both Parties shall devote attention to all aspects of international transport to ensure that they do not act as a barrier to the reciprocal expansion of trade.

Article 15

Cooperation in science and technology

1. The Parties shall agree to cooperate in the field of science and technology with the aim of promoting a lasting working relationship between their scientific communities and exchanging information and know-how regarding science and technology between the regions.

2. Cooperation in science and technology between the Parties shall be conducted as a matter of priority by means of:

(a) joint research projects in fields of common interest;

(b) exchanges of scientists in order to encourage joint research, prepare projects and provide high-calibre training;

(c) joint scientific conferences to exchange information, promote interaction and facilitate the selection of subjects for joint research;

(d) the publicizing of results and development of links between the public and private sectors.

3. Such cooperation shall involve the Parties' centres of higher education and research and their industries, particularly small and medium-sized enterprises.

4. The Parties shall agree between them the scope, nature and priorities of cooperation through a multiannual programme which can be adapted to suit the circumstances.

Article 16

Cooperation in telecommunications and information technology

1. The Parties shall agree to establish cooperation regarding telecommunications and information technology, with the aim of fostering economic and social development, driving the information society forward and making modernization of society easier.

2. Cooperation in this field shall seek especially to:

(a) facilitate the establishment of dialogue on the various features of the information society and promote the exchange of information on standards, inspection and certification in the field of information technology and telecommunications;

(b) disseminate new telecommunications and information technology, particularly in the fields of integrated services digital networks, data transmission and the establishment of new communications and information-technology services;

(c) stimulate the launching of joint research, industrial and technological development projects in the field of new communications technologies, telematics and the information society.

Article 17

Cooperation regarding environmental protection

1. With the aim of achieving sustainable development, the Parties shall encourage awareness of the issues of environmental protection and the rational use of natural resources in all fields of interregional cooperation.

2. The Parties shall agree to devote special attention to measures connected with the international dimension of environmental problems.

3. Cooperation could cover the following in particular:

(a) exchanges of information and know-how regarding matters including regulations and standards;

(b) training and education regarding the environment;

(c) technical assistance, the implementation of joint research projects and, where appropriate, institutional assistance.

TITLE IV

ENCOURAGING INTEGRATION

Article 18

Objectives and scope

1. Cooperation between the Parties shall seek to further the objectives of Mercosur's integration process and shall encompass all the areas of this Agreement.

2. To those ends, cooperation activities shall be considered in the context of the specific requests of Mercosur.

3. Cooperation should take any form which is considered appropriate, and particularly:

(a) arrangements for the exchange of information in any suitable manner, including the establishment of computer networks;

(b) training and institutional backing;

(c) studies and joint projects;

(d) technical assistance.

4. The Parties shall cooperate to ensure maximum efficiency in the use of their resources for the compilation, analysis, publication and dissemination of information, without prejudice to any steps which might be necessary to protect the confidential nature of some of that information. They shall also undertake to protect personal data in all instances in which there is provision for exchanging information via computer networks.

TITLE V

INTERINSTITUTIONAL COOPERATION

Article 19

Objectives and scope

1. The Parties shall promote closer cooperation between their respective institutions and shall particularly encourage regular contact between them.

2. Such cooperation shall have as wide a basis as possible and shall focus on:

(a) any means of fostering regular exchanges of information, including the joint development of computer networks for communication;

(b) the transfer of know-how;

(c) advice and information.

TITLE VI

OTHER AREAS OF COOPERATION

Article 20

Cooperation regarding training and education

1. Within the bounds of their spheres of competence, the Parties shall endeavour to find ways to improve education and training relating to regional integration, whether in the form of training for young people and vocational training or in the form of cooperation between universities or businesses.

2. The Parties shall pay particular attention to action which would promote the establishment of links between their specialist entities and encourage the use of technical resources and exchanges of know-how.

3. The Parties shall encourage the conclusion of agreements between training centres and the holding of meetings between bodies responsible for edcucation and training in the field of regional integration.

Article 21

Cooperation regarding information, communication and culture

1. Within the bounds of their spheres of competence, and with the aim of broadening knowledge of their political, economic and social realities, the Parties shall agree to strengthen the cultural links between them and encourage the dissemination of information on the nature, objectives and scope of their processes of integration to promote understanding of them within their societies.

The Parties shall also agree to expand exchanges of information between them on matters of mutual interest.

2. Such cooperation should seek to promote contact between the Parties' information and communications media in forms including technical assistance.

It could include the organization of cultural activities if their regional significance justifies such action.

Article 22

Cooperation in combating drug-trafficking

1. In accordance with their spheres of competence, the Parties shall promote the coordination and intensification of their efforts to combat drug-trafficking and its many ramifications, including financial ramifications.

2. Such cooperation shall include the promotion of consultation and greater coordination between the Parties at regional level and, where appropriate, between the relevant regional institutions.

Article 23

Future developments

1. The Parties may by mutual consent expand this Agreement with a view to enhancing the levels of cooperation and supplementing them, within the bounds of their respective laws, by means of agreements on specific sectors or activities.

2. With regard to the implementation of this Agreement, either of the Parties may put forward suggestions for widening the scope of cooperation, taking into account the experience gained in applying this Agreement.

TITLE VII

RESOURCES FOR COOPERATION

Article 24

1. In order to facilitate the achievement of the aims set out in this Agreement, the Parties shall make available, within the limits of their abilities and through their own channels, the appropriate resources, including financial resources.

2. Depending on the results obtained, the Parties shall call on the European Investment Bank to step up its activities within Mercosur in accordance with its own procedures and financing criteria.

3. The provisions of this Agreement shall not affect bilateral cooperation resulting from existing cooperation agreements.

TITLE VIII

INSTITUTIONAL FRAMEWORK

Article 25

1. A Cooperation Council is hereby established, with responsibility for the implementation of this Agreement; the Cooperation Council shall meet at ministerial level periodically and whenever circumstances require.

2. The Cooperation Council shall discuss important matters arising in connection with the Agreement and any other bilateral or international issues of common interest, with the aim of fulfilling the Agreement's objectives.

3. The Cooperation Council may also make appropriate proposals, with the agreement of the Parties. In carrying out its duties, the Cooperation Council shall undertake in particular to make recommendations which contribute to the ultimate objective of interregional association.

Article 26

1. The Cooperation Council shall be composed, on the one hand, of members of the Council of the European Union and members of the European Commission and, on the other hand, of members of the Mercosur Common Market Council and members of the Mercosur Common Market Group.

2. The Cooperation Council shall adopt its own rules of procedure.

3. The Cooperation Council shall be chaired in turn by a representative of the Community and a representative of Mercosur.

Article 27

1. The Cooperation Council shall be assisted in the performance of its duties by a Joint Cooperation Committee which shall be composed of members of the Council of the European Union and of members of the European Commission, on the one hand, and representatives of Mercosur, on the other.

2. The Joint Committee shall generally meet once a year, on a date and with an agenda agreed in advance, alternately in Brussels and in one of the Mercosur Party States. Extraordinary meetings may be convened by mutual agreement, at the request of either Party. The office of chairman of the Joint Committee shall be held alternately by a representative of each of the Parties.

3. The Cooperation Council shall set out the operating procedures of the Joint Committee in its own rules of procedures.

4. The Cooperation Council may delegate all or part of its powers to the Joint Committee; the latter shall provide continuity between meetings of the Cooperation Council.

5. The Joint Committee shall assist the Cooperation Council in the performance of its duties. In fulfilling its functions, the Joint Committee shall in particular:

(a) stimulate trade relations in accordance with the objectives of this Agreement and in compliance with provisions of Title II;

(b) exchange views on any matter of common interest which relates to trade liberalization and cooperation, including future programmes of cooperation and the resources available for their implementation;

(c) make proposals to the Cooperation Council, with the aim of stimulating preparations for the liberalization of trade and of intensifying cooperation, while taking due account of the need for coordination between the activities proposed; and

(d) in more general terms, make proposals to the Cooperation Council which contribute to achieving the ultimate aim of EU-Mercosur interregional association.

Article 28

The Cooperation Council may decide to set up any other body to assist it in the performance of its duties; it shall determine that body's composition, objectives and operating procedures.

Article 29

1. In accordance with the procedures laid down in Article 5 of this Agreement, the Parties shall establish a Joint Subcommittee on Trade, which shall ensure that the trade-related objectives of this Agreement are fulfilled and shall conduct preparatory work for the subsequent liberalization of trade.

2. The Joint Subcommittee on Trade shall be composed of members of the Council of the European Union and of members of the European Commission, on the one hand, and representatives of Mercosur, on the other.

It may commission any studies or technical analyses which it deems necessary.

3. The Joint Subcommittee on Trade shall report once a year to the Joint Cooperation Committee established under Article 27 of the Agreement on the progress of its work, and shall make proposals regarding the subsequent liberalization of trade.

4. The Joint Subcommittee on Trade shall submit its rules of procedure to the Joint Committee for approval.

Article 30

Consultation

Within the bounds of their spheres of competence, the Parties shall undertake to hold consultations on any issue referred to in this Agreement.

The procedure for the consultations referred to in the preceding subparagraph shall be laid down in the rules of procedure of the Joint Committee.

TITLE IX

FINAL PROVISIONS

Article 31

Other agreements

Without prejudice to the provisions of the Treaties establishing the European Community and Mercosur, neither this Agreement nor any action taken under it shall in any way affect the powers of the Member States of the European Community or the Mercosur Party States to undertake bilateral activities within their spheres of competence or where appropriate to conclude new agreements.

Article 32

Definition of the Parties

For the purposes of this Agreement, the term 'the Parties' shall mean, on the one hand, the Community or its Member States or the Community and its Member States, in accordance with their respective spheres of competence, as deriving from the Treaty establishing the European Community and, on the other hand, Mercosur or its Party States, in accordance with the Treaty establishing the Southern Common Market.

Article 33

Territorial application

This Agreement shall apply, on the one hand, to the territories in which the Treaty establishing the European Community is applied and under the conditions laid down in that Treaty and, on the other hand, to the territories in which the Treaty establishing the Southern Common Market is applied and under the conditions laid down in that Treaty and its additional protocols.

Article 34

Duration and entry into force

1. This Agreement shall be valid indefinitely.

2. The Parties shall determine the suitability, timing and conditions of the start of negotiations for Interregional Association in accordance with their own procedures and in the light of the work carried out and the proposals made within the institutional framework of this Agreement.

3. This Agreement shall enter into force on the first day of the month following that in which the Parties notify each other of the completion of the procedures necessary for this purpose.

4. Notification shall be sent to the Council of the European Union and the Mercosur Common Market Group.

5. The Secretary-General of the Council shall be the depositary of this Agreement for the Community and the

Government of the Republic of Paraguay shall be the depositary for Mercosur.

Article 35

Fulfilment of obligations

1. The Parties shall adopt any general or specific measure required for them to fulfil their obligations under this Agreement and shall ensure that they attain the objectives laid down in that Agreement.

If either Party considers that the other Party has failed to fulfil an obligation under this Agreement, it may take appropriate measures. Before doing so, except in cases of special urgency, it shall supply the Joint Committee with all relevant information required for a thorough examination of the situation with a view to seeking a solution acceptable to the Parties.

In the selection of measures, priority must be given to those which least disturb the functioning of this Agreement. These measures shall be notified immediately to the Joint Committee and shall be the subject of consultations within that Committee if the other Party so requests.

2. The Parties agree that the term 'cases of special urgency' in paragraph 1 of this Article shall mean a case of material breach of the Agreement by one of the Parties. A material breach of the Agreement shall consist in:

(a) repudiation of the Agreement not sanctioned by the general rules of international law, or

(b) violation of the essential elements of the Agreement, as referred to in Article 1.

3. The Parties agree that the 'appropriate measures' referred to in this Article are measures taken in accordance with international law. If a Party takes a measure in a case of special urgency as provided for under this Article, the other Party may ask that an urgent meeting be called to bring both Parties together within days.

Article 36

Authentic texts

This Agreement shall be drawn up in duplicate in the Danish, Dutch, English, Finnish, French, German, Greek, Italian, Portuguese, Spanish and Swedish languages, each of these texts being equally authentic.

Article 37

Signature

This Agreement will be open for signature in Madrid between 15 and 31 December 1995.

Hecho en Madrid, el quince de diciembre de mil novecientos noventa y cinco.

Udfærdiget i Madrid, den femtende december nitten hundrede og femoghalvfems.

Geschehen zu Madrid am fünfzehnten Dezember neunzehnhundertfünfundneunzig.

Έγινε στη Μαδρίτη, στις δέκα πέντε Δεκεμβρίου χίλια εννιακόσια ενενήντα πέντε.

Done at Madrid on the fifteenth day of December in the year one thousand nine hundred and ninety-five.

Fait à Madrid, le quinze décembre mil neuf cent quatre-vingt-quinze.

Fatto a Madrid, addì quindici dicembre millenovecentonovantacinque.

Gedaan te Madrid, de vijftiende december negentienhonderd vijfennegentig.

Feito em Madrid, em quinze de Dezembro de mil novecentos e noventa e cinco.

Tehty Madridissa viidentenätoista päivänä joulukuuta vuonna tuhatyhdeksänsataayhdeksänkymmentäviisi.

Som skedde i Madrid den femtonde december nittonhundranittiofem.

Pour le Royaume de Belgique

Voor het Koninkrijk België

Für das Königreich Belgien

Cette signature engage également la Communauté française, la Communauté flamande, la Communauté germanophone, la Région wallonne, la Région flamande et la Région de Bruxelles-Capitale.

Deze handtekening verbindt eveneens de Vlaamse Gemeenschap, de Franse Gemeenschap, de Duitstalige Gemeenschap, het Vlaamse Gewest, het Waalse Gewest en het Brusselse Hoofdstedelijke Gewest.

Diese Unterschrift verbindet zugleich die Deutschsprachige Gemeinschaft, die Flämische Gemeinschaft, die Französische Gemeinschaft, die Wallonische Region, die Flämische Region und die Region Brüssel-Hauptstadt.

På Kongeriget Danmarks vegne

Für die Bundesrepublik Deutschland

Για την Ελληνική Δημοκρατία

Por el Reino de España

Pour la République française

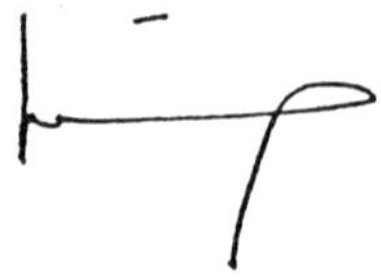

Thar ceann na hÉireann

For Ireland

Per la Repubblica italiana

Pour le Grand-Duché de Luxembourg

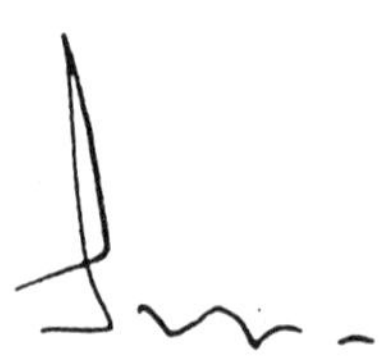

Voor het Koninkrijk der Nederlanden

Für die Republik Österreich

Pela República Portuguesa

Suomen tasavallan puolesta

För Konungariket Sverige

For the United Kingdom of Great Britain and Northern Ireland

Por la Comunidad Europea

For Det Europæiske Fællesskab

Für die Europäische Gemeinschaft

Για την Ευρωπαϊκή Κοινότητα

For the European Community

Pour la Communauté européenne

Per la Comunità europea

Voor de Europese Gemeenschap

Pela Comunidade Europeia

Euroopan yhteisön puolesta

För Europeiska gemenskapen

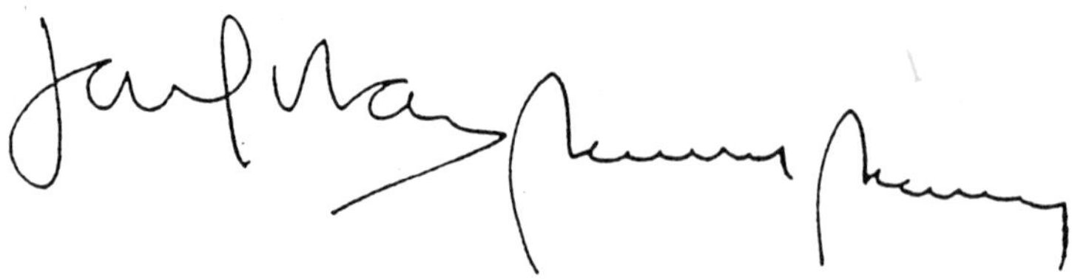

Por la República Argentina

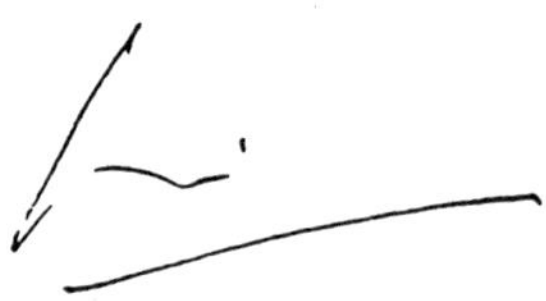

Pela República Federativa do Brasil

Por la República del Paraguay

Por la República Oriental del Uruguay

Por el Mercado Común del Sur:
Pelo Mercado Comum do Sul

Joint Declaration on political dialogue between the European Union and Mercosur

Preamble

THE EUROPEAN UNION AND THE MERCOSUR PARTY STATES,

— conscious of their historical, political and economic ties, their common cultural heritage and the bonds of friendship between their peoples,

— mindful that political and economic freedoms are fundamental to society in the European Union and the Mercosur countries,

— reaffirming human dignity and the promotion of human rights as cornerstones of a democratic society, in accordance with the United Nations Charter,

— reaffirming the essential role of the principles and democratic institutions based on the rule of law, respect for which governs the internal and external policies of the Parties,

— desiring to strengthen international peace and security in accordance with the principles of the United Nations Charter,

— sharing an interest in regional integration as a means of enabling their citizens to achieve sustainable and harmonious development predicated upon social progress and solidarity between their members,

— building upon the preferential relations formalized by the framework Cooperation Agreements which the European Community has signed with each of the Mercosur Party States,

— recalling the principles set out in the Solemn Joint Declaration signed by the Parties on 22 December 1994,

HAVE DECIDED to develop relations on a long-term basis.

Objectives

— Mercosur and the European Union solemnly reaffirm their commitment to progressing towards the establishment of an interregional association and to establishing greater political dialogue for that purpose,

— regional integration is one means of achieving sustainable and socially harmonious development, and a tool for ensuring competitiveness in the world economy,

— this dialogue is also intended to ensure closer consultation on issues affecting both regions and on multilateral issues, in particular by allowing the positions of the respective parties to be coordinated in the relevant multilateral organizations.

Mechanisms of the dialogue

— The parties will conduct this political dialogue by means of contacts, information exchanges and consultation, especially meetings at the appropriate level between the various Mercosur and European Union bodies as well as by making full use of diplomatic channels,

— in particular, with the aim of establishing and developing this political dialogue on bilateral and international issues of mutual interest, the Parties agree to hold:

(a) regular meetings, the detailed arrangements for which will be decided on by the Parties, between the Heads of State of the countries of Mercosur and the highest authorities of the European Union;

(b) an annual meeting of the Ministers for Foreign Affairs of Mercosur and of the Member States of the European Union, attended by the European Commission. These meetings will be held at a venue to be determined on each occasion by the Parties;

(c) meetings of other Ministers responsible for matters of mutual interest where such meetings are deemed necessary by the Parties in order to strengthen mutual relations;

(d) periodic meetings of senior officials from both Parties.

EUROPE
AGENCE INTERNATIONALE
D'INFORMATION POUR LA PRESSE
Agence Europe S.A. fondee le 2 decembre 1952

Redacteur en chef : Ferdinando Riccardi
Rédacteurs en chef adjoints :
Marina Gazzo et Michel Theys

Bureau de dépôt
Bruxelles X

SIEGE SOCIAL
2014 LUXEMBOURG - 32 rue Philippe II - BP 428
Tel. 22 00 32 - Telex 3431 - Telefax 46 22 77

DIRECTION ET RÉDACTION
Editeur responsable : Ferdinando Riccardi
1210 BRUXELLES - Bld Saint Lazare 10 - bte 13
Tel. 219 02 56 - Telex 21108 - Télefax 217 65 97

Imprimé à 1210 Bruxelles - Bld Saint-Lazare 10
par Imprimerie de l'Europe S.A.

N° 1912/13

30 November 1994

BULLETIN
QUOTIDIEN EUROPE

EUROPE© Documents

LONG TERM STRATEGY PROPOSED BY THE EUROPEAN COMMISSION FOR FUTURE EU RELATIONS WITH THE COMMON MARKET OF LATIN AMERICA (ARGENTINA, BRAZIL, PARAGUAY, URUGUAY)

During the meeting on 24 November between the European Commission and the foreign ministers of the four Mercosur countries, the latter welcomed the guidelines defined by the Commission in its October document on "strengthening European Union policy towards Mercosur". On 28 November, the General Affairs Council approved a report intended for the Essen Summit concerning future relations with Mercosur (and also with Mexico and Chile), a report which is based on the Commission document.

It can therefore be considered that this document now represents the base for future work and negotiations with Mercosur (even if some aspects, in particular the trade of agricultural products, will no doubt still give rise to difficulties). It is for this reason that we reproduce the document in full.

*** *** ***

THE EUROPEAN COMMUNITY AND MERCOSUR : AN ENHANCED POLICY

(Communication from the Commission to the Council and the European Parliament)

In its conclusions, the Corfu European Council of 24 and 25 June this year reaffirmed the importance it attached to its relations with Latin American countries and their regional groupings. It expressed its satisfaction with the progress achieved in the areas of democracy and respect for human rights, peace and disarmament, economic reforms and regional integration.

The European Council welcomed the accession of Mexico to the OECD and expressed its wish to strengthen its political and economic relations with this country. It also confirmed the intention of the European Union to strengthen its relations with Mercosur. It invites the Council and the Commission to pursue these questions further.[1]

These conclusions were foreshadowed by a statement issued by the Council at its general affairs meeting of 13 and 14 June, in which it expressed its willingness to strengthen

[1] The Commission will shortly transmit to the Council a discussion paper on the future of relations between the European Community and Mercosur.

relations between the European Union and that important Latin American regional grouping. The Council had also taken note, on this occasion, of the progress of the Commission's work on the matter and said that it would examine a Commission communication in the autumn.

Several months earlier the foreign ministers of the European Union, at a meeting with their Mercosur counterparts in São Paolo, had agreed to strengthen cooperation in pursuit of more ambitious goals. To that end, the Commission had been instructed to present a report to the Council soon.

This communication from the Commission to the Council and Parliament is in response to the requests of the European Council and the Council of Ministers. Its key components are:

- the strategic aspects of EC-Mercosur relations;

- the assessment of Mercosur's development and a review of its current relations with the Community;

- a proposal for a long-term strategy;

- a recommendation as to the short-term approach needed to establish a framework for relations conducive to the achievement of the long-term objective.

I. THE STRATEGIC INTEREST OF EC-MERCOSUR RELATIONS

(a) Progress towards regional integration

The international scene at the end of the twentieth century is dominated by two major trends: the end of the Cold War and increasing internationalization of economic and financial flows. The liberalization of international trade and the assertion of the rules of the market, as embodied by the Uruguay Round Final Act, reduce the margin for manoeuvre of individual countries.

There is therefore a risk that closed regional blocs may emerge in reaction to this process. It is in the Community's interest to ensure that moves towards integration and regionalization are outward-looking.

The increasing internationalization of economic and financial flows is coupled with a trend towards the regionalization of trade. The Community is, by virtue of its degree of integration, the oldest and most advanced example of this trend. The most recent is NAFTA, which is now attracting the interest of some Latin American countries. At the same time another regional group is asserting itself, namely Mercosur.

The decision to establish the Mercosur customs union from 1 January 1995 marks a qualitative leap forward of fundamental importance to the future development of the Southern Cone. Mercosur is already proving a magnet for other Latin American countries. Chile and Bolivia have already announced their intention to join Mercosur in the near future.

When conceived in a spirit of openness, regional integration - as European experience attests - is accompanied by growth in international trade (this is indeed a necessary condition for a regional trade arrangement to be authorized under Article XXIV of the GATT). It is also a way of bringing peoples closer together: the drawing-up of flanking policies, the spread of "regionalism" to such fields as standards and economic legislation, but also competition law, taxation and monetary matters, effectively creates solidarity. Last but not least, regional integration is an opportunity to rationalize external relations and international cooperation.

(b) Mercosur's place in relations between the Community and Latin America

The Community's relations with Latin America as whole have unfolded at three levels:

* at regional level, the Community has been conducting a formal political dialogue with the Rio Group since 1990,
* at subregional level, the San José dialogue with the Central American countries has been under way since 1984;
* at bilateral level, the Community has concluded "third generation" cooperation agreements with the different countries and groups of countries (the Andean Pact and Central America).

When dealing with a rapidly changing Latin America that offers new opportunities and challenges, the Community cannot limit itself to strengthening its relations with Latin America as a whole, but must also take account of regional or national specificities in its relations

Needless to say, a Union strategy aimed at strengthening relations with Mercosur, Mexico and other Latin American regions cannot be seen as an alternative to the dialogue with the Rio Group. It should instead be considered a means of deepening and extending that dialogue, within which the Community's interests demand that it recognize and take account of regional specificities. This means that the Community's proposed new strategy towards Mercosur must not be developed in isolation, but as part of a broader Community strategy towards all the Latin American countries, and in particular the Rio Group.

(c) Mercosur's specific nature

The strengthening of relations between the Union and Mercosur is in the interests of both.

The Union's interests in stronger relations are both political and economic. Politically, it has an interest in the consolidation of democratic systems, shared values and the desire of these countries to maintain a balance in their relations with the United States and Europe.

Embodying the radical changes that have occurred in the region in recent years, Mercosur - which is characterized by a desire to associate its development with that of the wider world - has set its sights higher than the liberalization of trade, aiming to become a key player on the international political stage.

The Community has recognized this, and has from the outset encouraged the four signatories to the Treaty of Asunción in their economic and political integration efforts. These efforts are all the more justified in economic terms. The countries concerned have 200 million inhabitants and Mercosur, with a GDP in excess of USD 600 billion, figures fourth in the league of major economic groupings:

List of economic powers in order of GDP
(USD million, 1992)

NAFTA	6 765
EC	6 744
Japan	3 507
Mercosur	642
Russia	397
ASEAN (minus Brunei)	375
Mexico	294
Maghreb	90

Source: World Bank

These countries are, moreover, market economies with great potential for economic growth (an emerging area of affluence), considerable natural resources and a growing demand for consumer products and capital.

Mercosur's interests are also political and economic: firstly, the four countries are hoping that the Community will give them support for democratization and the integration of their economies, and serve to counterbalance US influence in the area. In economic terms, the Community is an attractive market for Mercosur's products, offering relatively easy access (unlike other partners) and a source of capital, modern technology and cooperation.

Although much remains to be done, the consolidation of Mercosur is a crucial factor in the medium- and long-term progress of its members and the region as a whole. This consolidation does, however, depend on two conditions: the irreversibility of the undertakings given and uncontested international recognition

Both these conditions make the Community an obvious partner: firstly, because its integration offers the proponents of regional integration a model, secondly, because it can back them up with know-how, and lastly, and above all, because, notwithstanding the geographical distance, the members of the Community and Mercosur are bound by history and culture.

II. MERCOSUR'S DEVELOPMENT

Mercosur, the Southern Cone Common Market, came into being on 26 March 1991, when Argentina, Brazil, Paraguay and Uruguay signed the Treaty of Asunción. This move marked both a culmination and a new determination. It effectively enshrined the rapprochement under way between Argentina and Brazil since 1986 (the PICAB programme) and its ambitious goals reflect an increased will to build the future in a context of regional integration.

Mercosur's function is clearly to enhance its members' competitiveness in the face of increasing internationalization of economic and trade flows and its current priority is the introduction of a customs union on 1 January 1995.

Yet its remit is actually much broader, since the programme adopted by the Mercosur Council (which consists of the member countries' ministers for foreign and economic affairs) at its Las Leñas summit of 27 June 1992 included, for example, fiscal and monetary policies, industrial and technology policy, agricultural policy and the coordination of macroeconomic policies.

Despite some initial scepticism, the organization has achieved a lot in the past three years, even though its legal status will not be finalized for several months. The key decisions adopted in Buenos Aires on 5 August, at the Presidents' most recent summit, bear witness to this:

- a common customs tariff ranging for the most part from 0-20% (a top rate of 14% for capital goods with a uniform rate by 2001; a 16% top rate for computer products with a uniform rate by 2006; a list of exceptions etc.);
- origin rules for products not covered by the common customs tariff;
- the drawing-up of conditions for the operation of free zones;
- the setting-up of a trade commission to monitor the provisions adopted and negotiate trade agreements with third parties.

It was at that Buenos Aires summit that Chile and Bolivia expressed their wish to join Mercosur. The governments of these two countries took part in the summit and laid the foundations for the negotiation of "economic complementarity agreements" with a view to creating a free-trade area encompassing tariff and non-tariff matters, physical integration, investment protection and services, and ensuring their participation as observers in subsequent Mercosur meetings.

The deadline of 1 January 1995 is an ambitious step and one that will mark a turning-point in Mercosur's history. Institutions able to represent Mercosur internationally and manage its integration process will also have to be set up.

III. EC-MERCOSUR RELATIONS: BACKGROUND AND PROSPECTS

a) Trade flows

TOTAL MERCOSUR TRADE
(exports + imports)

	1985	1986	1987	1988	1989	1990	1991	1992
NORTH AMERICA	13089	13003	14654	16795	16429	16284	16624	17985
EEC	*12678*	*13772*	*15844*	*17289*	*18386*	*20414*	*21037*	*22478*
LATIN AMERICA	6648	7926	7853	9260	11707	11445	14553	18116
JAPAN	2756	3338	3294	4239	4422	4617	4919	4746
S.E. ASIA	1383	1590	1873	2840	3570	3829	4653	4857
REST OF WORLD	15239	11378	13015	14084	14377	14798	13470	15551
TOTAL	**51793**	**51007**	**56533**	**64507**	**68891**	**71387**	**75256**	**83733**

Source: Chelem-CEPII Million USD

The European Community has traditionally been Mercosur's largest trading partner with 26% of all trade in the period 1985-1992. This special relationship is also reflected in trade with individual Mercosur countries.

It is noteworthy that enlargement would increase the Community's market share by two percentage points, from 26% to 28% (1992 figures).

Although the balance of trade is very much in Mercosur's favour (a surplus of USD 46 billion for the period 1985-92), the Community's exports to Mercosur have increased dramatically (by more than 40% in the period 1992-93, for instance), making it by far the fastest growing market for European exporters.

MARKET SHARE IN 1992 (Exports + Imports)

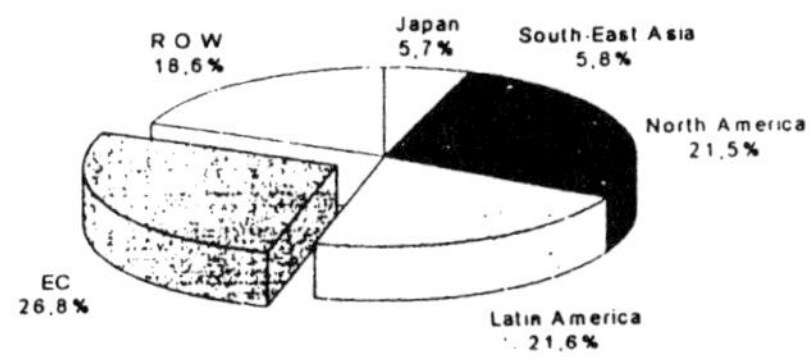

In terms of the size of its internal market, Mercosur already possesses a considerable number of high-income consumers. Coupled with its demographic potential, Mercosur's current economic dynamism prefigures the development in the medium term of a regional market of worldwide significance. In addition to demand for consumer goods, there is a demand for the intermediate and capital goods needed to develop industries to supply both local and export markets.

Mercosur's foreign trade has been growing by more than 10% a year since 1988; this exceptional rate far outstrips that of GDP growth. It is also a consequence of the priority accorded by Mercosur to opening up its economy.

This is illustrated by very high growth in trade within Mercosur (100% in the period 1990-93) as well as rapid growth in flows to the rest of Latin America (almost 20% a year since 1990).

As an exporter to highly industrialized regions, Mercosur continues to specialize basically in products of first-stage processing, save in the agro-industrial sector. Its exports to the rest of Latin America nevertheless contain an increasing proportion of value added, making it a supply hub for the entire subcontinent.

The implementation of the agricultural provisions of the Uruguay Round Final Act will bring improved access to Europe's market for some of the Mercosur countries' agricultural exports. Certain agricultural trade disputes have been resolved in the course of the Uruguay Round.

As an importer, Mercosur is diversifying its purchases and capitalizing on competition between Europe, North America and Asia. Its main imports from the Community are capital goods (machine tools, machinery, aerospace equipment etc.) and chemicals.

(b) Investment

The European Community is the leading foreign investor in Mercosur, which accounts for 70% of European direct investment in Latin America. Not only is European capital to be found in all four Mercosur countries, but in recent years the Community has been alone in increasing investment in Paraguay and Uruguay. The bulk (70%) of this investment has been in the industrial sector, though there has recently been an upturn in flows towards services and local financial markets. The financial markets in Buenos Aires, São Paolo and Rio de Janeiro have exercised a considerable attraction for some years now.

The privatization policies under way in Mercosur since 1988 have met with a favourable response from international investors, particularly in Europe, and they have made significant investments. For example, Europe has been the largest foreign investor in Argentina's privatization programme, accounting for almost a quarter of the incoming capital.

The trade in services is limited at the moment, since these activities are often conducted at a local level. This is undoubtedly a sector with considerable potential in the near future. Cooperation could, for example, involve major infrastructure, commercial distribution networks, transport, telecommunications and culture.

DIRECT INVESTMENT IN MERCOSUR IN 1990

Sources: ILPES, IDB/IRELA and the Commission

(c) EC-Mercosur cooperation

The Community was the first player on the international stage to engage in an informal political dialogue at ministerial level with Mercosur.[2]

In 1992 the Commission and representatives of Mercosur concluded an interinstitutional arrangement aimed at ensuring effective relations and, via two-way institutional support, pooling experience.

As part of its development policy, the Community has committed ECU 17 million for the transfer of integration experience in such key areas as agriculture, the harmonization of technical standards and customs legislation.

The Community is also helping finance the Hidrovía project, and particularly aspects relating to port infrastructure and administration, drawing on earlier European cooperation experiments concerning the administration of the Rhine and the Danube.

These regional programmes are buttressed by bilateral cooperation, which for some countries involves assistance for integration into Mercosur.

The Community also provides support for cultural links with the Mercosur countries, in particular through study programmes and programmes to train craftsmen working to conserve the cultural heritage. It also provides backing for schemes to promote Latin American writers in Europe. In a similar vein, an academic cooperation programme (ALFA) has recently been set up to encourage links between universities in the two regions.

It is worth underlining that Mercosur has been chosen as one of the main beneficiaries of the European Investment Bank's first ventures into Latin America.

In view of their importance to the regional integration process under way, the EIB will be helping to finance the Brazil-Northern Argentina-Buenos Aires and Uruguay-Buenos Aires roads.

In 1992 the aid granted by the Community and its Member States to the Mercosur countries totalled about USD 270 million, accounting for about 42% of all the official development aid received by those countries. In 1993 aid administered by the Commission exceeded ECU 60 million. This year that amount is set to rise to ECU 75 million.

(d) Political dialogue

The political dialogue, particularly at meetings with the Rio Group and in the UN General Assembly, has already borne fruit, underpinning the process of strategic integration and highlighting the mutual interest of strengthening relations between the two partners as emphasized by the foreign ministers at their meetings in Guimarães, Copenhagen and São Paolo.

The São Paolo meeting, in particular, was a milestone, with the Union's ministers and their Mercosur counterparts asking the Commission to draw up as soon as possible, in the light of what had already been achieved, a strategy for strengthening relations.

At their respective summit meetings (in Corfu in June and Buenos Aires in August), the heads of state and of government of both groupings echoed this desire to strengthen ties in pursuit of more ambitious objectives.

---

2 The four Mercosur countries are linked bilaterally to the Community by "third generation" agreements.

However, this dialogue, which originally focused on bilateral aspects of relations, is about to outgrow this framework. There are many synergies between the interests and viewpoints of Mercosur and the European Union; there are a great many multilateral issues which would lend themselves to closer consultation and, in particular, culminate in the coordination of positions in some multilateral organizations.

IV. TOWARDS STRONGER RELATIONS BETWEEN THE COMMUNITY AND MERCOSUR

(a) Two scenarios for the run-up to 2000

In the light of the views expounded above and in order to illustrate the advantages, both quantitative and qualitative, of liberalizing international trade between Mercosur and the European Community, two scenarios have been constructed for the period up to 2000 on the basis of trends observed over the last five years.

The first assumes no change in the trends, while the second takes account of the establishment of a free-trade area between the Community and Mercosur.

The main conclusions of these studies can be summed up as follows:

Scenario No 1: No change in current trends

In this scenario, Mercosur's export and import trade with its main partners continues at the average rates observed in the period 1988-92. This scenario involves:

- very high average growth of 11.5% a year in Mercosur's exports;
- considerable growth in the proportion accounted for by Latin America;
- a growth in the Community's trade deficit
- a doubling of Asia's market share.

MARKET SHARE - SUSTAINED TRENDS (EXPORTS and IMPORTS)

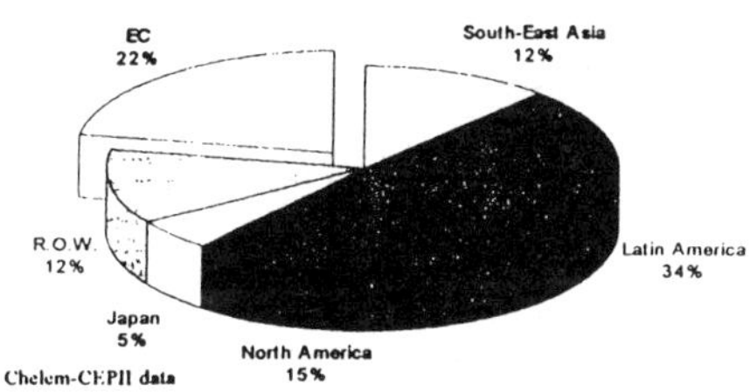

Source: scenario based on Chelem-CEPII data

This scenario would see the Community losing a considerable part of its market share.

Scenario No 2: Liberalization of trade between the Community and Mercosur

This scenario assumes the establishment of a free-trade area with Mercosur. The key results are:

- an increase in the Community's market share;
- growth of 11.5% in trade with Europe, compared with 7% for other regions;
- faster growth in European exports than in the first scenario.

In terms of product substitution, the scenarios show the considerable risks of high-value-added European exports gradually being marginalized.

Conversely, an agreement with Mercosur will potentially involve the Community transferring its custom for certain types of imports from other partners. The liberalization of trade would in fact create new opportunities, particularly in the aerospace, electronics, computer, electrical goods and automobile markets.

FREE TRADE WITH EC - MARKET SHARE (Exports+ Imports)

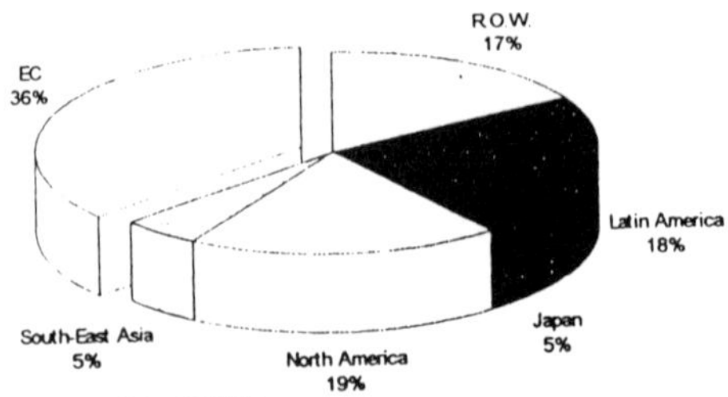

Source: scenario based on Chelem-CEPII data

Main conclusions

The Community currently enjoys a special position in Mercosur in terms of investment and trade. This state of affairs is also reflected in the existence of a shared technological and economic culture potentially favourable to outward expansion.

European economic operators warmly welcome the modernization and liberalization process launched by Mercosur and are playing an active part in it.

At the time of writing, Mercosur is already a significant consumer market and shows considerable potential for growth in this area and in the field of intermediate products.

Mercosur seems to be a new growth centre of worldwide importance and one of strategic importance to Europe.

The simulation exercises illustrate the adverse consequences of "going with the flow" for trade with Mercosur, since current trends, coupled with any extension of NAFTA, would lead, economically, to a loss of potential business and a continuation of the payments deficit.

(b) An inadequate cooperation instrument

As has already been pointed out, the present interinstitutional cooperation Agreement enabled Mercosur to be helped in its infancy, providing it with European experience in the area of integration.

Notwithstanding the achievements it has made possible, this Agreement is now too limited in scope, covering only administrative cooperation between the Commission and Mercosur. It would certainly not be a suitable framework for the development of cooperation in other fields, nor would it be able to adapt to the needs of European operators.

In view of the advantages and opportunities and of the shortcomings of existing cooperation instruments, relations between the Community and Mercosur have to be strengthened.

Moreover, as agreements and contacts with the Community's various partners multiply, agreements must be made more effective and the structural framework for relations and ministerial contacts improved.

The development of a regional framework for relations with Mercosur's member countries, replacing the present fragmented framework in the medium term, would help rationalize the Union's external relations system and improve its efficiency. This regional framework could become a blueprint for rationalizing relations with other groups of partners of a comparable nature.

The Commission is therefore proposing a dynamic two-stage strategy, the pace of which will be geared to Mercosur's development.

The ultimate goal is an EC-Mercosur interregional association founded on a balanced political, economic and trading partnership conducted in a spirit of solidarity, notably through the gradual establishment of a free-trade area for industrial products and services together with reciprocal and gradual liberalization of trade in agricultural products, taking account of the sensitivity of some products. Cooperation, including in the political sphere, could be deepened at the same time.

In the short term, there is a need to identify the best approach: one which, taking account of the progress of the integration process, lays down from the start the political and economic ground rules for enhanced cooperation culminating in interregional association.

The first step is to render existing cooperation instruments more operational and efficient, the object being to reduce to a minimum the gap between the present and the future by making the most of the Community's economic and industrial cooperation strategy.

(c) Interregional association

Objectives

- to foster interregional flows to the advantage of both partners and within the bounds of the Uruguay Round Final Act
- to promote strategic investment by firms
- to strengthen political cooperation at international level, in particular by seeking to reach joint positions in international forums on issues of mutual interest, including world peace and security
- to improve the efficiency of the Union's external activities by establishing a new framework for relations with partners of a similar nature.

Though it is too early to state in detail the components of such an association, the main lines would be:

- the gradual establishment of a free-trade area for industrial products and services, reciprocal and gradual liberalization of agricultural trade, taking account of the sensitivity of certain products,
- cooperation and dialogue on trade issues
- the liberalization of trade in services and capital
- joint financing instruments for regional projects
- cooperation on environmental issues and transport
- cooperation on research, science and technology
- cooperation on information, communications and culture
- interinstitutional cooperation
- political cooperation and coordination in international forums
- industrial cooperation
- cooperation regarding the information society, information technologies and telecommunications

The timetable for the implementation of the various components of interregional association would have to be agreed with Mercosur.

(d) Options

An intermediate stage, preceding interregional association, is warranted by Mercosur's newness and the fact that its structures are still incomplete. No such association would be possible until Mercosur has a full customs union and working institutions.
The response to the urgency and constraints may lie in a flexible and gradual short-term operation.
The following three options have been examined to this end:

- the conclusion of a trade cooperation agreement,
- the immediate establishment, without an intermediate stage, of an interregional association.

The ultimate objective of all three options is the establishment of an interregional association between the Community and Mercosur as soon as Mercosur has consolidated its position as a regional process and comprehensive partnership is possible. The options differ in their instruments and timetables.

Option No 1: A trade cooperation agreement

This option would give priority to the trade cooperation aspect.

While continuing the work begun under the existing interinstitutional cooperation Agreement, priority would be given to measures that will help strengthen Mercosur's structural capacity to manage effectively the trade-related aspects of its integration and the trade element of its cooperation with the Community in preparation for the liberalization of trade.

This option reflects the need to deepen trade links, with the political and structural side of relations taking second place.

Option No 2: A interregional framework agreement on trade and economic cooperation

This option would give relations in the short term a balanced approach simultaneously combining trade, substantial aid and greater consultation, including in the political sphere.

It therefore involves:

- preparations for the liberalization of trade between the Community and Mercosur,
- the extension of cooperation to all areas covered by Mercosur's integration process,
- reinforced political cooperation.

Compared with the previous option, this one offers the advantage of being a more active response to Mercosur, demonstrating the Community's express desire to contribute to Mercosur's consolidation process. This approach is genuinely political, and not simply economic.

Option No 3: An interregional association agreement

Set against the other options, this one preempts Mercosur's consolidation by proposing the immediate negotiation of an interregional association between the Community and Mercosur.

This agreement would include the provisions needed to bring about, according to a fixed timetable, a free-trade area of the type outlined above.

Cooperation under such an agreement would cover the same areas as the preceding option, but would be reinforced by the introduction of joint financial instruments through the raising of substantial funds by both parties.

Compared with the other options, this would be a proactive approach on the part of the Community aimed at accelerating the regional integration process by acting upstream even of initiatives by Mercosur and its members.

V. PROPOSAL AND PRACTICAL CONCLUSIONS

(a) Proposed option: the conclusion of an interregional framework agreement on trade and economic cooperation

The Commission believes that only the conclusion of an agreement of this type would be able to take account of the comparative advantage currently enjoyed by the European Community in the region and pave the way, in step notably with Mercosur's progress towards integration, for interregional association.

This agreement would, in particular, cover the following aspects:[1]

1. In terms of the liberalization of trade, its purpose would be to pave the way for the liberalization of trade along the lines set out in the above-mentioned interregional association agreement. In its proposals, the Commission will take care to reconcile the dictates of the CAP with the Community's international commitments, including those relating to the WTO.

2. In order to support integration, the Community would commit itself to substantial cooperation in three main areas:

2.1 Firstly, cooperation would have to focus on areas that would help Mercosur manage its own internal trade integration process as well as its foreign trade.

---

[1] The negotiating directives for the future agreement would obviously have to be specially geared to the bilateral "third generation" agreements currently in force.

A special effort would have to be made in such fields as: trade policy instruments (anti-dumping rules, safeguard measures etc.), harmonization of nomenclatures, rules for the administration of foreign trade, information system, origin controls, agreements on cumulative origin rules and agreements on quality recognition.

The Community and Mercosur will also have to step up efforts to establish cooperation between the relevant authorities on competition; this cooperation must enhance understanding of restrictive practices affecting trade between the two areas, with, in particular, a view to avoiding friction in their trade.

2.2 Secondly, Mercosur would have to be given integration support in areas other than trade. This broader cooperation would include support for regional administrative and decision-making authorities, increased technical assistance for the establishment of an internal market (harmonization of industrial, monetary and budget policies, harmonization of competition rules, investment protection, protection of intellectual property, macroeconomic coordination, regional balance, planning laws, environmental protection and cooperation regarding the information society) and Mercosur's participation in, for example, European R&D, information systems and telecommunications projects.

The resources devoted to European technical assistance to Mercosur as a regional integration process are currently modest. Enhanced cooperation in the above areas will, however, inevitably require increased funding from the Community and a practical commitment from the Community institutions, especially the Commission. It is inherent in cooperation of this type that technical assistance cannot always be contracted out. The Commission's departments possess the know-how needed for this type of technical assistance and provision should therefore be made for this agreement in Part A of the Community budget.[4]

2.3 The third area would consist of the establishment of several major regional projects (concerning, for example, transport, energy, the environment, telecommunications,information systems, town planning or other sectors of industry) which would be launched jointly, with technical, industrial and financial support from the Community (via the EIB, for instance).[5]

Such initiatives will help legitimize Mercosur and demonstrate to members of both groups the institutions' determination to obtain practical strategic results over and above trade in the traditional sense.

3. Broader consultation

In addition to the political dialogue already conducted offstage at the Union's meetings with the Rio Group, the dialogue between the Union and Mercosur should be stepped up. This could be done by making it more specific and deeper, both in terms of frequency and the choice of specific topics. This dialogue, conducted at ministerial level by the Mercosur countries and the various institutions of the Union, among them the Commission, could also take place at ad-hoc meetings.

In addition to subjects of common interest, the agenda could also include such issues as industrial cooperation, energy, the nuclear industry, security, environmental issues or drugs.

---

[4] The financial impact on Part A of the Community budget will be dealt with when the time comes to prepare the negotiating directives. It consists of mission expenses for staff from Community institutions sent to develop certain aspects of the technical assistance provided for. Provisional estimates suggest that this would amount to about ECU 200 000 per annum.

The financial impact on Part B of the Community budget will be studied when new guidelines are prepared for cooperation with the Asian and Latin American developing countries.

[5] Regional projects, such as Hidrovía, would serve as a good example of the opportunities that would open up for European investors.

(b) Practical conclusions

In the light of the above and in accordance with the conclusions of the Corfu European Council, the Commission calls on the Essen European Council to approve the proposed strategy, which is aimed, in the long term, at establishing an interregional association between the Community and Mercosur and, in the short term, at concluding an interregional framework agreement between the European Community and Mercosur on trade and economic cooperation.

To that end, the Commission will, in the first half of next year, be presenting to the Council draft negotiating directives for this new agreement.

The progress made in implementing this new long-term strategy will be regularly reviewed by the Council at its meetings on general affairs.